DEVELOPMENTS IN FOOD COLOURS—2

CONTENTS OF VOLUME 1

DEVELOPMENTS IN FOOD COLOURS—2

Edited by

JOHN WALFORD

*Organics Division, Imperial Chemical Industries PLC,
Blackley, Manchester, UK*

ELSEVIER APPLIED SCIENCE PUBLISHERS
LONDON and NEW YORK

ELSEVIER APPLIED SCIENCE PUBLISHERS LTD
Ripple Road, Barking, Essex, England

Sole Distributor in the USA and Canada
ELSEVIER SCIENCE PUBLISHING CO., INC.
52 Vanderbilt Avenue, New York, NY 10017, USA

British Library Cataloguing in Publication Data

Developments in food colours.—(The Developments
   series)
   2
   1. Coloring matter in food
   I. Walford, John   II. Series
   664′.06   TP456.C65

   ISBN 0-85334-244-X

WITH 38 TABLES and 35 ILLUSTRATIONS

© ELSEVIER APPLIED SCIENCE PUBLISHERS LTD 1984

The selection and presentation of material and the opinions expressed in this publication are
the sole responsibility of the authors concerned.

Printed in Great Britain by Galliard (Printers) Ltd, Great Yarmouth

PREFACE

The aim of this second volume is two-fold: to discuss technical advances in the food coloration field since the appearance of Volume 1 and to examine the progress made in understanding the need for regulating the use of and controlling the quality of colours permitted for use in foodstuffs.

In the technical field the emphasis of this volume is on current practice in the use of synthetic colours in the USA and on novel sources of naturally occurring colours. Insight into the influence of colour on food choice, adverse reactions to food colours, analytical methods for synthetic colours and current regulatory practice provide a rationale for the continued use of colours in food. A concluding contribution emphasises the continuing efforts made to improve our food supply, the use of food colours being one of a range of methods which can be called on to realise this aim.

I wish to express my thanks to the contributors who have made available the wide range of their experience for this project, particularly during a period when it has never been more difficult to set aside the required time.

JOHN WALFORD

v

CONTENTS

LIST OF CONTRIBUTORS

F. M. CLYDESDALE
Department of Food Science and Nutrition, University of Massachusetts, Amherst, Massachusetts 01003, USA.

F. J. FRANCIS
Department of Food Science and Nutrition, University of Massachusetts, Amherst, Massachusetts 01003, USA.

R. K. JOHNSON
Chemical Division, Hilton-Davis, 2235 Langdon Farm Road, Cincinnati, Ohio 45237, USA.

F. J. LICHTENBERGER
Chemical Division, Hilton-Davis, 2235 Langdon Farm Road, Cincinnati, Ohio 45237, USA.

K. MILLER
Department of Immunotoxicology, British Industrial Biological Research Association, Woodmansterne Road, Carshalton, Surrey SM5 4DS, UK.

S. NICKLIN
Department of Immunotoxicology, British Industrial Biological Research Association, Woodmansterne Road, Carshalton, Surrey SM5 4DS, UK.

L. E. PARKER

British Food Manufacturing Industries Research Association, Randalls Road, Leatherhead, Surrey KT22 7RY, UK.

A. J. TAYLOR

Department of Applied Biochemistry and Nutrition, School of Agriculture, University of Nottingham, Sutton Bonington, Loughborough, Leicestershire LE12 5RD, UK.

G. A. WADDS

D. F. Anstead Limited, Victoria House, Radford Way, Billericay, Essex CM12 0DE, UK. Present address: *Britvic Limited, Widford Industrial Estate, Westway, Chelmsford, Essex CM1 1BQ, UK.*

Chapter 1

REGULATORY APPROACHES TO FOOD COLORATION

L. E. PARKER

*British Food Manufacturing Industries Research Association,
Leatherhead, Surrey, UK*

SUMMARY

*Legislation on the use of colours in foods arose from the need to protect the
consumer from harm and from fraudulent practices. The regulations
promulgated by the various countries world-wide differ in detail rather than
concept, as all have the same ultimate goal. In Europe, the guiding principles
have been established by the EEC, and the function of the various bodies
concerned with EEC legislation is described. The EEC Directive on colours
and its implementation in the Member States is discussed, with particular
emphasis on the UK. Differences in attitude towards the use of colours in
foods in the Scandinavian countries and in the USA and Canada are also
considered.*

1. INTRODUCTION

The practice of colouring food has been with us for centuries. Today, the
food colours permitted in most countries are allowed only when a need has
been demonstrated and their safety assured. Before these colours are
authorised for food use we can be confident that they have been subjected
to rigorous toxicological testing and numerous debates between
Government officials, scientific advisers and usually representatives from
the food industry and consumer associations. We can also be sure that the
colours themselves have been manufactured to exacting standards resulting

1

in a high degree of purity. All this we now accept as normal. It has, however, taken many years of regulatory reform to develop the current legislation that enables us to place such trust in our food supply. The evolution of this sophisticated legislation has followed a similar pattern in most countries, and is reflected in the following observation:

> The life of the law has not been logic; it has been experience. The felt necessities of the time, institutions, of public policy, avowed or unconscious, even the prejudices which judges share with their fellow men, have a good deal more to do than the syllogism in determining the rules by which men should be governed.[1]

Up until the late 1800s there was no need for a food law; prior to this Britain was essentially an agricultural country, and people were accustomed to producing their own food or trading with trusted friends or neighbours. With the onset of the industrial revolution, however, a different situation evolved. People began to move to the new centres of industrialisation and had to rely totally on food produced and sold by others. With an ever-increasing demand for food in the growing towns and cities, particularly food at low cost, commercial competition became keen, and with no legal or administrative obstacles, it is not surprising that the adulteration of food flourished. Indeed, if we believe the records of the times, it was a very profitable business, and one upon which anyone might venture with little fear of detection.

Many people became concerned about the adulteration of their food. The situation was highlighted by the publication of F. C. Accum's *Treatise on the Adulteration of Food and Culinary Poisons* in 1820. This book included a list of traders who had been found guilty of selling adulterated food, and also some indication of analytical test methods that could be used to determine whether the food had been adulterated. Although the book caused quite a stir, it was impossible to achieve legislative reform at this time because of the ignorance of the general public, opposition from the influential trade sectors and totally inadequate enforcement.

The enforcement situation was resolved to some extent by the work of Dr A. H. Hassell, which gave support to the previously published methods of detecting adulteration. The analytical methods that he had developed were published in The Lancet, and the editor of this influential journal set up what was known as The Lancet Analytical Sanitary Commission, the scientific direction of which was under the control of Dr Hassell. The Commission examined and reported on samples of food which had been purchased on the open market and, where an adverse report was obtained, this was published in The Lancet along with full details of the offender. These reports received enough publicity, aided by The Times and other influential dailies and weeklies, to arouse the public to agitate for reform. If we recall Hassell's own conclusions, drawn from his studies regarding the average daily meal, it is not difficult to see why:

> Thus, with potted meat, fish and sauces taken at breakfast he would consume more or less Armenian bole, venetian red, red lead, or even bisulphuret of mercury. At dinner with his curry or cayenne he would run the chance of a second dose of lead or mercury; with pickles, bottled fruit and vegetables he would be nearly sure to have copper administered to him; and while if he partook of bon-bons at dessert, there was no telling of the number of poisonous pigments he might consume. Again his tea if mixed or green, he would certainly not escape without the administration of a little Prussian Blue.[2]

The public reaction to this led to the establishment of a Parliamentary Select Committee Inquiry into food adulteration in 1855–6. A Bill was introduced into Parliament in 1857, but was soon withdrawn due to opposition by the interested parties. Various 'anti-adulteration' groups were set up throughout the country, the most notable being the Social Science Association in Birmingham. Although this and other groups were vociferous in their demands for reform, it took a major incident to provoke any definite reaction from the Government.

In 1858 in Bradford 200 people were poisoned, 17 of them fatally, directly as a result of eating adulterated lozenges. This gave the pressure groups considerable ammunition, and as a result of extensive lobbying, the first general Act to prevent the adulteration of food and drink was passed in 1860. Unfortunately, the Act was, for all practical purposes, impossible to enforce. It had to be proven that the person who had sold the goods had done so knowing that they were adulterated. This *mens rea* proof, it was argued, was necessary to protect the small traders, who often had no alternative but to sell goods already adulterated at source by the larger and more powerful manufacturers. While it was no doubt true that these traders had little choice in the matter, it is hardly an attitude that would be condoned today.

Arguments raged around the inclusion of the *mens rea* clause in the Act for the next decade and a half, until finally, in 1875, the Sale of Food and Drugs Act was passed. This at last omitted the word 'knowingly', and became *the* influential food law governing the aspect of public health concerned with food and drugs for the next fifty years. The attitude of the trade had changed such that they now realised that it could be to their advantage to prevent unfair practices, as this encouraged fair competition.

There were several amendments to the 1875 Act over the next few decades, but the one with the most far-reaching consequences became law on 1 January 1900. For the first time the Act gave the Board of Agriculture (established in the early 1890s) the power to make binding rules regarding standards of composition of foods. The provisions of the Act held until 1938, when major amendments were effected as part of an overall consolidation of the food and drug law concerning public health. (The amendments repealed over 250 provisions scattered over 36 Acts dating as far back as Henry VIII[3].)

A new Act (the Food and Drugs Act, 1955) contained requirements fundamental to all food laws. These are that the food should not be injurious to health, and must be of the nature, substance and quality demanded by the purchaser. This Act, as amended by the Pharmacy Act of 1968 (to 'remove' the drugs) is the Act currently in force. It was reviewed in 1979, and, in January 1980, the Ministry of Agriculture, Fisheries and Food announced that no significant changes would be necessary.

2.   LEGISLATION ON COLOURS

Although the principles of food law are the same throughout the world, the specific regulations on food additives of all types and food colours in particular vary considerably between countries. In recent years there has been a good deal of research, the results of which are often ambiguous and open to interpretation, into the safety of chemicals, especially colours, used in foods. These differences in interpretation accepted by the various countries have led to the current situation in which a colour can be considered safe and acceptable in one country, but is prohibited in another.

2.1. EEC
There are three main principles underlying the function and purpose of the EEC as regards food law. These are:

1.   Protection of the health of the consumer.
2.   Prevention of fraud.
3.   Removal of non-tariff barriers to intra-community trade.

It is the third point that necessitates the changes in the laws of the Member States and requires that harmonisation ('approximation' in the language of the EEC) be carried out. Hence we have the introduction of the harmonisation programme which is intended to bring about uniformity in those laws that affect the functioning of the Common Market while still allowing for the differences in national customs, tastes and social systems. It was as part of the harmonisation programme that the Directive on colours was introduced. Directives are made under Article 100 of the Treaty of Rome, which is concerned with the harmonisation of legislation for the purpose of free movement of goods. They have no legal force in a Member State unless their provisions have been incorporated into the national legislation. The Directives usually stipulate a transition period of several years, by the end of which the Member States are expected to have implemented the provisions where necessary.

There are two types of EEC Directive, 'horizontal' and 'vertical'. The Colours Directive is an example of a 'horizontal' Directive, the provisions of which apply across the board and affect all foodstuffs. 'Vertical' Directives are more concerned with a particular group of foodstuffs, for example, cocoa and chocolate products, and apply only to those foods defined in it.

Directives are drawn up by the European Commission. (See Fig. 1.) Members of the Commission are appointed by agreement between the Governments of the Member States and take an oath of allegiance to the Community. They are expected to remain independent of both the European Council and their own Governments.

Although only the Commission can draw up a Directive, the incentive can come from anywhere, for example, other European or national bodies or industry. In cases involving complex legislation, it is usual for the Commission to consult groups of experts from national administrations who, without committing their Governments at this stage, will give their views on the shape that the legislation should take. Consultation with an advisory committee for food, which consists of both temporary and permanent representatives of European organisations, manufacturers and consumer groups, is also customary. The Commission may also take into account the recommendations of the Codex Alimentarius Commission, the Joint FAO/WHO Expert Committee on Food Additives and the EEC Scientific Committee for Food.

Once drafted, the proposed Directive is submitted to the Council of Ministers. The 'general' Council comprises the foreign ministers representing the various Member States. It also meets in specialised form, the ministers present reflecting the subject on the agenda (for example, if the meeting is on agriculture, then it will be the agriculture ministers that are

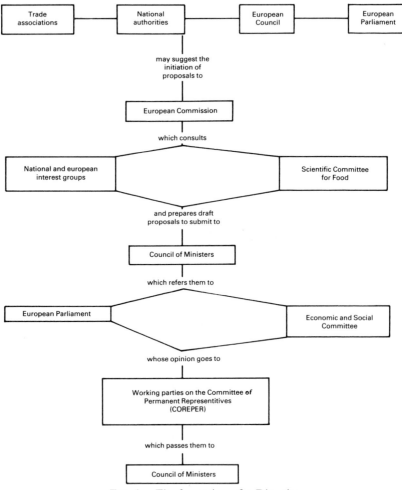

FIG. 1.   The formation of a Directive.

present). The Council Ministers are there to represent the interests of their own countries, but they also strive to achieve a solution in the interests of the Community as a whole.

When it receives a proposal, the Council circulates it to both the European Parliament and the Economic and Social Committee (ESC) for their views. It is also published in the 'C' series of the Official Journal of the European Communities, which is printed in all the official languages of the Community. The opinions of the European Parliament and the ESC are passed to the Committee of Permanent Representatives or COREPER (after its acronym in French), which comprises ambassadors from each of the Member States. The opinion of COREPER is a strong influence but the final decision remains firmly with the Council.

The Commission remains closely associated with the consideration of its proposals throughout the discussions, as it has the right to amend the proposals at any time before their final adoption by the Council. Once the final form of the Directive has been agreed by the Council, the Directive is published in the 'L' series of the Official Journal.[4,5]

2.1.1. The Colours Directive

The Council Directive on the approximation of the rules of the Member States concerning the colouring matter authorised for use in foodstuffs intended for human consumption, otherwise known as the Colours Directive, was published in the Official Journal of 11 November 1962. The Directive demands that the colours listed in Annex I 'shall not be subject to any general prohibition'. Colours listed in Annex II may be authorised if the Member State so wishes. The Directive does not specify the foods in which Member States must allow colours, nor does it establish any levels of use. It is left entirely to the discretion of the individual Member States to impose any restriction that they believe necessary. As this option is taken up to a greater or lesser extent in the various countries, manufacturers must consult national legislation to ensure that the use of a particular colour is permitted in the foods that they are producing.

In addition to listing the colours that the EEC have deemed to be suitable for food use, the Directive also establishes purity criteria. For the majority of substances, only the maximum permitted amount of insoluble material is given. There are also general purity criteria which restrict the levels of inorganic (heavy metal) and organic impurities. Substances authorised for diluting and dissolving the colouring materials are also laid down.[6]

The Directive has been amended a number of times to take into account results of more recent studies, as well as the requirements of new Member States. Provisions were included in the Treaty of Accession of Denmark, Eire and the UK to permit the use of colours that were allowed in these countries but were not authorised in the EEC. These provisions were only temporary, and expired at the end of 1977. Meanwhile, in 1974, the Scientific Committee for Foods (SCF) has been asked to review all the colours permitted for food use by the EEC and each of its Member States. In its final report, the SCF reaffirmed that, in principle, colours for which an Acceptable Daily Intake (ADI) could not be established should not be used. However, the Committee recognised that exemptions might be made in the case of compounds which are constituents of food and are derived from natural foods, provided the amounts ingested do not substantially exceed those quantities likely to be ingested as a result of the normal consumption of the foods in which they occur. In the event of widespread consumption of such a colour, it would become necessary to test for its safety and acceptability in foods. Other colours, prepared by synthesis or by physical means from sources that are not natural foods, are required to be tested for safety before acceptance.

Despite the fact that several of the colours used by the British food industry did not have an ADI assigned to them, work to assess their suitability was underway, and this, coupled with the submissions to the EEC on behalf of the manufacturers, was sufficient to persuade the EEC to amend the Colours Directive on 30 January 1978 and list most of these colours in Annex II, subject to further examination. Amongst the colours listed was Brilliant Blue FCF, and as an ADI has now been established for this colour, it has been proposed to promote it to Annex I.

While the UK was pressing for consideration of a number of colours not already on the EEC list, studies were being carried out in other parts of the world on amaranth, a colour to which an ADI had been assigned and which was on the EEC list of permitted colours. These studies resulted in the banning of amaranth in the USA, and a need to reconsider its status in the EEC. The SCF reviewed all the available data, and reaffirmed its earlier statement that, as a temporary ADI of 0–0·75 mg/kg body weight had been established for amaranth, it should remain on the EEC permitted list. The SCF did, however, recommend that further studies were desirable and necessary. The report was discussed in detail by the Member States and it was eventually agreed that amaranth should remain in Annex I, pending the completion and evaluation of the studies requested by the SCF. Some Member States argued that there should be restrictions on the use of amaranth throughout the Community, but eventually it was agreed that amaranth could not be considered in isolation. The situation was part of a much wider question as amaranth was one of the colours for which an ADI had previously been established and acceptance recommended. Instead, it was left to the discretion of the individual Member States to place restrictions as they saw fit. As we shall see later, this is precisely what has happened.

All Member States (with the exception of Greece, who has had little opportunity as yet) have incorporated the provisions of the Colours Directive into their national legislation. Hence, colours sold as such, either to the consumer or to the manufacturer, are required to be labelled in accordance with the provisions of the Directive. This means that the name and address of the manufacturer or seller established within the Community, the 'E' Number of the colour(s) present and the words 'colouring matter for foodstuffs' are required.

These declarations do not apply to foods in which the colours are present, as the labelling of foods is currently regulated entirely by separate regulations in each of the individual countries. These will be subject to considerable changes over the next few years, however, as the EEC Directive on the labelling of foodstuffs is incorporated into the national legislation of each Member State. This Directive requires that an ingredients list is present on the majority of foods, the ingredients being listed in decreasing order of weight as used. The presence of colours must be declared in the ingredients list by the generic term 'colours' followed by the specific name or the EEC Number of each of the colours present.[7]

2.1.2. United Kingdom

The first moves to discuss the use of food colours came in 1923 when the Minister of Health appointed a committee to consider all aspects of food coloration. On the basis of the report issued by this committee, regulations were drawn up and the Public Health (Preservatives etc. in Food) Regulations were made. Contrary to the advice of the committee, a 'negative' list approach was taken, and a list of colours prohibited for food use was incorporated into the regulations. It soon became obvious that this 'negative' list was a totally inadequate way of regulating colours, and following a Food Standards Committee report in 1954, new regulations incorporating a 'positive' list were issued. The Colouring Matter in Food Regulations, 1957 remained in force until 1966 when further regulations were made, again based upon recommendations arising from a formal Ministerial review.

The accession of the UK into the EEC made necessary still further changes to the food colour laws. A number of previously unlisted colours were added, and several delisted (see Table 1). In addition, a few colours used by the food industry prior to 1973 were permitted for use in the UK and Eire by the EEC on a temporary basis. The status of these colours was to be reviewed after 5 years. It was as a result of this review that several colours were added to Annex II of the EEC Colours Directive in 1978.

The Colouring Matter in Food Regulations 1973 are the regulations currently in force in the UK. The majority of the colours listed may be used in foods freely unless a compositional standard prohibits it. For example,

TABLE 1

HISTORY OF FOOD COLOURS PERMITTED IN THE EEC AND UK

Colour	E No.	Permitted in original EEC directive	Currently permitted by EEC	Permitted by 1966 UK regulations	Currently permitted in UK
Curcumin	E100	+	+		+
Lactoflavin	E101	+	+		+
Riboflavin-5'-phosphate			+[e,a]		+
Tartrazine	E102	+	+		+
Chrysoine S	E103	+		+	
Quinoline Yellow	E104	+	+		+
Fast Yellow AB	E105	+			
Sunset Yellow FCF	E110	+	+	+	+
Oil Yellow GG				+	
Oil Yellow XP				+	
Yellow 2G					+
Orange GGN	E111	+	+[e,a]	+	
Orange G				+	
Orange RN				+	
Cochineal (carminic acid)	E120	+	+	+	+
Orchil (orcein)	E121	+		+	
Carmoisine	E122	+	+	+	+
Amaranth	E123	+	+	+	+
Ponceau 4R	E124	+		+	
Ponceau 6R	E126	+			
Ponceau MX				+	
Scarlet GN	E125	+		+	
Fast Red E				+	
Red 10B				+	
Red 6B				+	
Red 2G			+[e,a]	+	+
Red FB				+	

Colour	E-number					
Erythrosine	E127	+	+	+		+[a]
Anthraquinone Blue	E130	+		+		+
Patent Blue V	E131	+	+	+	+	+
Indigo Carmine	E132	+	+	+[e,a]	+	+
Brilliant Blue FCF			+			
Violet BNP						
Chlorophylls	E140	+	+	+	+	+
Copper complexes of chlorophyll and chlorophyllins	E141	+	+	+	+	+[a]
Brilliant Green BS	E142	+	+	+	+	+
Caramel	E150	+	+	+	+	+
Brown FK			+	+[e,a]	+	
Chocolate Brown HT				+[e,a]	+	
Chocolate Brown FB						
Brilliant Black BN	E151	+	+	+	+	+
Black 7984	E152	+	+	+	+	+
Vegetable Carbon	E153	+	+	+	+	+
Carotenoids:	E160					
α-, β-, γ-Carotene	E160(a)	+	+	+	+	+
Annatto	E160(b)	+	+	+	+	+
Capsanthin	E160(c)	+	+	+	+	+
Lycopene	E160(d)		+	+	+	+
β-Apo-8-carotenal	E160(e)		+	+	+	+
Ethyl ester of β-apo-8-carotenoic acid	E160(f)			+	+	+
Flavine				+		
Xanthophylls:	E161					
Flavoxanthein	E161(a)	+	+	+	+	+
Lutein	E161(b)	+	+	+	+	+
Kryptoxanthein	E161(c)	+	+	+	+	+
Rubixanthein	E161(d)	+	+	+	+	+
Violoxanthein	E161(e)	+	+	+	+	+
Rhodoxanthein	E161(f)			+		
Canthaxanthein	E161(g)	+	+	+	+	+

(continued)

TABLE 1—contd.

Colour	E No.	Permitted in original EEC directive	Currently permitted by EEC	Permitted by 1966 UK regulations	Currently permitted by UK
Beet Red	E162	+	+		+
Anthocyanins	E163	+	+		+
Indigo				+	
Osage Orange				+	
Alkanet		+[a]		+	
Persian berry extract		+[a]		+	
Safflower				+	
Saffron				+	+
Sandalwood				+	+
Turmeric				+	+
Vegetable Carmeline		+[a]			
Ultramarine Blue		+[a,d]		+	
Pigment Rubine	E180	+[c]	+[c]		+[c]
Burnt Umber	E181	+[c]			
Calcium carbonate		+[b]	+[b]		
Titanium dioxide	E171	+[b]	+	+	+
Iron oxides and hydroxides	E172	+[b]	+[b]	+[f]	+[b]
Aluminium	E173	+[b]	+[b]	+[b]	+[b]
Silver	E174	+[b]	+[b]	+[b]	+[b]
Gold	E175	+[b]	+[b]	+[b]	+[b]

[a] Listed in Annex II as optional.
[b] For surface colouring only.
[c] For cheese rind only.
[d] For colouring sugar only.
[e] Permitted temporarily.
[f] Iron oxide only.

the Statutory Instrument that regulates bread prohibits the addition of any colour (except caramel to certain breads only).

2.1.2.1. How legislation is drawn up in the United Kingdom. For convenience, the UK is referred to here as if the same law applies throughout. As far as food law is concerned, however, there are three separate sets of regulations: one for England and Wales, one for Scotland and the third for Northern Ireland. Although the substance of the laws is generally the same, there may be differences in administrative procedure that necessitate the drawing up of separate regulations.

The usual procedure is as follows. The Ministry of Agriculture, Fisheries and Food (MAFF) jointly with the Department of Health and Social Security issue a press notice stating that the existing regulations are to be reviewed or that proposals to amend current regulations are to be circulated. In the case of a review, comments are invited and these are considered by the Food Additives and Contaminants Committee, which consists of representatives from the enforcement authorities, health authorities, industry, consumer groups and the academic world. The Committee may also consult any other sources that it deems necessary, such as studies carried out on behalf of the EEC or the US Food and Drug Administration. The report of the Committee is then published. MAFF is under no obligation to accept any or all of this report but it is unusual for a report to be totally ignored. Following the publication of the report, MAFF collects comments on the report from all interested parties before making up and circulating its proposals. If the need for an amendment to existing law or new legislation has already been established, proposals are drawn up and circulated to the appropriate parties. These include the enforcement authorities, trade and research associations and consumer groups. If the proposals are contentious, it is likely that the comments from these parties will necessitate new drafts of the proposals to be issued. Finally, the new regulations are laid before Parliament and a further press notice is sent out to announce the publication of the new law as a Statutory Instrument.

If it is necessary to amend an Act, the procedure is different in that it involves Parliament, such that a formal publication of a Bill is required rather than the simple 'laying before Parliament' which is all that is needed for regulations. The consultation with the interested parties would, of course, still take place.

2.1.2.2. Enforcement. As was demonstrated by the various Acts prior to

1875, there is no point in having a Food and Drug Act which cannot be enforced. Today, the enforcement of food legislation in the UK is effective because of the close cooperation that exists between the Government, its ministries, the food industry and the enforcement authorities themselves. The fact the legislation is drawn up only after consultation with the industries concerned usually means that the content of new laws is known to the manufacturers prior to enactment. This also means that they have had a fair amount of warning as to the likely effect of the new legislation and will have had a chance to prepare for it.

The Acts and regulations are enforced by Trading Standards Officers employed by the local authorities. They have the power to enter the premises of the manufacturer or seller and to remove samples for analysis. Their inspection is carried out on behalf of the local authority that they work for, and it is this local authority that brings prosecution in court against the offender if this is found to be necessary. Not all offences result in prosecution; in fact only a comparatively small percentage get this far. More usually, the manufacturer is given the opportunity to offer an explanation of the offence and an assurance that it will be corrected as soon as possible. Unless the offence is repeated, no action more stringent than a warning is taken.

The principles of food law enforcement in other countries are similar to those in the UK, although the detail and extent of the inspections vary considerably.

2.1.3. Belgium[8]

In Belgium, colours are regulated in the same way as all other food additives: by means of a single, comprehensive additives decree of 27 July 1978. This decree lists all additives allowed, and is divided into 14 chapters each concerned with a particular food group, such as sugar products, milk products, meat products and beverages. Each of these sections is then further divided to take into account different commodities, for example under the section on sugar products would be headings for sugars, sugar confectionery, jams and jellies, chewing gum and candied fruit. Under these headings are listed all the additives permitted in these foods, along with any restrictions. These restrictions may either be maximum levels of use (sugar confectionery may contain up to 100 ppm tartrazine, copper complexes of chlorophylls and chlorophyllins, and carotenoids; 50 ppm curcumin, erythrosine, Sunset Yellow FCF, Patent Blue V, carmoisine, Indigo Carmine and Brilliant Green BS; 20 ppm Brilliant Black BN and lactoflavin, and levels of caramel, Beetroot Red, anthocyanins, xanthophylls, Vegetable Carbon and chlorophylls in accordance with good manufacturing practice) or an indication that the additive is allowed in only very specific products (paraffin may only be used for enrobing gums and marzipan figures).

2.1.4. Luxembourg[9]

Permitted colours are listed and their use controlled by the 1969 regulation on colours. Only foods specifically mentioned in this decree are allowed to contain colours, and only the colours indicated may be used in the food. As in Belgium, maximum permitted levels are often laid down.

2.1.5. The Netherlands[10]

A regulation dated 29 December 1964 lists those colours that are permitted for food use. In addition to all those authorised by Annex I of the Directive, the Dutch also permit Brilliant Blue FCF, Chocolate Brown HT and riboflavin-5′-phosphate, thus taking advantage of the option laid down in the Directive and allowing some of the Annex II colours. The use of colours in foods is controlled entirely by compositional standards. Many of these permit the full range of authorised colours, but a number do restrict the use to certain selected colours or natural colours only. Only rarely are maximum levels of use laid down; for example the 'pudding powders' decree was amended in November 1981 to allow free use of caramel, Beet Red, anthocyanins and xanthophylls, but to limit the use of the other colours permitted to individual maxima of 20–100 mg/kg, depending on the colour concerned, and to a total maximum of 200 mg/kg. Restrictions of this nature are unusual at the moment, but are likely to become more common. Products that are not covered by a compositional standard may contain any of the permitted colours.

2.1.6. France[11]

France is considerably more restrictive than the Benelux countries over the use of colours. Most of the colours listed in Annex I of the EEC Directive are allowed in confectionery and patisserie products and instant desserts, but colours in other foods are severely restricted. There is a general preference for natural colours rather than synthetic ones.

Following the discussions in Brussels in 1976 on the fate of amaranth in the EEC, France decided that if there was to be no community-wide ban on this colour, she would restrict it. The result of this decision is, in effect, a ban on the use of amaranth for general food use, as it may only be used to colour caviar or caviar substitutes.

2.1.7. Germany[12]

The use of colours in foods in Germany is controlled by the permitted additives order of 22 December 1981. Caramel, lactoflavin, β-carotene, gold and silver may be used for foods generally unless a compositional standard prohibits it. Otherwise, all Annex I listed colours have an equal status and may be used in certain specified fish products, some fruit preserves and purées, artificial soft drinks, desserts (except those manufactured using cocoa, chocolate, coffee, eggs or caramel), artificial edible ices, candied fruit, confectionery (except liquorice and those products whose designation indicates that milk, butter, honey, egg, malt, caramel, cocoa, chocolate or coffee have been used), marzipan, certain liqueurs, and edible sausage casings. The foods specified in the regulation are the only foods in which these colours may be used unless specific permission has been obtained. No levels of use are laid down.

2.1.8. Italy[13]

Italy is probably the Member State that is the most restrictive over the use of food colours. Although sugar and flour confectionery may contain most of the permitted colours, the majority of foodstuffs are either not coloured at all, or may contain only a limited number of colours. Foods in which it is not expressly authorised to use colours must not be coloured. Authorisation is usually written into a standard of composition.

Like France, Italy would have welcomed a Community restriction of amaranth, but in the absence of such an example, followed the idea of France and now permits this colour only in caviar and caviar substitutes.

2.1.9. Denmark[14]

Like Belgium, Denmark regulates all its additives in the same way, that is by a single additives list. It is arranged in the same way as the Belgian list, by food category. The main difference between the two is that in addition to particular food groups, there is also a category to cover foods that are not included in any of the other groups. Colours listed in this latter group are annatto, Brilliant Black BN, Brilliant Blue FCF, β-carotene, copper complexes of chlorophyll and chlorophyllins, carmoisine, curcumin, erythrosine, Brilliant Green BS, Indigo Carmine, Patent Blue V, Ponceau 4R, lactoflavin, Beet Red, Sunset Yellow FCF, tartrazine, titanium dioxide, Vegetable Carbon and caramel. Most of these have maximum levels of use associated with them.

2.1.10. Eire[15]

In Eire, the situation is very much that of the UK. Any of the permitted listed colours may be used in amounts technologically necessary, provided that a compositional standard does not prohibit it. As there are very few compositional standards in Eire, this means that, in effect, colours may be used freely in the majority of foodstuffs.

2.1.11. Greece[16]

The current list of permitted food additives in Greece is similar to that of the EEC although there are several colours allowed by the EEC that are not listed for use in Greece. Under the terms of the Treaty of Accession, Greece has five years from the date which she joined the EEC (January 1981) to amend her food laws, where necessary, to implement the provisions of the EEC Directives already published.

Colours must only be used where a compositional standard allows. Synthetic colours may be added up to a maximum of 0·002 %, but natural colours can be added in amounts sufficient to achieve the desired effect.

2.2. Other Countries

The reasons behind regulating the use of colours in foods are to protect the health of the consumer and to prevent fraud. Hence the principles behind the promulgation of colours legislation is essentially the same throughout the world. The expertise and judgement of the Scientific Committee for Food is widely acknowledged, and the Committee has played a significant part in the shaping of legislation in many countries, particularly in other European countries. The major exceptions to this are the Scandinavian countries.

2.2.1. The Scandinavian Countries

The most extreme of the non-EEC Scandinavian countries is Norway,[17] which opposes the use of any synthetic colours in foods. The majority of natural colours authorised by the EEC are usually acceptable, as and when the additive list indicates that a product may be coloured. Any foods not covered by the additives list may contain any of the natural colours permitted in Norway. There are no levels of use set; amounts that are technologically necessary may be used.

Both Sweden[18] and Finland[19] also severely restrict the use of synthetic colours. The coal-tar colours amaranth, Ponceau 4R, tartrazine and Sunset Yellow FCF are allowed only in certain alcoholic beverages and, in the case of amaranth and Ponceau 4R, cocktail cherries. The use of natural colours is more strictly controlled than in Norway, and colours may only be used in foods where specified, and only up to the maximum levels indicated.

2.2.2. USA

The development of general food laws in the USA followed a similar pattern to that in Europe, although a number of years later. The arousal of Congress is attributed primarily to Dr Harvey Wiley, who was appointed chief chemist of the US Department of Agriculture in 1883. It was Dr Wiley who established the 'Poison Squad', a group of men who volunteered to eat foods that had been treated with suspect chemicals that were used in food, such as borax and salicylic acid. Much sensational publicity was given to the Poison Squad, which served to emphasise the need for a food law. By 1906, public opinion had become so vociferous that the first national law to protect the public from food adulteration was passed. This Act defined the terms 'food' and 'drug' and prohibited their trade if they were adulterated or misbranded.

Prior to the Act, there had been no Federal law against adulteration or misbranding, and individual States had exercised only limited action to prevent consumer deception. However, even these minimal restrictions had been sufficient to impede interstate trade, as the State laws that did exist were rarely compatible with each other, and trying to overcome the discrepancies was simply too much work for many of the traders.

It soon became apparent, however, that there were major faults in the 1906 Act. These were summarised in the report of the Chemist (of the US Department of Agriculture) in 1917:

While the accomplishments of the Food and Drugs Act have been considerable, it must be admitted that it has its serious limitations. Especially conspicuous ones are the lack of legal standards for foods or authority to inspect warehouses, and of any restriction whatever upon the use of many of the most virulent poisons in drugs; the limitations placed upon the word 'drug' by definition, which render it difficult to control injurious cosmetics, fraudulent medical devices used for therapeutic purposes, as well as fraudulent remedies for obesity and leanness; the limitation of dangerous adulterants to those that are added, so that the interstate shipment of a food that naturally contains a virulent poison is unrestricted. Furthermore, the law fails to take cognizance of fraudulent statements covering food and drugs which are not in or upon the food or drug package.[20]

Attempts were made to correct the deficiencies by amendments to the Act, but it soon became obvious that a new Act was necessary. In 1933, Walter G. Campbell, who was at that time Chief Chemist of the Food and Drug Administration (which had been established under that name in 1931), drafted a complete revision of the Act. Sections of the revision as it was introduced to Congress were highly controversial, and it was not until 1938 that an acceptable compromise was reached, and the Food, Drug and Cosmetic Act was passed.

This Act is currently in force, although it has been amended a number of times. The most famous amendment was the incorporation of the so-called 'Delaney Clause' in 1958. This was a result of the proposals of a Select Committee of the House of Representatives, headed by Delaney. The clause provides that a food additive should be considered unsafe 'if it is found to induce cancer when ingested by man or animal, or if it is found, after tests which are appropriate for the evaluation of safety of food additives, to induce cancer in man or animals....'

2.2.2.1. Regulations on food colours. Food colours were first controlled at Federal level in 1886 by an Act of Congress which allowed butter to be coloured. This was followed by authorisation to colour cheese, and by 1900, six years before the general food Act, colours had been specifically authorised in jellies, syrups, ketchup, wines, liquors, cordials, milk, ice-cream, confectionery, pastries, sausages, noodles, mustard, cayenne pepper and flavouring extracts. At the beginning of the 1900s, the US Department of Agriculture's Bureau of Chemistry was allocated funds to investigate the use of existing food colours. The view was taken that the synthetic 'coal-tar' colours should be allowed, provided they were harmless to health and could be shown to be necessary in a specific food application. Although this philosophy sounded simple and sensible, enforcement was practically impossible, owing in part to the sheer number of dyestuffs on the market at that time. After several years of investigations, seven colours were recommended for food use, and legalised under the Pure Food and Drug Act of 1906. The colours which were suggested are shown in Table 2. In addition it was recommended that safety testing of new colours should be carried out and sanitary manufacturing practices and purity criteria be adhered to.

These recommendations were arrived at very early in the evolution of American food legislation, and many years ahead of other countries. For example, the UK, which was a leader in general food law, did not seriously consider the use of food colours until the 1920s.

TABLE 2
FOOD COLOURS LEGALISED BY THE USA PURE FOOD AND
DRUG ACT, 1906

Common name	FD & C Number (given later)
Ponceau 3R	FD & C Red No. 1
Amaranth	FD & C Red No. 2
Erythrosine	FD & C Red No. 3
Orange I	FD & C Orange No. 1
Naphthol Yellow S	FD & C Yellow No. 1
Light Green SF Yellowish	FD & C Green No. 2
Indigo Carmine	FD & C Blue No. 2

These and other principles were upheld by the courts under the Food Inspection Decision of 1907 which stated that:

The use in food for any purpose of any mineral dye or coal-tar dye except those coal-tar dyes hereinafter listed, will be grounds for prosecution. Pending further investigations now underway, and the announcement thereof, the coal-tar dyes hereinafter named, made specifically for use in foods, and which bear a guarantee from the manufacturer that they are free from subsidiary products and represent the actual substance, the name of which they bear, may be used in foods. In every case, a certificate that the dye in question has been tested by competent experts and found to be free from harmful constituents must be filed with the Secretary of Agriculture and approved by him.

This ruling established, in effect, a voluntary certification of food colours.

By 1938, eight more colours had been added to the list, and the Food, Drug and Cosmetic Act of 1938 consequently included all 15. It also established certification of these artificially produced dyes as mandatory.

Another important development introduced by the 1938 Act was the use of FD & C numbers. The 'FD & C' indicated that they were suitable for use in foods, drugs and cosmetics, and were manufactured to a higher degree of purity than colours intended for other purposes. Dyes for industrial use could still be produced and referred to by their common names.[21]

In 1960, Congress enacted the Colour Additives Amendments to the 1938 Act, which considerably affected the laws relating to food colours. Colours were now taken out of the definition of additives, a separate term 'colour additive' being defined as 'any dye, pigment, or other substance made or obtained from a vegetable, animal, mineral or other source, and capable of colouring a food, drug, cosmetic, or the human body'.[22] All the coal-tar colours previously listed were considered to be provisionally listed and would only be allowed temporarily while further studies were undertaken. The provisional listing was valid only for a period of $2\frac{1}{2}$ years, after which the FDA Commissioner could extend the period if studies were still in progress. Most of the currently authorised synthetic colours are still only provisionally listed, a fact that caused a certain amount of confusion in the early part of 1981. The recently inaugurated President Reagan directed that a 60-day freeze on all regulations would take place. During this period, the provisional listing of most of the permitted synthetic colours expired, and the FDA Commissioner was unable to extend the time of the listing. Theoretically, this meant that for a few weeks, a vast number of food products throughout America contained 'illegal' colours and should have been confiscated. The provisional listing was, of course, re-established immediately the freeze had expired.

REFERENCES

References to national legislation include all amendments up to July 1982.

1. Holmes, O. W., *The Common Law*, 1881, Little Brown, Boston.
2. Amos, A. J. (Ed.), *Pure Food and Pure Food Legislation*, 1960, Butterworths, London.
3. Paulus, I., *The Search for Pure Food*, 1974, Martin Robertson, London.
4. Noel, E., *Working Together; The Institutions of the European Economic Community*, 1979, Commission of the European Communities, Luxembourg.
5. Jackson, R. and Fitzmaurice, J., *The European Parliament*, 1979, Penguin, London.
6. *Official Journal of the European Communities*, **5**, 82–5, 11 November 1962.
7. *Official Journal of the European Communities*, **22**, L33, 1–4, 11 February 1979.
8. Belgium. Royal arrêté fixing the list of additives authorised for foodstuffs, 27 July 1978 and Royal arrêté of 2 October 1980 concerning the trade and labelling of additives.
9. Luxembourg. Grand ducal regulation of 27 June 1969 relating to colouring materials authorised for use in foods destined for human consumption.
10. The Netherlands. Colours decree (Commodity Law), 29 December 1964.
11. France. The regulations on foodstuffs and others, R. A. Dehove, 10th edn, 1981.
12. Germany. Permitted additives order, 22 December 1981.
13. Italy. Permitted additives. Ministerial decree of 31 March 1965.
14. Denmark. List of approved food additives, National Food Institute, October 1980.

15. Eire. Health (Colouring Agents in Food) Regulations 1973, Statutory Instrument 1973 No. 149.
16. Greece. Food Code, Chapter III, Article 35, 1972.
17. Norway. List of approved food additives, 1981.
18. Sweden. List of approved food additives, 1980, SLV; FS 1980: 13.
19. Finland. Decree No. 988 of the Food Committee concerning additives for food products, 30 October 1979.
20. Middlekauff, R. D., '200 Years of US Food Law; A Gordian Knot', *Food Technology*, 1976, **30**, 48–54.
21. Anon., 'Food Colours. A Scientific Status Summary', *Food Technology*, 1980, **34**, 77–84.
22. USA. The Colour Additives Amendments of 1960, Commerce Clearing House.

Chapter 2

ANALYSIS OF SYNTHETIC FOOD COLOURS

G. WADDS†

D. F. Anstead Ltd, Billericay, Essex, UK

SUMMARY

At the present time, when food colour specifications are being widely reviewed, there is still a shortage of published, official analytical methodology, particularly within the EEC. For permitted water-soluble food dyes, their corresponding aluminium lakes and the inorganic food pigments, the analytical considerations are different in each category. Those methods which are published for different types of colourants conforming to different specifications, are distributed throughout the technical literature and are often difficult for the analyst to locate.

Food colour additive regulations frequently make special demands upon the supporting analytical methods and on the equipment needed to perform those methods. A selection of useful methods is reviewed and some tried and tested approaches are offered. A collection of analytical reference data which should be of value in both qualitative and quantitative aspects of food colourant analysis is also given.

1. INTRODUCTION

In most countries of the world the coloration of food is regulated by Government statute. This is usually achieved by the publication of permitted lists and purity specifications for each colourant and sometimes by the limitation of permitted colourant levels in certain food products.

† *Present address:* Britvic Ltd, Chelmsford, Essex, UK.

There are four major bodies currently active in the formulation of food additive regulations and specifications. These are the American Food and Drug Administration (FDA), the EEC Scientific Committee for Food (SCF), the UK Food Additive and Contaminants Committee (FACC) and the Joint FAO/WHO Expert Committee on Food Additives (JECFA). These bodies not only recognise the need to safeguard the health of the consumer, but they also recognise the need to avoid barriers to trade which may be caused by differences in regulatory controls. It is therefore in the interests of all countries to strive ultimately towards a common list of permitted food additives conforming to internationally acceptable purity specifications, which are both stringent enough to protect the consumer and reasonably attainable by industrial manufacturers.

Proper control of colourants (by all interested parties) depends on the implementation of suitable qualitative and quantitative analytical methods. Food colours are analysed at all levels of complexity, ranging from the cursory examination for confirmation of identity, to the exhaustive purity determination that might be carried out by a public analyst or Government laboratory. The testing procedures that are used depend on the regulations that are in force and the specifications implicit in those regulations.

1.1. EEC Requirements
In the EEC most permitted food colourants carry an 'E' specification, which is made up of two parts:

1.   General criteria for organic and inorganic impurities defined in the same way for all permitted colours.
2.   Specific purity criteria which relate to each individual colour.

Thus, the colour must comply with all the general and specific purity requirements in order to qualify as a food colour with an 'E' number. It is a major problem within the EEC that virtually no official methods are published for the analysis of food colourants against their legal specifications.

1.2. FDA Requirements
By way of contrast, in the US, FDA specifications for food, drug and cosmetic colourants are supported by published methods, many of which are acknowledged as official methods and reported as such by the Association of Official Analytical Chemists.[1] Other publications also carrying useful summaries of American methodology are by Marmion[2] and

Venkataraman.[3] FDA colour additive specifications tend to differ from their European counterparts by placing lower limits on a smaller number of heavy metals (usually including lead and arsenic) and by limiting a smaller number of organic contaminants. Moisture and diluent limits are usually included and a minimum pure colour content is required.

1.3. FAO/WHO Requirements
Although food colour specifications recommended by the Food and Agriculture Organisation and the World Health Organisation (FAO/WHO) carry no legal mandate, they are intended to have an international application and are often adopted by countries having no alignment with either the USA or the EEC. FAO/WHO recommended specifications[4] frequently contain analytical methods which are designed to support specified parameters. These methods of identification and purity determination are usually quite basic and classical in nature, intended for the analyst who may not have access to advanced instrumentation. The methods are not intended to be referee methods, but are generally applicable to materials available in international commerce.

It is not intended that this chapter should catalogue all official and unofficial methods for the analysis of synthetic colourants. Any attempt to do this would undoubtedly confuse the reader with a surfeit of alternatives. With the shortage of up-to-date official methodology (particularly within the EEC) there is felt to be a need to summarise those methods which are considered most useful and which are most generally applied throughout industry.

2. SYNTHETIC DYES

2.1. Qualitative Identification
A variety of methods for colour additive identification have been reported in detail,[2,3] but this is commonly achieved by spectrophotometric or chromatographic methods, or by a combination of both.

2.1.1. Spectrophotometry
Most of today's laboratories possess scanning UV/visible spectrophotometers for a wide range of analytical applications. Solutions of food dyes in 0·02% ammonium acetate buffer at pH 6 exhibit reproducible characteristic absorption spectra, which offer the most convenient means of identification (see Appendix). Such curves yield both qualitative and quantitative information which is valuable to the analyst.

The distinguishing features of these spectra may be significantly affected by careful adjustment of the pH of the dye solutions towards acid or alkali, thus providing a valuable additional degree of discrimination.[5] For example, it is important to be able to distinguish between Patent Blue V (CI 42051) and Blue VRS (CI 42045) because only the former is permitted as a food colour in certain areas of the world. These two dyes are structurally very similar and are difficult to differentiate from one another by most test procedures. Their absorption spectra under neutral and acidic conditions are essentially identical. However, unlike Blue VRS, Patent Blue V contains a phenolic hydroxyl group, which dissociates in alkali beyond pH 10 to form a phenolate anion. This species has a λ_{max} at 630 nm, enabling it to be distinguished from Blue VRS which does not exhibit the same wavelength shift in alkaline conditions.[6]

The following scheme is recommended as a simple means of identifying most water-soluble dyestuffs:[1]

Prepare a neutral solution of the dye at a concentration suitable for spectrophotometric analysis (0·001–0·01 %). Divide the solution into three portions and to one portion add a few crystals of ammonium acetate. To the second and third portions add dilute hydrochloric acid and dilute sodium hydroxide respectively to make them about 0·1 N. Determine the spectrophotometric curves of these solutions and compare them with the corresponding curves of known dyes under the same conditions.

If the spectrophotometric data cannot be correlated with a known colour, the unknown colour may be a mixture requiring chromatographic separation. For absolute confirmation of identity, a spectroscopic identification usually requires the support of a suitable chromatographic technique, particularly if spectrally interfering substances may be present.

2.1.2. Simple Chromatography
Paper chromatography (PC) has been used for very many years for the identification of food dyes,[3,6,7] and some suitable separation systems are shown in Table 1. Reports of effective thin-layer chromatographic systems (TLC) are also plentiful in the literature.[3,7,8] Some satisfactory examples may be found in Table 2. It should be remembered that the Rf values of water-soluble food dyes are affected by a number of variables, and a positive identification should only be achieved against a standard substance chromatographed in several different systems.

More recently, the sulphonic and carboxylic acid functions of food dyes

TABLE 1
PAPER CHROMATOGRAPHY OF FOOD
DYES—SOME USEFUL SOLVENT SYSTEMS

1. Butanone	70 ml
Acetone	30 ml
Water	30 ml
2. Butanone	70 ml
Acetone	30 ml
Water	30 ml
SG 0·88 ammonia	0·2 ml
3. Trisodium citrate	2 g
Water	95 ml
SG 0·88 ammonia	5 ml
4. Isobutanol	25 ml
Ethanol	50 ml
Water	25 ml

TABLE 2
TLC OF FOOD DYES ON SILICA GEL G—
SOME USEFUL SOLVENT SYSTEMS

1. Isopropanol	70 ml
SG 0·88 ammonia	20 ml
Water	10 ml
2. Ethyl acetate	65 ml
Pyridine	25 ml
Water	10 ml
3. n-Butyl acetate	30 ml
Pyridine	45 ml
Water	25 ml
4. n-Butanol	60 ml
Ethanol	10 ml
Glacial acetic acid	0·5 ml
Water	20 ml

have been exploited by their extraction and separation as ion-pairs. The use of ion-pair TLC on reverse-phase systems[9] has allowed faster and more efficient separations of anionic dyes to be carried out (see Table 3). Paired-ion extraction has also been demonstrated as a useful means of isolating acidic dyes from foodstuffs.[9]

An evaluation of PC, TLC and High Pressure Liquid Chromatographic (HPLC) techniques for the separation of food colours, both as free dyes and as their ion-pairs, has been reported.[10]

TABLE 3
PAIRED-ION TLC OF FOOD DYES (SILICA
GEL/CTMA)—SOME USEFUL SOLVENT
SYSTEMS[9]

1. Methanol	90 ml
Acetone	10 ml
Glacial acetic acid	1 ml
CTMA counter ion	0·1 M
2. Methanol	50 ml
Acetone	50 ml
CTMA counter ion	0·1 M

Reverse-phase plates prepared by immersion for 1 min in fresh 0·1 M counter ion (cetyltrimethylammonium bromide) in methanol, followed by careful drying in hot air.[9]

2.1.3. HPLC

The rapid development of HPLC instrumentation in recent years has resulted in the publication of various procedures for the separation, identification and determination of mixed food dyes. Reasonably effective separations have been achieved on ion-exchange columns[11] and by paired-ion chromatography on reverse-phase systems,[12,13,14] but both approaches have inherent disadvantages. Because of the complex equilibria involved in paired-ion HPLC and the long re-equilibration times that are sometimes necessary between gradient elution programmes, repeatability of retention data can be a problem.

Very efficient and repeatable separations of quite complex dye mixtures can be achieved using reverse-phase gradient elution of the unpaired colours on 7·5 × 0·5 cm columns packed with spherical 3 μm octadecyl silica.[15] This ion-suppression technique appears to allow more selectivity than the alternative approaches and is ideal for identification purposes (see Figs 1, 2 and 3). The operating conditions for these separations were as follows:

HPLC conditions for the analysis of food dyes
   Sample: A mixture of dyes at a concentration of approximately 300 mg/ml of each. 5 ml injected.
   Column: 7·5 × 0·5 cm Ultrasphere ODS 3 μm.
   Solvent A: 0·1 M sodium sulphate adjusted to pH 2·5 with phosphoric acid.
   Solvent B: 15 ml solvent A
           70 ml water
           220 ml methanol
   Gradient Programme:

Time	Function	Value	Duration
0	%B	100	20
30	%B	0	5
55	Stop		

   Flow Rate: 1·5 ml/min.
   Chart Speed: 0·5 cm/min.

Modern equipment (see Fig. 4) permits the rapid spectral scanning of component peaks as they elute, thus providing an unequivocal identification of mixed colours in one operation via their spectral and retention characteristics. 'On the fly' spectra may be scanned in 8–12 s without stopping the solvent flow.

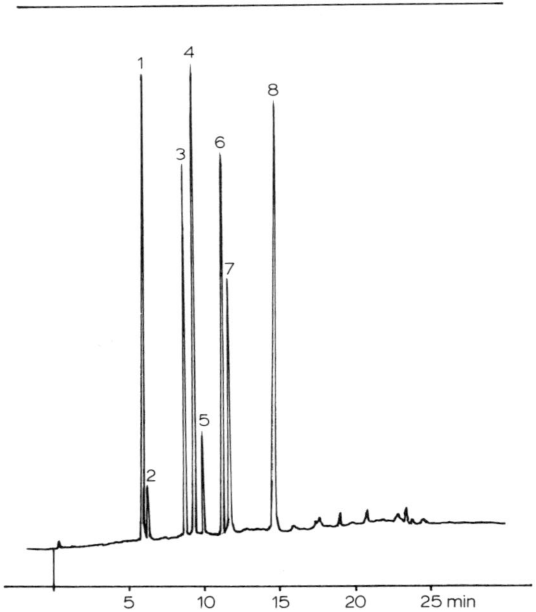

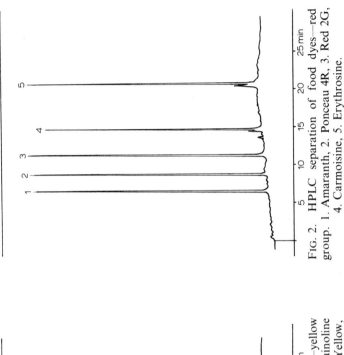

FIG. 2. HPLC separation of food dyes—red group. 1. Amaranth, 2. Ponceau 4R, 3. Red 2G, 4. Carmoisine, 5. Erythrosine.

FIG. 1. HPLC separation of food dyes—yellow group. 1. Tartrazine, 2. Quinoline Yellow, 3. Quinoline Yellow, 4. Sunset Yellow FCF, 5. Quinoline Yellow, 6. Yellow 2G, 7. Quinoline Yellow, 8. Brown HT.

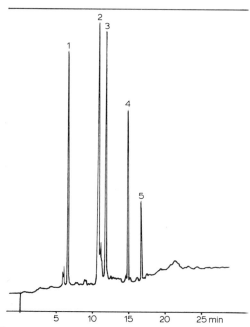

FIG. 3.   HPLC separation of food dyes—blue group. 1. Indigo Carmine, 2. Black PN, 3. Green S, 4. Brilliant Blue FCF, 5. Patent Blue V.

FIG. 4.   High pressure liquid chromatograph. Courtesy of Altex Beckman.

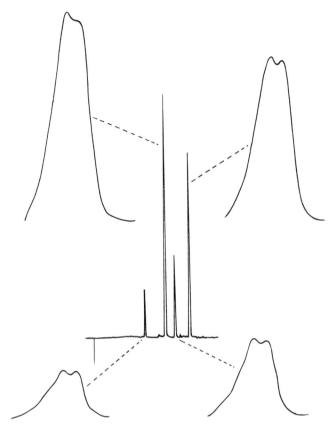

FIG. 5. HPLC separation/spectrophotometry of Quinoline Yellow components.

By continually reverting back to a fixed solvent or air reference, these curves are electronically compensated for concentration changes that take place in the detector cell during the scan. Providing the peaks are large enough, they are more than adequate for qualitative purposes (see Fig. 5). With the growing power and reliability of HPLC equipment, such systems are expected to be more widely used in future for the identification and determination of colourants.

2.2. Quantitative Analysis of Major Components

The major components of full strength synthetic water-soluble food colours are active dye (including subsidiary dyes), inorganic salts and moisture. Summation of the analytical determinations for these three constituent

TABLE 4
TITRATION WITH 0·1 N TITANOUS CHLORIDE

Dye	FD & C No.	CI No.	E No.	Molecular weight	Milliequivalent weight	F ml/g	Buffer
Yellow 2G	—	18965	—	551·3	0·1378	72·56	Citrate
Tartrazine	Yellow No. 5	19140	E 102	534·4	0·1336	74·85	Tartrate
Sunset Yellow FCF	Yellow No. 6	15985	E 110	452·4	0·1131	88·42	Citrate
Ponceau 4R	—	16255	E 124	604·5	0·1511	66·17	Citrate
Carmoisine	—	14720	E 122	502·4	0·1256	79·62	Tartrate
Amaranth	—	16185	E 123	604·5	0·1511	66·17	Citrate
Red 2G	—	18050	—	509·4	0·1274	78·52	Tartrate
Ponceau SX	Red No. 4	14700	—	480·4	0·1201	83·26	Tartrate
Allura Red	Red No. 40	16035	—	496·4	0·1241	80·58	Tartrate
Patent Blue V	—	42051	E 131	1159·5	0·2899	34·50	Tartrate
Indigo Carmine	Blue No. 2	73015	E 132	466·4	0·2332	42·88	Tartrate
Brilliant Blue FCF	Blue No. 1	42090	—	792·8	0·3964	25·23	Tartrate
Green S	—	44090	E 142	576·6	0·2883	34·69	Tartrate
Fast Green FCF	Green No. 3	42053	—	808·9	0·4045	24·72	Tartrate
Brown HT	—	20285	—	652·6	0·0816	122·6	Tartrate
Black PN	—	28440	E 151	867·7	0·1085	92·20	Concentrated HCl

classes should give a result in the region of 100 %, after making allowances for cumulative experimental error. Food dye samples which fail to answer this characterisation should be more exhaustively examined for the presence of other components. These other constituents may be permitted (or non-permitted) diluents which are deliberately added for standardisation purposes or to ease the incorporation of the dye for certain applications.

2.2.1. Dye Content

2.2.1.1. Titrimetry.

Monoazo, disazo, indigoid and triarylmethane (TAM) dyes are generally readily reducible by titanous chloride reagent and this has formed the basis of the traditional assay method for most food dyes.[1,2,4,16] Notable exceptions are erythrosine (xanthene type) and Quinoline Yellow (quinophthalone type), which are not reducible and have to be assayed by other means. The theoretical milliequivalent weights and titration factors against 0·1 N titanous chloride for the remaining food colours are shown in Table 4. The method is as follows:

Preparation of 0·1 N titanous chloride solution. Add 100 ml of 15–20 % titanous chloride concentrate to 100 ml concentrated hydrochloric acid and boil briefly to expel oxygen. Dilute the mixture to 1 litre with freshly boiled water and transfer it to a suitable aspirator. Bubble carbon dioxide through the solution for a few minutes and store the reagent under carbon dioxide to prevent oxidation.

Standardisation procedure. Accurately weigh 3 g ferrous ammonium sulphate into a titration flask which is continuously guarded by a stream of carbon dioxide. Add 50 ml freshly boiled water and 25 ml 10 N sulphuric acid followed by 50·0 ml 0·1 N potassium dichromate. Back-titrate the excess dichromate until the end point is almost reached, then add 5 ml 20 % w/v ammonium thiocyanate solution as indicator. Continue titrating until the red colour of the iron thiocyanate complex is permanently discharged. Carry out a reagent blank determination and correct for it, then calculate the strength of the titanous chloride.

$$\text{Normality} = \frac{50 \times \text{normality potassium dichromate}}{\text{ml titanous chloride (corrected)}}$$

Titration procedure. Accurately weigh a quantity of dye sample, equal to about 2 milliequivalents, into a carbon dioxide guarded titration flask (see Table 4). Weigh 10 g of appropriate buffer salt (trisodium citrate or sodium hydrogen tartrate—see Table 4) into the flask and add 150 ml water. Pass carbon dioxide through the flask, bring the solution to boiling, and titrate the dye under carbon dioxide while on the boil until the colour disappears.

Dye content

$$= \frac{\text{ml titanous chloride} \times \text{normality titanous chloride} \times 1000}{\text{sample weight} \times \text{titration factor } F} \%$$

Colour manufacturers usually find it convenient to use titanous chloride titration as a regular method of dye strength determination. On the other hand, colour users seldom carry out enough pure dye determinations to warrant specialised titration equipment and preparation of the titrant.

2.2.1.2. Spectrophotometry. Spectrophotometric methods are commonly used for the assay of food dyes. The procedures are simple, but some care is necessary to achieve dependable results. The spectrophotometer should be a UV/visible instrument, and preferably with a scanning and recording facility for it to be of maximum use in other aspects of colour additive analysis (see also Sections 2.1 and 2.3). Good photometric

TABLE 5
SPECTROPHOTOMETRY IN pH BUFFER

Dye	FD & C No.	E No.	λ_{max} (nm)	$E_{1\,cm}^{1\%}$
Yellow 2G	—	—	400	450
Quinoline Yellow	—	E 104	414	800
Tartrazine	Yellow No. 5	E 102	426	527
Sunset Yellow FCF	Yellow No. 6	E 110	480	551
Brown FK	—	—	435	457
Brown HT	—	—	462	367
Ponceau SX	Red No. 4	—	502	540
Allura Red	Red No. 40	—	502	556
Ponceau 4R	—	E 124	505	431
Carmoisine	—	E 122	515	545
Amaranth	—	E 123	523	438
Red 2G	—	—	(504)/528	620
Erythrosine	Red No. 3	E 127	526	1 154
Black PN	—	E 151	568	553
Indigo Carmine	Blue No. 2	E 132	610	489
Fast Green FCF	Green No. 3	—	625	1 560
Brilliant Blue FCF	Blue No. 1	—	629	1 637
Green S	—	E 142	632	1 720
Patent Blue V	—	E 131	635	2 000

FIG. 6.   Scanning UV/visible spectrophotometer. Courtesy of Pye Unicam Ltd.

accuracy ($\pm 1\%$), wavelength accuracy (± 1 nm) and overall stability
(0.001 A/h) are essential. A maximum effective bandwidth of 2 nm is also
desirable. Most modern instruments of this type (see Fig. 6) have the
necessary performance requirements but periodic maintenance and
calibration checks are recommended for maximum reliability. The method
is as follows:

Accurately weigh about 0.1 g finely ground dye sample, transfer
quantitatively to a 500 ml volumetric flask with water and dilute to
standard volume. Ensure that dissolution is complete at this stage.
Pipette 10 ml of this solution to a 100 ml volumetric flask and dilute to
standard volume with 0.02% ammonium acetate solution. (Stronger
dyes such as Patent Blue V or Green S may require greater dilution to
bring their absorbance within the measuring range of the spectrophotometer).

Measure the absorbance of the dye solution in a 1 cm cell at the
absorption maximum and make solvent/cell blank corrections as
necessary. Calculate the dye content of the sample using the $E_{1\,cm}^{1\%}$ value
corresponding to 100% pure dye (see Table 5).

$$\text{Dye content} = \frac{\text{absorbance} \times \text{dilution factor } (\%)}{\text{standard } E_{1\,cm}^{1\%} \times \text{sample weight}}$$

2.2.1.3. Gravimetry. Erythrosine is the only commonly used food dye
which is insoluble in dilute acid, and which can consequently be assayed

gravimetrically. In the US it is the convention to calculate the pure dye as the disodium salt monohydrate. Elsewhere in the world, the pure dye content is expressed as the anhydrous disodium salt. The gravimetric factors for converting from the precipitated acid form to 'pure dye' are 1·074 and 1·053 respectively.

The AOAC[1] describes a method whereby 0·5 g colour is dissolved in 100 ml water, 25 ml dilute hydrochloric acid (2 %) is added and the solution is boiled for several hours to coagulate the precipitate. After cooling and transferring to a tared Gooch crucible with dilute hydrochloric acid (1 %), the precipitate is washed with water (2 × 15 ml) and dried for 3 h at 135 °C. The crucible is finally cooled in a desiccator and weighed.

$$\text{Dye content} = \frac{\text{precipitate weight} \times 1 \cdot 074 \times 100 \%}{\text{sample weight}}$$

The FAO/WHO method[4] requires the dissolution of 1 g erythrosine sample in 250 ml water and the addition of 8·0 ml of 1·5 N nitric acid to precipitate the acid form of the dye. This is then filtered through a sintered glass crucible (porosity 3) which has been tared containing a small glass stirring rod. The precipitate is washed with dilute nitric acid (0·5 %) until the filtrate gives no turbidity with 0·25 N silver nitrate solution and is then washed with 30 ml water. After drying at 135 °C to constant weight, using the glass rod to break up the precipitate, the crucible is cooled and weighed.

$$\text{Dye content} = \frac{\text{precipitate weight} \times 1 \cdot 053 \times 100 \%}{\text{sample weight}}$$

2.2.2. Inorganic Salts

Inorganic salts, either added deliberately or present as by-products, may be significantly large components of water-soluble food colours. Sodium chloride is most commonly found, but some dyes such as Green S and Indigo Carmine often contain substantial amounts of sodium sulphate. Food colours which assay at 70 % dye content or less have usually been further diluted by addition of an extender. Apart from sodium chloride and sodium sulphate such extenders may include sodium carbonate, sodium bicarbonate and various carbohydrates, oils, fats and organic acids.

The classical method for the determination of chloride is the Volhard method:

Accurately weigh about 2 g dye into a 250 ml beaker and dissolve in water. Add 10 g activated carbon and boil gently for 2–3 min before allowing to cool to room temperature. Add 3 ml 2 N nitric acid and stir vigorously. Transfer the mixture to a 200 ml volumetric flask, washing out the beaker thoroughly, and dilute to standard volume with water. Filter the solution through a dry filter paper into another flask. If the dye is not completely absorbed, add further 2 g portions of carbon until the filtrate is colourless. Pipette 50 ml filtrate into a 250 ml stoppered conical flask and add 6 ml 2 N nitric acid. Then add 10 ml standard 0·1 N silver nitrate solution (or sufficient to give a 2–5 ml excess depending on the chloride content) and 2 ml nitrobenzene. Stopper the flask and shake it vigorously until the precipitate coagulates and then add 1 ml saturated ferric ammonium sulphate solution as indicator. Titrate the excess silver nitrate with standard 0·1 N ammonium thiocyanate solution until a red colour persists for 1 min with shaking. (The calculation assumes that 10 g activated carbon occupies 5 ml):

$$\text{Sodium chloride} = \frac{[(10 \times N_1) - (\text{titre} \times N_2)] \times 0·005\,85 \times 195 \times 100\,\%}{\text{sample weight} \times 50}$$

N_1 is normality of silver nitrate solution
N_2 is normality of ammonium thiocyanate solution.

This traditional method is adequate for analysing chloride in dyes, but can be tedious and time-consuming, especially for just one or two determinations. Electrometric methods obviate the need to decolorise the sample solution and are much more convenient in practice.

The automatic potentiometric titration described by Graichen and Bailey[17] represents a worthwhile improvement, but still requires the use of a silver nitrate solution which has to be standardised beforehand.

A most satisfactory method involves the use of a dedicated chloride analyser which depends upon the coulometric liberation of silver to precipitate silver chloride. The determination runs automatically to a dead-stop end point and requires little or no calibration. The sample requirements of different models vary, but the equipment illustrated (see Fig. 7) accepts 0·5 ml samples containing up to 0·165 % sodium chloride. For most dyes, it is only necessary to prepare a 1 % aqueous solution of the sample to be treated. Then,

$$\text{Sodium chloride} = \frac{\text{Result displayed (mg\%)}}{10}\ \%$$

Sodium sulphate is usually present below the 1 % level in most full strength food dyes, but can occasionally be found as a major component.

FIG. 7.   Chloride analyser. Courtesy of Corning Ltd.

Like sodium chloride, it may also be determined by gravimetric or electrometric means.

One gravimetric method depends on decolorising the dye sample (2 g) with activated carbon, using the same procedure as described for sodium chloride.

Take 50 ml of the colourless filtrate in a 250 ml beaker and add 20 ml 0·2 N barium chloride solution dropwise, with stirring. Boil the suspension and keep it hot on a steam bath for 3 h. Allow the beaker to cool overnight and filter the precipitate through a tared sintered glass crucible (porosity 3). Wash the precipitate with water and then with small volumes of ethanol. Remove the solvent on a vacuum line and dry the crucible in an oven to constant weight. Calculate the sodium sulphate content from the precipitate weight.

$$\text{Sodium sulphate} = \frac{\text{precipitate weight} \times 0\cdot6086 \times 195 \times 100}{\text{sample weight} \times 50}\%$$

The gravimetric method for determination of sulphates quoted by the British Standards Institution[16] and the FAO/WHO[18] avoids the use of activated carbon, but depends on a salting out process to remove excess dye. The procedure is as follows:

Accurately weigh about 5 g dye sample into a 250 ml conical flask and dissolve it in about 100 ml hot water. Add 35 g sodium chloride, stopper the flask and swirl frequently during 1 h. Cool, transfer with saturated sodium chloride solution to a 250 ml standard flask and dilute to volume. Shake the flask and filter the solution through a dry filter paper. Pipette 100 ml filtrate into a 500 ml beaker, dilute to 300 ml with water and acidify with concentrated hydrochloric acid, adding 1 ml in excess. Boil the solution and add an excess of 0·25 N barium chloride solution dropwise with stirring. Heat the mixture on a hotplate for 4 h or leave overnight at room temperature, then bring it to 80 °C and allow the precipitate to settle. Filter the precipitated barium sulphate, wash with hot water and ignite to constant weight in a tared sintered glass crucible. Carry out a blank determination, correcting the precipitate weight as necessary and calculate the sodium sulphate content of the dye.

$$\text{Sodium sulphate} = \frac{2 \cdot 5 \times \text{corrected precipitate weight} \times 0 \cdot 6086 \times 100 \%}{\text{sample weight}}$$

It is possible to titrate soluble sulphate with a standard solution of lead nitrate, detecting the end-point electrometrically. A selective ion electrode can achieve this in principle but the electrode is rapidly poisoned by large excess of dye. A potentiometric titration method using lead nitrate and a recording autotitrator has been published.[19] This correlates quite well with the official FDA method[1] and requires little sample preparation, but is not applicable to erythrosine (FD & C Red No. 3).

2.2.3. Moisture
The standard procedure for volatile matter or loss on drying is as follows:

Accurately weigh about 2 g dye sample into a tared squat-form weighing bottle with a ground-glass lid. Heat the open bottle in an oven at 135 ± 5 °C until constant weight is obtained. Express the weight loss as a percentage of the sample weight.

This method is universally used but takes at least a few hours to perform and requires repeated heating, cooling and weighing to be certain of the correct result. Not only is this labour intensive, but the time delay in quality control is sometimes unacceptable in the industrial environment.

The Karl Fischer technique of moisture determination has been shown to

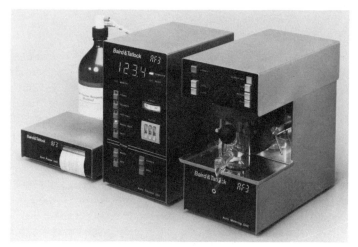

FIG. 8. Karl Fischer Autotitrator. Courtesy of Baird and Tatlock Ltd.

correlate closely with drying loss measurements for most food dyes and is frequently used as an alternative method. The introduction of the direct reading Karl Fischer Autotitrator makes it possible to determine moisture content in 1 or 2 min once the instrument has been standardised. (See Fig. 8). Time-saving aspects of such equipment can make it quite cost-effective in a busy laboratory where several moisture determinations form part of the daily routine. Samples containing 2–100 mg water can be analysed with a precision of 0·3 % at moisture levels of 50 mg or more. For powdered dye samples the procedure is:

Calibrate the instrument to determine the water equivalent of Karl Fischer reagent using a 50 μl water sample from a micro-pipette. This is necessary at least daily or prior to a series of analyses because of the instability of the reagent.

Accurately weigh (preferably by difference on a top-pan balance) 0·3–1 g dye sample, introduce it into the titration cell by briefly raising the top of the unit, and start the titration. When the determination is finished, read the mg water determined and calculate it as a percentage of the sample weight.

$$\text{Moisture content} = \frac{\text{result displayed (mg)} \times 100\,\%}{\text{sample weight (mg)}}$$

2.3. Quantitative Analysis of Minor Components

Quantitative methods are required for those impurities (organic or inorganic) for which a maximum limit is declared in the colour additives specification. These limits may vary from one regulatory authority to another and also from one colourant to another. Uncoloured organic impurities are generally described as intermediates whereas those that are coloured are regarded as subsidiary dyes. The latter are structural variants of the main dye and make some contribution to the dye content assay. Methods for the analysis of subsidiary dyes therefore depend on a chromatographic separation of one form or another.

2.3.1. Subsidiary Dyes

For many years, ascending paper chromatography has been effectively used to separate subsidiary dyes in food colours and this technique is still adequate for most purposes. It is more time consuming than most HPLC methods, but has the advantage of using inexpensive equipment. The most suitable solvent system depends on the dye under examination,[16,18,20,21] but solvent mixtures 2 and 3 shown in Table 1 can be used for most permitted dyes. The basic procedure is as follows:

At least 2 h before commencing the separation, equilibrate the atmosphere in the chromatographic tank with the appropriate solvent mixtures using suitable drapes or liners. With a micro-pipette apply 0·1 ml of a 1 % aqueous dye solution (i.e. 1 mg dyestuff) as a narrow stripe 2·5 cm from the bottom of a sheet of Whatman No. 1 chromatography paper. Thoroughly dry the sample stripe and develop the chromatogram in the equilibrated tank alongside a blank reference sheet of chromatography paper. After development, dry the chromatogram and cut off the separated subsidiary bands. Cut a corresponding strip for each band from the reference sheet, extract each strip (cut into pieces) in a separate tube with 10·0 ml of 50 % aqueous acetone and filter each extract through a small filter paper. With a suitable spectrophotometer, measure the absorbance A of each coloured extract at its peak wavelength using the corresponding reference extract as a blank.

Using the $E^{1\%}_{1\,cm}$ value for the main dyestuff, calculate the subsidiary dye content as a percentage of the total dyestuff. In each 10 ml extract,

$$\text{Subsidiary dye} = \frac{100 \times A}{E^{1\%}_{1\,cm}} \text{ mg}$$

Therefore,

$$\text{Total subsidiaries extracted} = \frac{100(A_1 + A_2 + \cdots)}{E^{1\%}_{1\,cm}} \text{ mg}$$

$$= \frac{10\,000(A_1 + A_2 + \cdots)}{E^{1\%}_{1\,cm}} \%$$

Many TLC systems for the separation and determination of subsidiary colours in synthetic food dyes have been reported, but a useful summary covering all the American colours is given by Venkataraman.[3] A collection of various methods for the analysis of subsidiaries in certain individual colourants has been made by Marmion.[2]

Idealised HPLC chromatograms for most EEC permitted food dyestuffs have been published[22] showing the elution order of most expected minor components including subsidiary dyes. These separations were carried out using gradient elution anion exchange techniques very similar to those employed by FDA.[1,2,3] Variations on this approach using, for instance, paired-ion or ion-suppression chromatography, can also give separations which are suitable for the determination of subsidiary dyes.[23,24,25] The ion-suppression technique described in Section 2.1.3 shows sufficient resolving power to be useful for the determination of minor components in most synthetic food dyes.

2.3.2. Synthetic Intermediates

The traditional method of analysing synthetic intermediates is classical column chromatography/UV spectrophotometry, although in recent years HPLC has become the method of choice.

The classical technique is widely described[1,2,3,18] and readily gives fairly dependable results, but is slow to perform. This column chromatographic procedure may be carried out as follows:

Prepare the column by slurrying 12 g Whatman CF 11 cellulose powder (or equivalent) with about 100 ml water and transferring it to a glass column approximately 50 cm long and 2 cm in diameter. After settling, wash the packing through with 100 ml water followed by 40 ml ammonium sulphate eluent solution (25 % w/v).

Slurry 2 g cellulose powder with 10 ml eluent solution and 5 ml aqueous 1 % dye solution (= 50 mg dye) and quantitatively transfer the slurry to the top of the column using small amounts of the eluent solution. Continue to pass the ammonium sulphate diluent solution through the column, collecting 50 ml fractions until the colour begins to elute.

Using ammonium sulphate eluent solution as a blank, scan the UV absorption spectrum of each collected fraction and measure the absorbance A at each significant absorption peak. Divide each fraction into two halves, making one acidic and one alkaline by the addition of concentrated hydrochloric acid and SG 0·88 ammonia respectively.

From the $E_{1\,cm}^{1\%}$ value of each identified intermediate (see Table 6), calculate the amount of intermediate in each fraction.

$$\text{Weight of intermediate found} = \frac{A \times 500}{E_{1\,cm}^{1\%}}\,\text{mg}$$

$$\text{Total intermediates} = \frac{\text{Sum of weights found}}{50} \times 100\,\%$$

If $E_{1\,cm}^{1\%}$ values are not available for the intermediates detected, standard solutions of the purified individual compounds should be made up in the ammonium sulphate eluent, examined spectrophotometrically and used for comparative purposes.

HPLC techniques for the determination of synthetic intermediates in anionic dyes usually employ separation on strong anion exchange (SAX) columns with a gradient elution programme.[2,3,22] Invariably the primary eluent is 0·01 M sodium tetraborate and the secondary eluent is 0·01 M sodium tetraborate incorporating sodium perchlorate at concentrations of 0·1 M–0·5 M, depending on the dye under examination. Anion exchange HPLC procedures have been reported for the determination of intermediates in tartrazine,[26,27] Sunset Yellow,[28,29] amaranth,[26] Allura Red[30,31] and Indigo Carmine.[32] These methods are typical of those used by the FDA to control the quality of certified dyestuffs, but such procedures are limited in selectivity, especially with closely related substances.

The use of reverse-phase HPLC with buffered eluents and composition gradients can produce impressive separation of dye components in a shorter analysis time and has the potential for automation. Reverse-phase HPLC methods for the determination of intermediates in Indigo Carmine[25] and erythrosine[33] have been reported and evaluated. It is expected that similar methods will become more widely used in future for the separation and quantitation of intermediates closely resembling one another in terms of structure, λ_{max} and $E_{1\,cm}^{1\%}$ value. (See Table 6.)

2.3.3. Primary Aromatic Amines

The content of unsulphonated primary aromatic amines in synthetic food dyestuffs is limited to 0·01 % by European colour additives specifications.[22,34,35,36]

Various methods have been reported for the determination of primary aromatic amines in food colours, but a number of these are unsuitable for monitoring amine levels below the regulatory limit.[37] No official EEC method has yet been published, although the British Standard method[38] of

TABLE 6

DETERMINATION OF INTERMEDIATES

Dye	FD & C No. (E No.)	Intermediate	$E_{1\,cm}^{1\%}$	λ_{max} (nm)	pH
Yellow 2G		Sulphanilic acid	856	249	
		3-Methyl-1-(2,5-dichloro-4-sulphophenyl)-5-pyrazolone			
Quinoline Yellow	(E 104)	4,4'-Diazoaminodi(benzene sulphonic acid)	760	360	
		Quinaldine	700	315	
		Quinaldine-8-sulphonic acid	480	318	Acidic
		Phthalic acid	450	228	Acidic
Tartrazine	Yellow No. 5	Sulphanilic acid	856	249	
	(E 102)	4-Hydrazinobenzene sulphonic acid	730	253	Basic
		3-Carboxy-1-(4-sulphophenyl)-5-pyrazolone	640	257	Acidic
		4,4'-Diazoaminodi(benzene sulphonic acid)	760	360	
Sunset Yellow FCF	Yellow No. 6	Sulphanilic acid	856	249	
	(E 110)	2-Naphthol-6-sulphonic acid	2 850	232	
		6,6'-Oxybis(naphthalene-2-sulphonic acid)	1 740	240	
		4,4'-Diazoaminodi(benzenesulphonic acid)	760	360	
		2-Naphthol-3,6-disulphonic acid	2 370	235	
Ponceau 4R	(E 124)	Naphthionic acid	360	320	
		2-Naphthol-6-sulphonic acid	2 850	232	
		2-Naphthol-3,6-disulphonic acid	2 370	235	
		2-Naphthol-6,8-disulphonic acid	1 806	235	
		2-Naphthol-3,6,8-trisulphonic acid	1 729	239	
Carmoisine	(E 122)	Naphthionic acid	360	320	
		1-Naphthol-4-sulphonic acid	740	247	

Colour	Index	Compound			
Amaranth	(E 123)	Naphthionic acid	360	320	
		2-Naphthol-6-sulphonic acid	2850	232	
		2-Naphthol-3,6-disulphonic acid	2370	235	
		2-Naphthol-6,8-disulphonic acid	1806	235	
		2-Naphthol-3,6,8-trisulphonic acid	1729	239	
		1-Naphthol-8-amino-3,6-disulphonic acid	1170	240	Acidic
Red 2G		1-Naphthol-8-acetamido-3,6-disulphonic acid			
Ponceau SX	Red No. 4	1-Naphthol-4-sulphonic acid	740	247	
		2,4-Xylidene-6-sulphonic acid	390	237	
Allura Red	Red No. 40	5-Amino-4-methoxytoluene-2-sulphonic acid	470	250	
		2-Naphthol-6-sulphonic acid	2850	232	
		6,6'Oxybis(naphthalene-2-sulphonic acid)	1740	240	
		2,2'-Dimethoxy-5,5'-dimethyl-diazoaminobenzene-4,4'-disulphonic acid	460	383	
Erythrosine	Red No. 3	Sodium iodide	910	223	
	(E 127)	Phthalic acid	450	228	
		2-(2,4'-Dihydroxy-,3'5'-diiodobenzoyl)benzoic acid	470	348	Acidic
		2,4,6-Triiodoresorcinol			
Patent Blue V	(E 131)	3-Hydroxybenzaldehyde			
		3-Hydroxybenzoic acid			
		3-Hydroxy-4-sulphobenzoic acid			
		N,N-Diethylaminobenzene sulphonic acids			
Indigo Carmine	Blue No. 2	Isatin	310	367	Basic
	(E 132)	Isatin-5-sulphonic acid	890	244	
		5-Sulphoanthranilic acid	530	260	Basic
Brilliant Blue FCF	Blue No. 1	Benzaldehyde-2-sulphonic acid	440	252	
		N-Ethyl-N-(3-sulphobenzyl)-sulphanilic acid	470	274	Basic
		N-Ethyl-N-(3-sulphobenzyl)aniline	470	252	Basic

(continued)

TABLE 6—contd.

Dye	FD & C No. (E No.)	Intermediate	$E_{1cm}^{1\%}$	λ_{max} (nm)	pH
Green S	(E 142)	2-Naphthol-3,6-disulphonic acid	2 370	235	
		4,4′-Bis(dimethylamino)benzhydrol			
		4,4′-Bis(dimethylamino)benzophenone)			
Fast Green FCF	Green No. 3	Benzaldehyde-3-sulphonic acid	495	246	Basic
		4-Hydroxy-2-sulphobenzaldehyde	900	335	Basic
		N-Ethyl-N-(3-sulphobenzyl)aniline	470	252	
Brown FK		Sulphanilic acid	856	249	
		m-Phenylenediamine			
		4-Methyl-m-phenylenediamine			
Brown HT		Naphthionic acid	360	320	
		2,4-Dihydroxybenzyl alcohol			
Black PN	(E 151)	Sulphanilic acid	856	249	
		4,4′-Diazoaminodi(benzene sulphonic acid)	760	360	
		1-Aminonaphthalene-7-sulphonic acid			
		5-Naphthol-4-acetamido-1,7-disulphonic acid			
		5-Naphthol-4-amino-1,7-disulphonic acid			

extraction, diazotisation and coupling has been extensively used for over 20 years. A modification of this procedure[39] confers greater sensitivity using N-1-naphthylethylenediamine (NED) as a coupling agent and p-toluidine as a convenient reference compound. The method is as follows:

Accurately weigh about 2 g dye sample and transfer it into a 250 ml separating funnel with 100 ml water. Ensure complete dissolution of the dye, add 5 ml N sodium hydroxide solution and extract with 2 × 50 ml quantities of toluene. Wash the combined toluene extracts with 10 ml portions of 0·1 N sodium hydroxide solution to remove traces of dye. Extract the washed toluene with 3 × 15 ml portions 0·5 N hydrochloric acid and combine the acid extracts in a 50 ml standard flask. Dilute the solution to volume with water and mix well.

Pipette 5·0 ml of this solution into a stoppered test tube and cool it for 10 min in an ice bath. Add 0·05 ml of 5 % sodium nitrite solution to the tube, mix and allow it to stand a further 15 min in the ice bath. Add 0·25 ml of 10 % ammonium sulphamate solution, stopper the tube and shake it vigorously. Allow the tube to stand for one min and add 1 ml of 50 % w/v sodium acetate solution. Develop the colour by adding 0·1 ml of a solution of N-1-naphthylethylenediamine hydrochloride (1 % in 9:1 ethanol/water). Allow the tube to stand for 10 min at room temperature and finally add 0·5 ml concentrated hydrochloric acid. Mix the solution and scan the absorption spectrum from 500–550 nm in a 1 cm cell against a corresponding blank solution.

Prepare the blank by carrying 5·0 ml of 0·5 N hydrochloric acid through the diazotisation and coupling procedure in a stoppered tube. Prepare suitable standards by pipetting 0·05 ml and 0·10 ml aliquots of a 0·040 % solution of p-toluidene into stoppered tubes and carrying them through the same procedure used for the blank solution. Measure the absorbances A_1 and A_2 of these standards against the blank solution and calculate the amine content of the dye sample from the calibration. A_1 corresponds to 0·000 02 g amine and A_2 corresponds to 0·000 04 g amine.

$$\begin{array}{l} \text{Amine content} \\ \text{(calculated as } p\text{-toluidine)} \end{array} = \frac{\text{amine found} \times 10 \times 100 \%}{\text{sample weight}}$$

A method has been described for the reverse-phase HPLC separation and quantitation of various primary aromatic amines (aniline, 4-amino-biphenyl, benzidine, o-toluidine, α- and β-naphthylamine) in synthetic food dyes.[37] The method uses an Extrelut Kieselguhr column for the preliminary extraction of the amines from the organic dyestuff, and has shown itself to be capable of determining amines at the ppm level using UV detection. The alternative use of an electrochemical detector improves the sensitivity by up to 30 fold, and such methodology may well form the basis by which future food colour additive legislation is enforced.

2.3.4. Leuco-base

Triarylmethane food dyes (such as Brilliant Blue FCF, Patent Blue V, Green S and Fast Green FCF) are prepared by condensation reactions which produce the uncoloured leuco-base as an intermediate. The leuco-base is oxidised to the fully conjugated, coloured dyestuff with an oxidising agent such as lead dioxide, manganese dioxide or dichromate. Levels of residual leuco-base are normally limited to 5 % or 6 % by most food colour specifications for triarylmethane dyes.

Determination of leuco-base depends on its further oxidation to produce the corresponding coloured species and measuring the subsequent increase in absorbance of the parent dyestuff:[40]

Dissolve 0·10–0·13 g triarylmethane dye, accurately weighed, in water and dilute to 1 litre in a standard flask. Pipette 10·0 ml of this primary dye solution into a 250 ml standard flask and add to it 50 ml of 1 % solution of copper chloride in N,N-dimethylformamide (DMF). Bubble a rapid stream of air through the solution for 30 min and dilute to standard volume with water. Measure the absorbance of this solution (A_x) at the appropriate maximum (see Table 5), using as a blank a solution of 1 % copper chloride in DMF (50 ml) diluted to 250 ml with water.

Pipette a further 10·0 ml of the primary dye solution into another 250 ml standard flask, add 50 ml DMF and dilute to volume with water. Measure the absorbance of this solution (A_y) at the appropriate peak using as a blank 50 ml DMF diluted to 250 ml with water.

TABLE 7
DETERMINATION OF LEUCO-BASE

Dye	Molecular weight of dye	Molecular weight of leuco-base	Ratio R
Patent Blue V (calcium)	582·7	606·7	0·960 4
Patent Blue V (sodium)	1 159·4	1 201·4	0·965 0
Brilliant Blue FCF	792·8	816·8	0·970 6
Green S	576·6	600·6	0·960 0
Fast Green FCF	808·9	832·9	0·971 2

Calculate the leuco-base content of the dye using the $E_{1\,cm}^{1\%}$ and R values for the dye under examination (see Tables 5 and 7).

$$\text{Leuco-base} = \frac{(A_x - A_y) \times 250 \times 100\%}{E_{1\,cm}^{1\%} \times \text{sample weight} \times R}$$

where R is the molecular weight ratio of the dye to the corresponding leuco-base (see Table 7).

2.3.5. Water-insoluble Matter

Insoluble material in food dyestuffs is usually regulated to a maximum of 0.2% although there are some variations, e.g.

Patent Blue V	0.5% max. (SI 1973 No. 1340 specification)
Red 2G	0.1% max. (SI 1973 No. 1340 specification)
FD & C Blue No. 2	0.4% max. (FDA specification)
FD & C Yellow No. 6	0.5% max. (FDA specification)
FD & C Green No. 3	0.5% max. (FDA specification)

Methods vary slightly[1,18] but usually give similar results. The method given in British Standard 3210:1960[16] is widely used and simple to perform:

Accurately weigh 4.5–5.5 g of dye sample into a 250 ml beaker and dissolve it in about 200 ml hot (80–90 °C) distilled water. Cool the solution to room temperature and filter it through a tared No. 4 sintered glass crucible. Wash the filter until the washings are colourless and then dry at 135 °C to constant weight. Express the residue as percent insoluble matter in the dye sample.

2.3.6. Ether Extractable Matter

This requirement is applicable to all sulphonated food dyes (i.e. all except erythrosine) regulated by European specifications, and is usually limited to a maximum of 0.2%. American food colour specifications, with the exception of FD & C Yellow No. 6, do not contain a maximum limit for ether extractable material.

Although other methods have been published previously,[16,18] the following official method has been reported[41] for the enforcement of EEC specifications with respect to ether extractable matter in sulphonated food dyestuffs:

Accurately weigh about 10 g of dye sample onto a filter paper. Fold the paper and insert it into a Soxhlet thimble, closing the thimble with a piece of fat-free cotton wool. Extract for 6 h with dry, peroxide-free diethylether in a Soxhlet extraction apparatus. Evaporate the ether extract in a tared Soxhlet flask and then dry the flask for 20 min in an oven at $85 \pm 2\,°C$. Allow the flask to cool in a desiccator and weigh it. Repeat the drying and weighing process until constant weight is obtained, i.e. successive weighings differ by less than 0·5 mg. Report the ether extractable matter by expressing the weight of the residue as a percentage of the sample weight taken.

2.3.7. Trace Heavy Metals

Classical wet methods for the determination of lead, arsenic, chromium and copper in water-soluble food dyes have been available for many years,[2,16,18] and sulphide screen limit tests for heavy metals have also been described.[16,18] These methods have severe limitations and some are time-consuming to perform. Flame atomic absorption spectrophotometry (AAS) is now a widely used technique (see Fig. 9) which has almost entirely superseded the use of wet methods for the determination of heavy metals.

In spite of its suitability for trace metal measurements, AAS analysis of food dyestuffs is still faced with two major difficulties:

1. Interferences from non-specific absorption and matrix effects.
2. Low regulatory levels for some elements require optimum sensitivity.

Consideration of these two aspects has an important bearing on both the

FIG. 9. Atomic absorption spectrophotometer. Courtesy of Instrumentation Laboratory (UK) Ltd.

choice of analytical instrument and the adopted procedure for sample preparation.

Before choosing an AAS instrument, it is a good idea to submit the most difficult samples that can be found to the applications laboratories of the candidate instrument manufacturers. Hard scrutiny of the results will often reveal shortcomings in equipment performance. Food colours usually need to be analysed for a number of heavy metals at a time, so a multi-lamp turret is useful but a double beam configuration instrument is seldom necessary for such work. A background correction device (usually. a deuterium arc lamp) is essential, as is a hydride generator and cold vapour kit (for mercury). Both air/acetylene and nitrous oxide/acetylene burner heads will be required for the metals which are limited by most food colour specifications. Instruments with good electronic stability and good optical transmission characteristics will generally perform best at very low levels. Optical systems with lenses rather than mirrors tend to scatter less light and allow hollow cathode lamps to be run at low currents, thus improving the signal/noise ratio.

In order to reduce potential interferences in the trace metal analysis of dye solutions, it has been widely advocated that the sample is prepared either by dry ashing or wet digestion procedures.[2,3] However, such treatment can result in losses of volatile elements such as arsenic and mercury, and also takes valuable time to carry out. In most cases it is quite possible to analyse a simple dye solution by AAS provided that a background correction device is used and that the calibration is made by a standard addition method. Only in rare cases is an interference effect so difficult to overcome that it becomes necessary to resort to a digestion technique to produce a valid result. The following approach is recommended initially for all food dyestuffs:

Prepare the analytical solution by dissolving 2·0 g of sample in the minimum volume of distilled water or dilute acid, heating if necessary, and diluting the solution with water to 100 ml in a standard flask.

Calibrate by the method of standard additions, adding 50 μl aliquots of a suitable spiking solution to 10·0 ml portions of the sample solution. The sample, the spiked sample(s) and the blank should then be aspirated into the AAS instrument in sequence. If the sample absorbance reading is set to zero and the spiked sample absorbance(s) attenuated to display the level(s) added, the blank solution then directly displays the concentration in the sample, but as a *negative* quantity. This procedure avoids the need to draw calibration graphs or to calculate response factors.

TABLE 8
APPROXIMATE DETECTION LIMITS REASONABLY ATTAINABLE IN FOOD COLOURS BY
ATOMIC ABSORPTION SPECTROPHOTOMETRY

Element	Wavelength (nm)	Flame system	Detection limit (ppm)
Lead	217·0	Air/acetylene	1
Arsenic	193·7	Argon/hydrogen	0·2 (hydride)
Antimony	217·6	Argon/hydrogen	0·2 (hydride)
Copper	324·8	Air/acetylene	1
Chromium	357·9	N_2O/acetylene	2
Zinc	213·9	Air/acetylene	0·2
Barium	553·5	N_2O/acetylene	2
Mercury	253·7	Cold vapour	0·05
Selenium	196·0	Argon/hydrogen	0·2 (hydride)
Cadmium	228·8	Air/acetylene	1

A standard solution which is suitable for spiking purposes may contain 200 ppm each of lead, copper, zinc, cadmium, barium and chromium, and 1000 ppm of antimony. Addition of a 50 μl spike to 10 ml of sample solution then effectively adds 5 ppm of antimony and 1 ppm of each of the other elements.

Determine lead, copper, zinc, cadmium and antimony in an air/acetylene flame (2300 °C) at the wavelengths shown in Table 8.

Determine barium and chromium at the recommended wavelengths using a fuel-rich nitrous oxide/acetylene flame with a red cone. In order to achieve the requisite sensitivity for barium it may be necessary to add to the sample solutions 0·2–0·5 % potassium chloride as an ionisation suppressant. In difficult matrices, the absorption signal may also be enhanced by the addition of 0·5 % ethylenediaminetetraacetic acid (EDTA) to the sample solution.

Determine arsenic and selenium at the appropriate wavelengths, using a hydride generator to flush the hydride into a cool, argon or nitrogen entrained hydrogen flame from a 10 ml or 20 ml quantity of acidified sample solution. Calibrate the response by the addition of 0·5 μg and 1 μg amounts of arsenic or selenium to corresponding volumes of blank solution. Since the absorbance readings are transient, it is more convenient to record the peak heights by outputting the display to a chart recorder. Other elements which can, if required, be determined by this technique are antimony, tin, bismuth, lead and tellurium.

Determine mercury at 253·7 nm using a closed-loop, cold vapour accessory, measuring the absorbance of the vapour in a quartz cell after

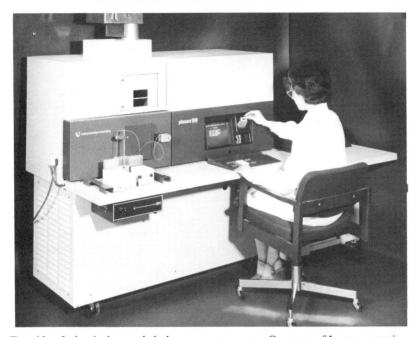

FIG. 10.   Inductively coupled plasma spectrometer. Courtesy of Instrumentation
Laboratory (UK) Ltd.

addition of 0·5 ml stannous chloride to the acidified sample solution.
Calibrate the equipment by spiking known amounts of standard mercury
solution to fixed quantities of acidified blank.

Table 8 shows those trace metal detection limits which are reasonably
attainable in most food colours using conventional flame AAS equipment.
Lower detection limits can undoubtedly be achieved by using superior
specification equipment or by flameless atomisation techniques, but the
additional cost of such equipment is not usually justified by the currently
regulated levels of heavy metals in food colours.

Other techniques which have been used for the determination of trace
metals in food colour additives include ion-selective electrodes, polar-
ography, X-ray fluorescence (XRF) and neutron activation analysis
(NAA). Because of their limitations or high cost, none of these methods has
yet attained widespread popularity in the colour field.

An emergent technique is inductively coupled plasma spectroscopy
(ICPS) which can simultaneously analyse all the regulated heavy metals
with a high sample throughput (see Fig. 10). ICP spectrometers are at least

five times more costly than conventional flame AAS instruments and can be less sensitive than AAS for some elements, notably lead and cadmium. Use of such computer controlled equipment is very wasteful for small numbers of determinations, but can prove cost effective in central laboratories or large companies where the workload is high and a number of trace metals routinely monitored. For this reason it is thought probable that future food colour additive regulations will be enforced via centralised government laboratories operating ICPS equipment.

3. ALUMINIUM LAKES

Lake colours are the insoluble salts (usually aluminium salts) of water-soluble food dyestuffs, precipitated on to a substrate of alumina hydrate. With the notable current exception of Denmark, aluminium lakes are usually permitted for food use in those countries where the corresponding water-soluble dyes are also permitted.

Apart from the USA, where special requirements apply, the impurity specifications for food lake pigments are very similar to those required for the water-soluble dyes, and similar methods of analysis are often used. From the analyst's point of view, the major components of a food lake are dye, moisture and alumina hydrate, but none of these is limited by regulation and the alumina content is rarely, if ever, determined.

3.1. Qualitative Identification
While food lakes are characteristically insoluble in water, they are generally soluble in dilute ammonia solution with a little heat. All aluminium lakes except erythrosine lake dissolve readily in hot dilute hydrochloric acid and the solutions give the identifiable reactions of aluminium with base and with alizarin.

3.1.1. Chromatography
Hydrochloric acid solutions of aluminium lakes may be examined chromatographically by using any of the PC or TLC systems suggested in Table 1 or Table 2 and comparing the sample with an authentic dye specimen. A sample which is suspected to contain erythrosine lake should first be dispersed in dilute ammonia solution and then chromatographed against authentic material. For blended products, whose first appearance can occasionally be quite misleading, the chromatographic approach is most reliable.

3.1.2. Spectrophotometry

Spectrophotometric identification of aluminium lakes (except erythrosine) is best achieved by boiling 50 mg of lake sample with 100 ml of 15 % sodium tartrate solution to release the dye. Cool the solution and dilute to volume in a 200 ml standard flask. Scan the absorption spectrum and compare the result with standard reference spectra (see Appendix). To confirm the identity of erythrosine lake, weigh 50 mg of sample and dissolve in 10 ml N sodium hydroxide solution. Dilute to volume with water in a 250 ml standard flask and examine the spectrum against suitable standards.

3.2. Quantitative Analysis of Major Components

3.2.1. Dye Content

3.2.1.1. Titrimetry. The dye content of aluminium lakes may be determined by titanous chloride titration, using the same buffer material as recommended for the corresponding water soluble dyes. For lakes of azo and TAM dyes:

Accurately weigh about 1·0 g of lake colour into a flask and dissolve it in 30 ml 5 N hydrochloric acid with gentle heating. Add 10 g of the appropriate buffer salt (see Table 4) with 150 ml water and continue to boil. Pass carbon dioxide through the flask and titrate the dye under carbon dioxide with standard 0·1 N titanous chloride until the colour disappears. Calculate the dye content as described in Section 2.2.1.

For indigo Carmine lake:

Dissolve 1–1·5 g sample, accurately weighed, in 100 ml water containing 10 g sodium hydrogen tartrate, using gentle heat. Upon total dissolution, pass carbon dioxide through the flask and titrate the dye with standard 0·1 N titanous chloride as described above. Calculate the dye content of the lake as described in Section 2.2.1.

3.2.1.2. Gravimetry. The dye content of erythrosine lake may be determined gravimetrically by the following procedure:

Disperse about 2·0 g, accurately weighed, of lake colour in 200 ml water and add 20 ml concentrated hydrochloric acid. Simmer the suspension for several hours to coagulate the precipitate, then cool and filter through a tared, sintered glass crucible (porosity 3). Wash the precipitate with dilute hydrochloric acid (1 %), then with water and finally dry at 135 °C to constant weight. Cool the crucible in a desiccator and weigh.

$$\text{Dye content (as Al salt)} = \frac{\text{precipitate weight} \times 1 \cdot 019 \times 100 \%}{\text{sample weight}}$$

3.2.1.3. Spectrophotometry. For all food lakes except erythrosine, adopt the procedure described in Section 3.1.2 and measure the absorbance value of the solution at the appropriate absorption maximum. Using the spectrophotometric data given in Table 5, calculate the dye content of the lake sample.

For erythrosine lakes, accurately weigh about 50 mg of sample into a flask and dissolve in 10 ml N sodium hydroxide solution as described in Section 3.1.2. Dilute to suitable standard volume and calculate the dye content of the sample from the maximum absorbance value and the data given in Table 5.

3.2.2. Moisture Content

Because of the non-stoichiometric nature of the substrata used for the production of aluminium lake pigments, large drying losses of up to 25 % or so are occasionally obtained. Provided that the lake pigment has the colouring power expected of it, there is nothing intrinsically wrong with apparent moisture contents of this order.

Unless otherwise specified, moisture content (or volatile matter) is usually accepted as that weight loss which occurs on heating at 135 °C until constant weight is obtained. For some materials, including those based on alumina hydrate, constant weight can be somewhat elusive, and it is often much quicker to determine moisture via Karl Fischer titration. The following method is recommended for lake pigments:

Accurately weigh 0·2–0·3 g of lake pigment into a tared weighing bottle and dispense onto the sample 10 ml of anhydrous methanol to abstract the moisture. Shake the mixture for 1 min and transfer the suspension to the reaction vessel of the Karl Fischer Autotitrator. Read the moisture content directly and correct this value by subtracting the reading obtained from a 10 ml blank portion of anhydrous methanol.

$$\text{Moisture content} = \frac{\text{corrected mg displayed} \times 100\%}{\text{sample weight (mg)}}$$

3.3. Quantitative Analysis of Minor Components

The minor organic components of aluminium lakes are determined by the same general methods that are applied to the water-soluble dyes.

Subsidiary colours and synthetic intermediates may be determined chromatographically after heating the lake with a 15 % solution of sodium tartrate to release the dye. (See Sections 2.3.1 and 2.3.2.) Primary aromatic amines may be extracted from the powdered lake using toluene in a Soxhlet extraction apparatus. Since the levels of any amines detected in lake pigments are likely to be extremely low, it is advisable to concentrate the extract as much as possible at this stage, before back-extracting into dilute hydrochloric acid. Carry out the colorimetric procedure as described in Section 2.3.3.

Trace heavy metals are determined by AAS as detailed for water-soluble dyes in Section 2.3.7. Prepare the solution by dissolving about 2 g of the lake, accurately weighed, in 30 ml of 5 N hydrochloric acid, using gentle heat. Cool and make the solution to standard volume with water in a 100 ml flask. Aspirate the sample solution as previously described for the elements of interest, calibrating the instrument response by the method of standard additions where applicable.

For erythrosine lakes and other lake colours which may prove difficult to dissolve, adopt the following procedure:[1]

Weigh 2 g sample into a 500 ml Kjeldahl flask, add 10 ml sulphuric acid and 10 ml nitric acid, and digest over a low flame until sulphur trioxide fumes appear. Add 5 ml portions of nitric acid (wait until sulphur trioxide fumes appear before adding each succeeding portion) until all the organic matter is in solution. Slowly add 5–10 ml of a mixture of nitric acid and 60–70 % perchloric acid (1 + 1), and continue digestion until the white precipitate formed shows first signs of spattering. Let the flask cool and cautiously add 5 ml water and then a few drops of ammonium hydroxide. Swirl the flask vigorously and cool under running water. Add 20 ml citric acid solution (50 % special grade—low in lead) and adjust to pH 3·0–3·4 (bromophenol blue) with ammonium hydroxide.

Determine trace heavy metals in this solution by AAS, calibrating the response by the method of standard additions.

3.3.1. Water-soluble Salts

In order to be certified for use in food in the USA, aluminium lakes may not contain more than 2·0 % of soluble chlorides and sulphates, calculated as sodium salts. This requirement has also been adopted for food lake colours used in Japan and is likely to become part of European colour additive legislation governing lakes. The following procedure is effective:

Accurately weigh about 5 g of pigment sample and boil it with 200 ml water for 2–3 min. Allow the suspension to separate as far as possible, overnight if necessary. Decant the supernatant and centrifuge it or pass it through a 0·2 μm microfilter if further clarification is needed.

To determine sodium sulphate, take 50 ml of the clear filtrate in a 250 ml beaker and add 20 ml 0·1 M barium chloride solution dropwise with stirring. Boil the suspension and keep it hot in a steam bath for 3 h. Allow the beaker to cool overnight and filter the precipitate through a tared No. 3 sintered glass crucible. Wash the precipitate with water and dry the crucible to constant weight in an oven at 135 °C. Calculate the sodium sulphate content as follows:

$$\text{Sodium sulphate} = \frac{\text{precipitate weight} \times 0\cdot6086 \times 4 \times 100\,\%}{\text{sample weight}}$$

To determine sodium chloride in the lake pigment, pipette 0·5 ml of the clear supernatant liquid from the extraction stage described above, into the sample cell of the chloride meter. Titrate the sample to the usual dead-stop end point and read off the concentration of chloride in the solution. Calculate the sodium chloride content of the sample as follows:

$$\text{Sodium chloride} = \frac{\text{result displayed (mg \%)}}{5 \times \text{sample weight}}$$

3.3.2. Acid-insoluble Inorganic Matter

The American requirement for FD & C lakes to contain no more than 0·5 % acid-insoluble inorganic material has also been adopted for Japanese food lakes. This requirement is likely to be incorporated into other national specifications for food-grade aluminium lakes in the fairly near future. In the absence of an official FDA procedure, the following method is valid for all food lakes including that of erythrosine (which gives an acid-insoluble residue of *organic* material):

Accurately weigh about 5 g of lake colour into a 500 ml beaker and add 200 ml of 5 N hydrochloric acid. Heat the mixture almost to boiling and stir thoroughly to ensure maximum dissolution. Add 100 ml distilled water and allow the beaker to cool. Filter the entire contents of the beaker through an ashless filter paper (Whatman 542) and dry the filter in an oven at 130 °C. Transfer the dried filter and its contents to a tared silica crucible and ignite at 600 °C for 30 min to destroy any acid-insoluble organic matter. Allow the crucible to cool in a desiccator and weigh the residue as inorganic matter insoluble in hydrochloric acid.

$$\text{Insoluble matter} = \frac{\text{residue weight} \times 100\,\%}{\text{sample weight}}$$

4. INORGANIC PIGMENTS

Synthetic inorganic pigments which are becoming more widely accepted for use in food products throughout the world are titanium dioxide and the iron oxides and hydroxides. Vegetable Carbon is also sometimes put in this category although it is manufactured by the carbonisation of vegetable material, usually peat.

Neither Vegetable Carbon nor the iron oxide pigments are currently permitted for food use in the USA, and some countries still only permit the use of iron oxides in the surface coating of certain foodstuffs. The attraction of inorganic pigments is that they are both cheap and effective, and since their absorption in the gastrointestinal tract is negligible, their toxic potential is practically zero.

It is necessary to enforce rigorous specifications for inorganic food colours in order to prevent the usage of cheaper, paint-grade materials, which can contain substantial levels of impurities detrimental to the human consumer. The most widely encountered specifications are those of the EEC and the FAO/WHO, but the American specification for titanium dioxide[42] sets a high international standard and also gives an acid extraction method for analysing trace metals.

4.1. Titanium Dioxide
4.1.1. Qualitative Identification
Titanium dioxide is a white, odourless, infusible powder which is insoluble in water and dilute acids. When a small sample is heated strongly in a tube, the material becomes pale yellow, but the colour disappears on cooling. The following method can be used to confirm the identification:

Heat about 50 mg of sample in a tube with 1 ml concentrated sulphuric acid until white fumes appear, and then allow to cool. Dilute cautiously with about 20 ml water and filter the suspension into a few drops of dilute hydrogen peroxide solution. An immediate orange coloration of peroxytitanium sulphuric acid complex confirms the identification of titanium.

4.1.2. Quantitative Analysis
Titanium dioxide may be assayed volumetrically by passing the sample solution through a Jones reductor and then titrating with ceric ammonium nitrate solution.[43] The following spectrophotometric method is adequate for most purposes and is considerably more convenient:

Accurately weigh about 0·25 g of titanium dioxide into a 500 ml conical flask, add 25 g ammonium sulphate and 50 ml concentrated sulphuric acid. Rest a filter funnel in the neck of the flask to prevent sample loss, and heat until the solid material dissolves completely. Cool the solution and transfer quantitatively to a 100 ml standard flask, diluting to volume with water. Use this solution for the determination of trace metals and for the titanium dioxide assay.

Pipette 5 ml of the sample solution into a 250 ml standard flask containing 60 ml concentrated sulphuric acid and 100 ml water. Add 4 ml of 30 % hydrogen peroxide and mix well. Dilute the solution cautiously to volume with water, while cooling in a cold bath. Allow the flask to stand for exactly 15 min and measure its absorbance A at 405 nm in a 1 cm cell. Calculate the pigment purity by comparing with the absorbance from a standard of known purity or by using the following formula:

$$\text{Titanium dioxide} = \frac{A \times 250 \times 100\%}{91\cdot4 \times 5 \times \text{sample weight}}$$

where 91·4 is the $E_{1\,cm}^{1\%}$ value for pure titanium dioxide.

4.1.2.1. Trace metals. Determine the trace metal content of the material by direct introduction of the sample solution into the AAS instrument. Calibrate the instrument response using the method of standard additions as previously described and use a background corrector where applicable.

It is worth noting here that the American 21 CFR 1.1 specification[42] for titanium dioxide states that lead, arsenic and antimony shall be determined in the solution obtained by boiling 10 g of the colourant for 15 min in 50 ml of 0·5 N hydrochloric acid. The West German DFG specification[36] advises that mineral pigments including titanium dioxide and iron oxides should be analysed for inorganic impurities using an extract made with 0·1 N hydrochloric acid. On the other hand, in its interim report,[22] the Food Additives and Contaminants Committee suggested some mineral pigments specifications which particularly required trace contaminants to be determined by total dissolution. It is felt that any treatment other than total dissolution may eventually allow the use of low-grade colours which are not fit for human consumption.

4.1.3. Acid-soluble Matter
The determination of acid-soluble material and/or water-soluble material in titanium dioxide pigments occasionally gives trouble because very fine

pigment particles pass the analytical filter and are weighed as though they constitute soluble matter. Cloudy filtrates undoubtedly produce high results and should be discarded if they are encountered. Use of asbestos-mat filtration in a Gooch crucible is recommended if conventional filtration methods are ineffective.

The UK Colouring Matter in Food Regulations 1973[34] contains the following method for determination of acid-soluble substances in titanium dioxide:

Suspend 5 g of colouring matter in 100 ml of 0·5 N hydrochloric acid and heat for 30 min in a water bath, shaking occasionally. Filter through a Gooch crucible containing a filter bed of three layers—the first, coarse asbestos, the second, pulped filter paper, and the third, fine asbestos. Wash with three successive 10 ml portions of 0·5 N hydrochloric acid. Evaporate the filtrate to dryness in a platinum evaporating dish and heat to a dull red until the residue weight is constant. The weight of the residue shall not exceed 0·0175 g (0·35 %).

4.1.4. Water-soluble Matter

Water-soluble material may be determined using the method described in Section 4.1.3, but substituting water for 0·5 N hydrochloric acid. Alternatively, the method described in Section 3.3.1 is suitable, evaporating 100 ml of the clear filtrate in a tared platinum dish before drying to constant weight at a dull red heat.

4.1.5. Soluble Barium Compounds[18]

The following method can be used to determine whether soluble barium compounds are present:

Heat the residue obtained in the test for acid-soluble matter (see Section 4.1.3) with 20 ml 0·1 N hydrochloric acid in a boiling water bath. Filter the solution and add 1 ml dilute sulphuric acid to the clear filtrate. A negative result is indicated if no turbidity or precipitate is produced after allowing to stand for 30 min.

4.2. Iron Oxides

4.2.1. Qualitative Identification

Iron oxides are fine, odourless, red, black, brown or yellow powders. They are insoluble in water, ethanol and dilute acids but dissolve readily in

TABLE 9
SYNTHETIC IRON OXIDE PIGMENTS

	Red	Yellow	Black
CI No.	77 491	77 492	77 499
Particle shape	Spherical	Acicular	Cubical
General formula	Fe_2O_3	$FeO(OH).nH_2O$	$FeO.(Fe_2O_3)_n$
Maximum ignition loss (%)	1	14	1
Minimum iron content (%)	68·5	60·2	69·9
FeO content (%)	—	—	20–25

concentrated hydrochloric acid under gentle heating. The following tests confirm the presence of iron:

1. Make a solution of powdered sample in hydrochloric acid and add a few drops of dilute ammonium thiocyanate solution. A positive result is indicated by an immediate blood red coloration.
2. To a hydrochloric acid solution of the sample, add a few drops of potassium ferrocyanide solution. A positive result is indicated if a deep blue precipitate forms.

It is seldom that naturally occurring iron oxides meet the purity requirements for food grade colourants. High specification brown iron oxides are best prepared by blending the synthetic red, black and yellow primary components to the required shade. Such blends then exhibit total iron content and ignition loss values which are intermediate between those of the respective primes. (See Table 9.)

4.2.2. Quantitative Analysis
All iron oxide pigments contain iron (III) but only red iron oxide (CI 77491) is a stoichiometric compound of anhydrous ferric oxide with a minimum purity of 98%. Yellow iron oxide (CI 77492) is a hydrated ferric oxy hydroxide with a minimum ferric oxide content of 86%. The remainder can be driven off as water upon ignition. Black iron oxide (CI 77499) is a ferrosoferric oxide of general formula $FeO.(Fe_2O_3)_n$, where n may be between 1 and 2. Material with the best pigmentary properties has a FeO content of 20–25%, and the empirical formula is certainly not Fe_3O_4 as textbooks often suggest.

The iron (III) content of oxide pigments may be conveniently determined by the following volumetric method:

Accurately weigh into a stoppered conical flask about 0·2 g of sample and dissolve in 10 ml concentrated hydrochloric acid under gentle heat. Allow the solution to cool and add 30 ml distilled water. Then add 3 g of potassium iodide and 1 ml of 0·005 M copper sulphate solution as catalyst. Stopper the flask and allow the mixture to stand for 10 min. Add a further 20 ml distilled water and titrate the liberated iodine with 0·1 N sodium thiosulphate solution, adding the starch indicator towards the end of the titration. Perform a blank titration using the same reagent quantities carried through the procedure, and make any necessary corrections. Calculate the iron (III) content of the sample as follows:

$$\text{Iron (III)} = \frac{\text{ml sodium thiosulphate} \times \text{normality} \times 55 \cdot 85 \times 100\%}{\text{sample weight} \times 1000}$$

For red and yellow iron oxides this result amounts to the total iron content of the pigment and enables the overall purity to be calculated. In the case of black iron oxide it is necessary to oxidise the iron (II) completely before titrating the total iron as follows:

Accurately weigh into a silica crucible about 0·2 g of black iron oxide. Ignite the sample at red heat for 30 min and allow to cool. Dissolve the residue by heating with 5–10 ml concentrated hydrochloric acid and transfer the solution quantitatively to a stoppered conical flask using distilled water. Add 10–12 drops 30 % hydrogen peroxide solution and boil gently for 5 min to allow excess peroxide to decompose. Allow the solution to cool, then add 3 g of potassium iodide and 1 ml of 0·005 M copper sulphate solution. Stopper the flask and allow the mixture to stand for 10 min. Add 20 ml distilled water and titrate the liberated iodine with 0·1 N sodium thiosulphate solution, adding the starch indicator towards the end of the titration. Carry out a blank titration using the same reagent quantities and make any necessary corrections. Calculate the total iron content of the sample and then use the iron (III) content previously determined to calculate the pigment purity.

Total iron content

$$= \frac{\text{ml sodium thiosulphate} \times \text{normality} \times 55 \cdot 85 \times 100\%}{\text{sample weight} \times 1000}$$

Then,

Iron (II) content = Total Iron − Iron (III)
Pigment purity = FeO content + Fe_2O_3 content
= Iron (II) × 1·286 + Iron (III) × 1·430 %

4.2.2.1. Trace metals. The determination of trace metals in iron oxide pigments is best carried out via total dissolution of the sample and AAS as follows:

Accurately weigh 5 g of sample into a conical flask and dissolve under gentle heat in 50 ml concentrated hydrochloric acid. Cautiously dilute with distilled water and transfer the solution quantitatively to a 200 ml standard flask, diluting to standard volume with water. Use 10·0 ml portions of this sample solution to prepare the standard addition calibration for AAS as described in Section 2.3.7. Spray these spiked standards alongside the sample and a suitable solvent blank, using background correction if appropriate.

Maximum sensitivity is not usually required for the determination of antimony in iron oxides. This element is routinely monitored in an air/acetylene flame rather than with a hydride generator. When determining traces of lead in iron oxides, interference is frequently encountered at the 217·0 nm resonance line. Under these circumstances it is preferable to analyse for lead at the alternative 283·3 nm line where the signal is not greatly reduced but the interference is usually eliminated. The analytical conditions for other trace metals are as listed in Table 8.

4.2.3. Water-soluble matter
Iron oxides do not show quite such a pronounced tendency as titanium dioxide to pass filters, but nevertheless the remarks concerning this procedure under Sections 4.1.3 and 4.1.4 may be helpful. Use a Gooch crucible/asbestos filter (or microfilter) in case of difficulty and note that the limit for water-soluble material may be as high as 1 % in some specifications for iron oxides.

4.2.4. Loss on Ignition
To find the weight loss on ignition:

Ignite about 2 g of sample, accurately weighed, to a dull red heat (about 800 °C) until constant weight is attained. Yellow iron oxide loses up to 14 % of its weight upon ignition whereas black iron oxide may actually gain weight due to atmospheric oxidation.

4.3. Vegetable Carbon
This is the description given to the black food pigment prepared from vegetable matter. It should not be confused with Vegetable Black which is a

furnace black of coarse structure derived from vegetable oil, or with Carbon Blacks which are made from hydrocarbon fuels. Both of these types of carbon pigments can be contaminated with tar products or polynuclear hydrocarbons which should be absent from food-grade colour additives. The chemical inertness of carbon colourants makes them difficult to characterise and to distinguish from one another. The purity requirements for food-grade Vegetable Carbon include test methods for the specific absence of higher aromatic hydrocarbons and tar products.[18,34]

4.3.1. Qualitative Identification

Vegetable Carbon is a fine, bulky, black powder, practically insoluble in all usual solvents. If a 500 mg sample is ignited at red heat until it burns slowly away without flame, the residue should weigh no more than 20 mg (4 %).

4.3.2. Quantitative Analysis

No specific chemical methods are published, but the carbon content is usually taken as the dry bulk powder less the ash content determined after ignition to constant weight.

4.3.3. Moisture Content

To determine the moisture content:

Accurately weigh about 2 g of sample and dry in an oven at $140 \pm 5\,°C$ to constant weight. Express the loss in weight as percent moisture.

4.3.4. Higher Aromatic Hydrocarbons

The UK Colouring Matter in Food Regulations 1973[34] contains the following requirement:

Weigh 1 g of Vegetable Carbon and extract it with 10 g of pure cyclohexane for 2 h. The extract shall show no colour and shall exhibit practically no fluorescence under ultraviolet light. The extract shall leave no residue on evaporation.

4.3.5. Tar Products

The UK Colouring Matter in Food Regulations 1973[34] contains the following requirement:

Boil 2 g of Vegetable Carbon with 20 ml N sodium hydroxide and filter the suspension. The filtrate shall be colourless.

4.3.6. Trace Metal Content

To determine the trace metal content:

Weigh 10·0 g of Vegetable Carbon into a flask and add 100 ml distilled water and 10 ml concentrated nitric acid. Boil the extract under reflux for 1 h and filter the hot mixture on a Buchner funnel through a slow, ashless (Whatman 542) filter paper. Wash the filter with 3 × 25 ml portions of water and make up to 250 ml in a standard flask. Determine the trace metal content of this extract by AAS as previously described, using a background corrector where necessary and calibrating the instrument response by the standard addition method.

ACKNOWLEDGEMENTS

I would like to thank the staff of the Technical Department of D. F. Anstead Ltd for their valuable help in preparing this chapter, and in particular, Mrs J. Mitchell for her care and tenacity in typing the manuscript.

REFERENCES

1. *AOAC Methods*, 13th edn, 1980, 34. Colour Additives, p. 568. Association of Official Analytical Chemists, Washington, DC.
2. Marmion, D. M., *Handbook of US Colorants for Foods, Drugs and Cosmetics*, 1979, John Wiley and Sons, New York.
3. Venkataraman, K., *The Analytical Chemistry of Synthetic Dyes*, 1977, John Wiley and Sons, New York.
4. *Specifications for the Identity and Purity of Some Food Colours, Flavour Enhancers, Thickening Agents and Certain Food Additives*, WHO Food Additives Series No. 7, 1976, World Health Organisation, Geneva.
5. *Separation and Identification of Food Colours Permitted by the Colouring Matter in Food Regulations 1957*, 1960, Association of Public Analysts, London.
6. Allavena, S., *Boll. Laboratori Chim. prov.*, 1960, **11**, 738.
7. Endean, M. E. and Bielby, C. R., *The Extraction and Identification of Artificial Water-soluble Dyes from Foods*, Leatherhead Food R.A. Res. Rep. No. 214, 1975, Leatherhead Food R.A.
8. Hoodless, R. A., Pitman, K. G., Stewart, T. E., Thomson, J. and Arnold, T. E., *J. Chromatog.*, 1971, **54**, 393.
9. Van Peteghem, C. and Bijl, J., *J. Chromatog.*, 1981, **210**, 113.

10. Puttemans, M. L., Dryon, L. and Massart, D. L., *J. Assoc. Off. Anal. Chem.*, 1982, **65**, 730.
11. Passarelli, R. J. and Jacobs, E. S., *J. chromatog. Sci.*, 1975, **13**, 153.
12. McKone, H. T. and Ivie, K., *J. Chem. Ed.*, 1980, **57**(4), 321.
13. Lawrence, J. F., Lancaster, F. E. and Conacher, H. B. S., *J. Chromatog.*, 1981, **210**, 168.
14. Puttemans, M. L., Dryon, L. and Massart, D. L., *J. Assoc. Off. Anal. Chem.*, 1982, **64**, 1.
15. Heal, R. L. and Chaytor, J. P., Altex Scientific, unpublished work.
16. British Standard 3210:1960, *Methods for the Analysis of Water-soluble Coal Tar Dyes Permitted for Use in Foods*, 1960, British Standards Institution, London.
17. Graichen, C. and Bailey, J. E., *J. Assoc. Off. Anal. Chem.*, 1974, **57**, 356.
18. *Specifications for Identity and Purity of Food Additives, Vol. 2 Food Colours*, 1963, Food and Agricultural Organisation of the United Nations, Rome.
19. Bailey, J. E. and Graichen, C., *J. Assoc. Off. Anal. Chem.*, 1974, **57**, 353.
20. British Standard 4138:1967, *Specification for Erythrosine BS for Use in Foodstuffs*, 1967, British Standards Institution, London.
21. British Standard 4354:1968, *Specification for Black PN for Use in Foodstuffs*, 1968, British Standards Institution, London.
22. Ministry of Agriculture, Fisheries and Food, *FACC Interim Report on the Review of the Colouring Matter in Food Regulations 1973*, FAC/REP/29, 1979, HMSO, London.
23. Calvey, R. J. and Goldberg, A. L., *J. Assoc. Off. Anal. Chem.*, 1982, **65**, 1080.
24. Lancaster, F. E. and Lawrence, J. F., *J. Assoc. Off. Anal. Chem.*, 1982, **65**, 1305.
25. Bailey, J. E., *J. Assoc. Off. Anal. Chem.*, 1980, **63**, 565.
26. Bailey, C. J., Cox, E. A. and Springer, J. A., *J. Assoc. Off. Anal. Chem.*, 1978, **61**, 1404.
27. Calvey, R. J., Goldberg, A. L. and Madigan, E. A., *J. Assoc. Off. Anal. Chem.*, 1981, **64**, 665.
28. Singh, M., *J. Assoc. Off. Anal. Chem.*, 1974, **57**, 358.
29. Bailey, J. E. and Cox, E. E., *J. Assoc. Off. Anal. Chem.*, 1975, **58**, 609.
30. Singh, M., *J. Assoc. Off. Anal. Chem.*, 1974, **57**, 219.
31. Cox, E. A. and Reed, G. F., *J. Assoc. Off. Anal. Chem.*, 1981, **64**, 324.
32. Singh, M., *J. Assoc. Off. Anal. Chem.*, 1975, **58**, 48.
33. Goldberg, A. L. and Calvey, R. J., *J. Assoc. Off. Anal. Chem.*, 1982, **65**, 103.
34. Ministry of Agriculture, Fisheries and Food, The Colouring Matter in Food Regulations 1973 (SI 1973 No. 1340), HMSO, London.
35. EEC Council Directive of 23 October 1962, *J. Off. Commun. Europ.*, 1962, **5**, 2645.
36. Deutsche Forschungsgemeinschaft Farbstoff-Kommission, *Farbstoffe für Lebensmittel*, 1978, p. 40. DFG, Bonn.
37. Hunziker, H. R. and Miserez, A., *Mitt. Gebiete Lebensm. Hyg.*, 1981, **72**, 216.
38. British Standard 3611:1963, *Specification for Red 2G for Use in Foodstuffs*, 1963, British Standards Institution, London.
39. Wadds, G. A. and Thamby, S. B. K., unpublished work, 1979.

40. Dantzman, J. and Stein, C., *J. Assoc. Off. Anal. Chem.*, 1974, **57**, 963.
41. EEC Council Directive of 28 July 1981, *J. Off. Commun. Europ.*, 1981, **24**, 6.
42. US Code of Federal Regulations, Title 21, Parts 1 to 99, 1979, 73.575, US Government Printing Office, Washington.
43. *British Pharmacopoeia 1980*, Volume I, p. 457. HMSO, London.

APPENDIX

The following pages show UV/visible absorption spectra which may be found useful for identification of the following colours:

E102	Tartrazine
E104	Quinoline Yellow
E110	Sunset Yellow FCF
	Yellow 2G
	Brown HT
	Brown FK
E122	Carmoisine
E123	Amaranth
E124	Ponceau 4R
E127	Erythrosine
	Red 2G
E131	Patent Blue V
E132	Indigo Carmine
	Brilliant Blue FCF
E142	Green S
E151	Black PN

G. WADDS

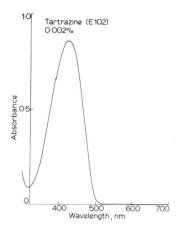

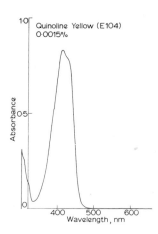

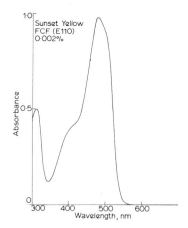

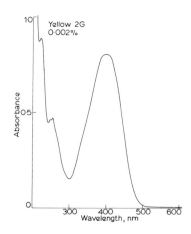

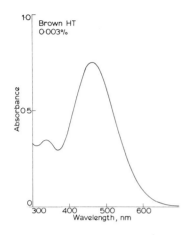

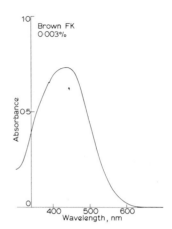

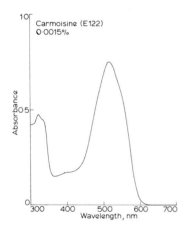

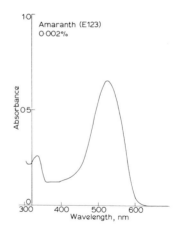

72 G. WADDS

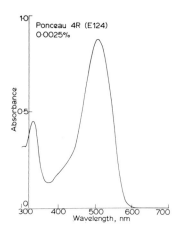

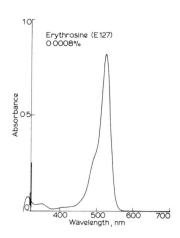

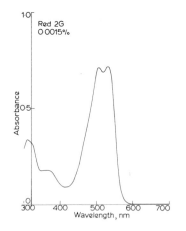

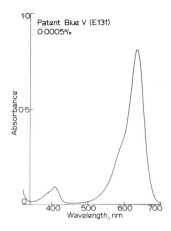

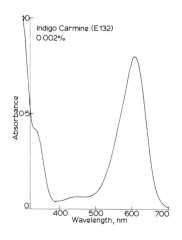

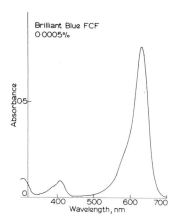

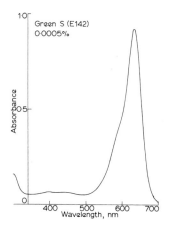

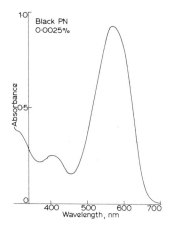

Chapter 3

THE INFLUENCE OF COLOUR ON SENSORY PERCEPTION AND FOOD CHOICES

F. M. Clydesdale

*Department of Food Science and Nutrition,
University of Massachusetts, Amherst, USA*

SUMMARY

Colour is associated with every aspect of our lives and plays an integral role in all our behavioural decisions. From birth, nature teaches us to make value judgements on our environment based in large measure on colour. Since the act of eating represents an extremely personal behaviour, in that we take part of our environment into us, it is not surprising that colour conditions our choices. Colour affects our overall judgements on the worth of food from both an aesthetic and a safety point of view. It plays an important role in taste thresholds, flavour identification, food preference, pleasantness, acceptability and ultimately food choice.

However, its role is elusive and difficult to quantify. This creates problems in a technologically oriented society because if numbers cannot be assigned to a cause–effect relationship, there is a tendency to deny the existence of that relationship. That has often led to a situation where the role of colour is either ignored or minimised which, unfortunately, has placed colour in a secondary role to the other sensory characteristics; a position which is not consistent with the facts. Indeed, the importance of colour in food choices is so unquestionable that it is often taken for granted, a situation which must be re-evaluated in view of the need for the creation of new and different foods to feed a hungry world.

1. INTRODUCTION

And when these days were completed, the king gave for all the people
present in Susa the capital, both great and small, a banquet lasting for
seven days, in the court of the garden of the king's palace. There were
white cotton curtains and blue hangings caught up with cords of fine
linen and purple to silver rings and marble pillars, and also couches of
gold and silver on a mosaic pavement of porphyry, marble, mother-of-
pearl and precious stones. Drinks were served in golden goblets, goblets
of different kinds, and the royal wine was lavished according to the
bounty of the king.[1]

Thus does the Bible in the Book of Esther describe a great banquet with
abundant references to colour. Indeed, even from the earliest times colour
has been a thing of beauty, wonder and mystery. Primitive man associated
colours with dramatic events. Red was associated with life due to the colour
of flowing blood and evidence exists that the dead were painted this colour
100 000 years ago. Manipulation of colourants by primitive man to
produce crude paintings is known to have existed about 80 000 years ago
and the Upper Cave Man of prehistoric China wore red ornamental beads.
Today it is obvious that colour is an important ingredient in almost every
manufactured object, as well as being an inspiration in works of art, both
man-made and natural. Our colour conditioning has even taught us to
associate physical responses, such as pain, with colour. Early work by
Coriat[2] described an adult patient where different types of pain produced
different colours: hollow pain, blue colour; sore pain, red colour; and
superficial headache, white colour. More recent exploratory work[3] has
suggested that children's synaesthetic response to pain generally correlated
with the so-called warm colours (red, orange, yellow) more than others and
the colour red was the one most often singled out.

A consideration of colour as a science began in the era of Greek
civilisation with the teachings of Aristotle and with continuous refinement
evolved into modern colour theory. This chapter is not an appropriate
vehicle for a discussion of colour theory, but the interested reader may
consult any one of several references[4-7] for a description of theory and
measurement, and others for a discussion of vision[8] and psychological
aspects.[9]

However, in the terms of reference of this chapter, it is important to stress
that colour is not merely a physical phenomenon. In fact, colour is a
sensation experienced by an individual when energy in the form of

radiation within the visible spectrum falls upon the retina of the eye.[4] That colour is a sensation dependent upon what a person sees cannot be overemphasised.

The question at hand is, what effect does the sensation, which we call colour, have on sensory perception of food, food choices and therefore food intake and enjoyment? This effect is difficult to assess. It might be compared to defining the worth and importance of 'goodwill' in the total selling price of a business. It is an extremely important factor but is difficult to quantify exactly.

The visual sense, which we often take for granted, may be more appreciated if we analyse our daily behaviour and how it is affected by what we see. Also, when we consider the complexity of the light patterns that strike the eye and the amount of signal sorting necessary to convert the nerve impulses to identification of objects, space, location, and movement, we begin to realise how sophisticated the visual sense is. There is no doubt that experience plays a large part in our evaluation of how we interpret what we see and at an early age we probably developed our ability to discriminate visually by using other senses to confirm visual analysis. However, as adults we have learned to structure behaviour solely on what is seen without even being aware that other senses were involved at an earlier time to help us achieve this result.

Usually we examine an object with our eyes to determine its desirability or usefulness to us. Is it old or new, fresh or stale, beautiful or ugly, unused or worn? Almost always the judgement is made without being aware of the actual optical process that led us to the final conclusion.

As Hunter[5] has pointed out:

The driver of an automobile on a highway appraises the surface of the highway ahead, but not for its darkness of color or for its gloss. Instead, he is looking for the presence of water or ice on the highway revealed by dark color or gloss. A farmer looks at the soil in his field to determine its readiness for plowing, planting, or cultivating. He is not trying to determine color and texture, although these are the specific optical attributes that reveal to him the soil quality. A man examines a shirt in his closet for cleanness as an all-inclusive quality. He does not look consciously for patterns and degrees of yellowness and grayness that, nevertheless, are the appearance attributes used to judge lack of cleanness. It is obvious that very little conscious analysis is made by a person of his actual visual sensations of the appearance of things about him. He simply comes to a conclusion based on an untold number of previous experiences. He enjoys the glossiness of his new car without associating it with any particular phenomenon involving the interaction of light and object, just as he picks the 'freshest' meat without consciously realizing that the redness of the meat influenced his choice.

Thus, it may be seen that the visual senses are often first funnelled through the subconscious before conscious decisions are made. Therefore, it would appear that the visual sense and all that implies might be the most important sense in terms of governing our daily behaviour.

The visual sense utilises the appearance of an object, which is composed not only of colour, but of texture, gloss, lustre, translucency. However, colour must be considered as a major, if not the major attribute in evaluating the appearance of food. Yet there are some who will admit to the role of taste and smell in food acceptance but refuse to acknowledge colour, claiming that because it is a learned association we can unlearn it.

Let us examine this claim a little more thoroughly. The argument generally goes something like this. We colour foods and, therefore, teach people to associate food wholesomeness and taste with a particular colour. If we stopped colouring foods, then people would learn that colour is not important in discriminating between levels of food wholesomeness and taste and ultimately food choice and consumption.

I believe there might be some merit in this argument if food processing was the only way that food attained coloration. However, this is not the case; nature has the biggest crayons and the largest colouring book and the food manufacturer just cannot compete. Witness the foliage on a New England autumn day. Now you are faced with the problem of convincing nature not to colour oranges 'orange' so that people will not associate an orange colour with degree of ripeness and, therefore, taste and texture, nor red colour with the palatability of a tomato. The list of natural products and the relationship between colour and overall acceptability goes on and on. Indeed, nature has been a harsh and consistent teacher of the need to examine colour prior to eating and I believe that it would be an awesome task to convince people that colour should be ignored in certain foods and yet achieve a prominent place in evaluating overall quality in others. Certainly, the USDA recognises the importance of colour in grading frozen concentrated orange juice, since it receives 40 quality points in a 100 point scale. Should we ignore this 40 percent contribution of colour in a simulated orange drink? It would seem absurd to do so and, in fact, would simply make the simulated orange beverage non-competitive in the market place.

With these facts at our disposal, it is somewhat difficult to imagine why the use of colour in food raises such emotional responses. As Dember and Warm[9] point out, first impressions of food are visual and our willingness to accept them is dependent, for the most part, on colour. Later, acceptance or rejection of foods by colour scrutiny becomes a more complicated behavioural response incorporating all of the other processes that determine behaviour such as learning, memory, motivation and emotion.

However, antagonism does arise. Some of the questions posed are valid and fall into the category of honest scientific disagreement, while others may be motivated by the choice of a diet which bolsters self-image and sends messages to the rest of the world. Sadalla and Burroughs[10] conducted a study in which they attempted to correlate eating preferences with how people see themselves and how others see them. They found that there was some correlation between food preferences, their own personality ratings and ratings on objective tests. Also, they found considerable agreement in the subject's characterisation of personality traits with food preferences. They saw fast-food lovers as patriotic, pronuclear, conservative, antidrug and dressed in polyester suits. They saw vegetarians as pacifist, hypochondriacal, drug-using, weight-conscious, liberal and likely to drive foreign cars. This, of course, means that symbolism as well as food quality is important in trying to get an affluent people to change their eating habits. I am not certain, however, how much symbolism is involved in food choice when starvation is close at hand.

2. VISUAL APPEARANCE AND COLOUR IN FOOD CHOICES

Prior to discussing the role of colour in foods, it is important to first recognise the fact that colour is only one attribute of appearance, albeit a very important attribute particularly in relation to food.

Hunter[5] suggests that our ability to see red light on a piece of paper and still describe the paper as white, or to see a light and dark area of the same surface and still recognise the surface as being uniform, has produced a need for a means of characterising appearance situations. He further suggests that we do this by classifying the apparent visual condition or 'mode' of each thing seen as follows:

1.   The illuminant mode—the stimulus is a source of light.
2.   The object mode—the stimulus is illuminated by a source of light.
3.   The aperture mode—the stimulus is seen simply as light, e.g. seeing a glimmer of light through a crack in a door.

TABLE 1

THE MOST IMPORTANT APPEARANCE ATTRIBUTES OF OBJECTS

Class of object	Colour attributes	Geometric attributes
Diffusion surfaces ('surface colours')	Colour by diffuse reflection: Lightness Hue Saturation	Glossiness by specular reflection
Metallic surfaces	Colour by specular reflection: Glossiness Hue Saturation	Reflection haze by diffuse reflection
Translucent specimens	Colour by diffuse transmission: Translucency Hue Saturation	Glossiness by specular reflection
Transparent specimens	Colour by specular transmission: Clarity Hue Saturation	Transmission haze, or turbidity by diffuse transmission

Reprinted from Reference 5 with permission.

However, our visual process does not evaluate appearance by these modes but goes further and allows us to evaluate object appearance in terms of attributes or specific visual qualities of the object which may be classified into four major groups[5] as shown in Table 1.

Hutchings[11] in discussing visual appearances of foods versus colour states that,

The first impression of a food quality is usually visual, and a major part of our willingness to accept a food depends on its appearance. Appearance is a compound of all the information about the product and its environment which reaches the eye.

Unfortunately, the word 'color' has superseded 'appearance' as the description of the total visual perception of foods. This was almost tolerable in the food industry as long as the food technologist was concerned with the changes accompanying relatively minor manipulations of natural foods.... The technologist is now concerned with the fabrication of foods like steak made from vegetable protein; thus he is

TABLE 2

PRODUCT APPEARANCE ATTRIBUTES AND IMAGES

	Optical properties ←	┌ Colour ├ Translucency ├ Gloss ├ Uniformity └ Visual flavour
On-shelf image ┐ Preparation image ┤ ← ├ Physical form ←	┌ Shape and size ├ Surface texture └ Visual consistency
On-table image ┘	Mode of presentation ←	┌ Product description ├ Wrap package ├ Contrast phenomena └ Illumination

Reprinted from Reference 11 with permission.

concerned even more with total appearance, including factors like size and shape, and not with color alone.

Based on Kramer's[12] product attribute circle, Hutchings[11] goes on to describe in some detail the appearance zone of that circle which Kramer had not done. He proposes to divide appearance into three headings as shown in Table 2. All of these have an obvious overlap but it is a very interesting classification and emphasises the point that colour, although dependent on many other physical and optical attributes, is still only a part of total appearance.

Although others have reviewed the 'optical properties' classification, Hutchings introduces a novel term which he calls 'visual flavour' in this category. He proposes that the optical properties, particularly colour, occur at the appearance/flavour interface of the Kramer attribute circle whereby an anticipation of flavour is gained from the separate factors of appearance. Thus the term, visual flavour, which aptly describes an important function of colour in food choice.

Having given the total appearance factor of foods due recognition, I will now try to focus on the colour of foods, and all that implies, and its effect on food preferences and food choices. Some of the evidence for such interrelationships is qualitative and almost anecdotal in nature while other evidence is more quantitative. An attempt will be made in the following sections to separate such evidence into loose classifications which hopefully might provide a clearer understanding of the relationship between colour, other sensory attributes, preference and food choices.

3. QUALITATIVE INDICATIONS OF THE IMPORTANCE OF COLOUR

The colour blue means fidelity in Austria, indifference in Brazil, fright in Italy, anger in France and jealousy in Portugal. The social associations of colour with emotions have counterparts in the act of eating and food choices. Clydesdale[13] has pointed out that the food service industry has taken advantage of such associations in designing different types of eating environments for different types of restaurants. The fast-food service outlet where one may pick up a quick coffee and doughnut in the morning is quite often painted a bright, almost bilious yellow colour. This colour imparts an impression of cleanliness but also imparts a feeling of psychological activity which really does not enhance the mood for sitting around and enjoying one's coffee. However, it does provide a motivating force for removing oneself from such an atmosphere as quickly as possible. High volume is the secret in this case, and the colour provides the impetus for movement along with a feeling of cleanliness. If one looks further at food service areas, one can recall other eating establishments where the bright yellows are toned down by blues and browns. These would be the cafeterias where the meals are slightly more expensive, and yet, it is imperative to move people through in a fairly rapid fashion. Then we have the very expensive 'exclusive' type of food service establishments which use deep reds, deep browns, along with subdued lighting, which is nearly always incandescent or candlelight. There is a very good reason for this, since it provides not only an atmosphere aesthetically pleasing to the senses, so people may linger over cocktails or after-dinner drinks (which of course creates a profit), but in addition, it is known that cosmetics look particularly good under candlelight or incandescent light.

Kostyla and Clydesdale[14] quote several sources which verify the influence of experience on colour and further suggest that context also influences colour. Northern New England (north of Hartford, Connecticut, and east of Springfield, Massachusetts) is the only part of the US where brown eggs are preferred to white eggs, except at Easter when white eggs increase in sales.

The Joint FAO/WHO Expert Committee on Food Additives[15] recognised that colour has an effect on food choices, 'The value of color in food products lies mainly in the fact that the interest of consumers in a food may decrease if it does not have the color to which they have become accustomed'. Obviously such interest will have a very large effect on subsequent food preferences and choices. A report by the Institute of Food Technologists[16] supports this observation by quoting studies that show that food does not taste 'as it should' when it is not coloured 'right'.

Rolls et al.[17] investigated food intake and variety in food and obtained some interesting results. Presentation of a series of different yogurts to a group of male and female subjects created a greater intake compared to the intake when only one yogurt was offered. In this experiment the three different yogurts differed in flavour, colour, and texture. In order to assess the effect of flavour alone, they eliminated most of the colour and texture differences and re-evaluated intake on the same subjects. Interestingly, no enhancement of intake was noted in this case, indicating that flavour alone without colour and texture did not influence the consumption of yogurt. Another study with chocolates[17] also indicated that foods of the same basic type differing only in flavour do not enhance intake.

Wheatley[18] presented panel members with a dinner consisting of steak, peas and french fries abnormally coloured but served under colour masking conditions. During the meal, normal lighting was resumed revealing blue steaks, red peas and green french fries, which caused most of the subjects to become ill.

It seems to be obvious from these and other studies that abundant qualitative evidence exists to prove the existence of a direct link between colour, food preference and food choice.

4.   QUANTITATIVE INDICATIONS OF THE IMPORTANCE OF COLOUR

The basis of choice for distinguishing some studies as qualitative and some as quantitative is admittedly arbitrary. The distinction does not imply anything other than the fact that the studies which have been assigned a quantitative designation in this section seemed to be concerned with numerical data to a greater extent than the others. However, in any given instance, it is recognised that a study could easily be reclassified.

Hall[19] tested a panel's reaction to sherbets which had their flavour and colour mismatched. When the sherbets were white and made with any of the six test flavours (lemon, lime, orange, grape, pineapple, and almond), the panel was unable to identify correctly the individual flavours. When the same sherbets were deceptively coloured, most of the same judges also made wrong identifications. For instance, when lime-flavoured sherbet was coloured green, 75 % of the judges said it was lime, but when it was coloured purple, like grape, only 47 % identified it correctly. From these studies these researchers concluded that:

1. In this case colour far outweighs flavour in the impression it makes on the consumer, even when the flavours are pleasant and the food is a popular one.

2. Colour influences not only the consumer's ability to identify flavour but also to estimate strength and quality.

These results seem to be in agreement with Rolls' study,[17] discussed in the last section, with colour clearly playing a significant role over and above flavour in food choice.

Earlier studies[20] by Foster also confirmed this observation. In a study with forty consumers, who evaluated a speckled versus an unspeckled dry snack food, a significant preference for the unspeckled dry product was found. This is an interesting observation in light of the popularity of the speckled, mint-like confections currently on the market. However, it does point out that colour and appearance effects on food preference cannot be generalised and are often product specific. Indeed, Foster[20] found an opposite effect when evaluating a speckled 'charcoal grilled' sample. Schutz[21] demonstrated the importance of colour by raising the flavour score of an inferior juice by simply adding colour and Ringo[22] showed significant colour–flavour interaction in hedonic responses to milk shakes. In this study, milk shakes containing 3 %, 6 % or 8 % sucrose were utilised as carriers of different flavours and were either correctly coloured, incorrectly coloured or had the colours masked prior to flavour evaluation. Samples which contained 6 % sucrose and were correctly flavoured and coloured generally received the highest hedonic measurements. As well, the more concentrated sucrose samples were reported to have more intense flavours than the corresponding 3 % sucrose samples. Panelists found it more difficult to identify the uncoloured samples than those with colour cues. It was concluded that colour had a significant influence on flavour recognition, perceived flavour intensity and on the overall degree of preference of the milk shakes.

The significant role of colour in correct identification of food flavours and hedonic quality was also investigated by DuBose et al.[23] They found that colour masking dramatically decreased flavour identification of fruit-flavoured beverages, while atypical colours induced incorrect flavour

TABLE 3

PERCENTAGES OF FLAVOUR RESPONSES TO EACH OF THE 16 BEVERAGES COLLAPSED ACCORDING TO FLAVOURS WITH SIMILAR COLOUR ASSOCIATIONS ($N = 27$)

Flavour responses	Test beverages															
	Cherry flavoured				Orange flavoured				Lime flavoured				Flavourless			
	Red	Orange	Green	Colourless	Red	Orange	Green	Colourless	Red	Orange	Green	Colourless	Red	Orange	Green	Colourless
Cherry/strawberry/raspberry	92·6	51·8	44·4	55·5	44·7	3·7	—	3·7	33·3	—	—	—	33·3	—	—	11·1
Orange/apricot	—	29·6	3·7	3·7	33·3	81·5	29·6	29·6	3·7	59·2	—	3·7	—	29·6	—	3·7
Lime/lemon–lime	—	3·7	37·0	14·8	11·1	3·7	40·7	22·2	33·3	22·2	85·1	66·7	—	—	40·7	—
Lemon/grapefruit/apple	—	7·4	3·7	18·5	—	3·7	14·8	29·6	3·7	11·1	3·7	14·8	14·8	14·8	11·1	22·2
Blueberry/grape/other	3·7	7·4	11·1	7·4	7·4	3·7	11·1	3·7	7·4	3·7	7·4	7·4	11·1	11·1	7·4	14·8
No flavour	3·7	—	—	—	7·4	3·7	3·7	7·4	18·5	3·7	3·7	7·4	40·7	44·4	40·7	48·1

Reprinted from Reference 23. Copyright © by Institute of Food Technologists.

responses that were characteristically associated with the atypical colour, as shown in Table 3. In this table all flavour categories which are normally associated with the same predominant colour are combined along with the same collapsed percentage of responses. It is apparent that inappropriate colouring of the four flavoured beverages induced flavour responses that are normally associated with that colour. For example, the orange-coloured, cherry-flavoured beverage was most frequently mis-identified as having an orange or apricot flavour, the green-coloured, cherry-flavoured beverage was most frequently mis-identified as lime or lemon/lime, and the colourless, cherry-flavoured beverage was most frequently mis-identified as lemon, grapefruit or apple. Similar patterns can be seen elsewhere in Table 3.

In addition, the colour level of beverages had significant effects on their overall acceptability, acceptability of colour and flavour, as well as on flavour intensity. The same results were shown with cake samples, with the exception that a significant interaction of colour and flavour level was observed on overall acceptability. It should be noted that, although colour was extremely important, correlational analysis showed the overall acceptability of both the beverage and cake products was more closely associated with ratings of flavour acceptability than with ratings of colour acceptability. Interestingly, the inclusion of colourant safety information did not affect any aspect of a product's acceptability.

5. EFFECT OF COLOUR ON TASTE THRESHOLDS

At this point it would seem that ample evidence has been offered to document the role of colour in the enjoyment of food, quality of life, food choices, food preference and even appropriate flavour identification. Based on these observations, it could be assumed that colour may play an even more basic role from both a physiological and psychological view in our relationship to food. Pangborn[24] has suggested that parotid flow may be stimulated by the sight as well as the feel and odour of a lemon and she saw slight changes in salivary secretions in response to 1·6% sodium chloride solution upon changing illumination and background noise.[25] Therefore, it is reasonable to assume that colour might affect taste thresholds and, in fact, several workers have studied this phenomenon. Pangborn[26] evaluated the influence of colour on sweetness discrimination, which might be considered as being potentially indicative of threshold discrimination. In the initial part of this study, beverages were prepared with various concentrations of sucrose, citric acid and artificial flavouring and colouring in distilled water. On different days, the beverages were presented for evaluation under overhead, daylight or red illumination to mask colour differences. It was found that the untrained panelists had a slight tendency to ascribe greater sweetness and greater flavour to orange- and red-coloured solutions containing apricot and cherry flavouring respectively, especially when sucrose differences were very small. Under red illumination the untrained panelists were more accurate than the highly trained, who Pangborn suggests may have been distracted by the red light. Interestingly, both panels showed a tendency to ascribe more sweetness and more flavour to the first sample within a pair. In the second part of this study, the effect of specific colours on the discrimination of sucrose levels was examined and it was found that sweetness discrimination was not influenced by red, green or yellow colouring in unflavoured aqueous solutions. However, in pear nectar there was a tendency to designate the green-coloured samples as the least sweet. Pangborn speculated that the green colour was associated with tartness or lack of sweetness.

Schutte and Zubek[27] evaluated the effect of visual deprivation on taste sensitivity to salt and sucrose and found it to be significant within one day after normal visual stimuli were resumed. The influence of ambient light on the intensity of acid taste was studied by Gregson[28] utilising three concentrations of citric acid and four illumination levels. He concluded that ambient light had a tendency to increase acid taste intensity slightly and that the intensification effect was not easily explained as a simple threshold shift.

Maga[29] designed a study to investigate specifically the possible interaction of colour (colourless, red, green and yellow) with the threshold concentrations of the four basic tastes (salty, sour, bitter, and sweet) on a simple model system of water. The investigator concluded that, 'this study clearly demonstrated that color can influence a person's ability to distinguish threshold levels of the four basic tastes'. The study showed that in most cases coloured solutions needed to be more concentrated before subjects were capable of identifying the specific taste. This was especially true for sour and bitter tastes but the insensitivity varied with colour, thus implicating the psychological role of specific food association with specific colours.

Each basic taste was affected by colour as follows:

Sour—A red-coloured sour solution was detected at a slightly higher concentration than the colourless sour solution. However, the sour flavour in yellow and green solutions was detected at significantly higher concentrations than in the colourless sour solution.

Bitter—Yellow and green bitter solutions were detected at significantly higher concentration than the colourless bitter control, but red bitter solutions required the highest concentration of all. Thus, people apparently do not associate a red colour with a bitter taste.

Sweet—The yellow sweet solution was detected at significantly higher concentration than the colourless control. Thus, people did not associate yellow colour with a sweet taste. However, the green-coloured sweet solution was detectable at a concentration significantly below that of the control.

Salt—No coloured salt solutions were detected at concentrations significantly different from that of the colourless control. The investigator explained this by citing the fact that numerous foods of varying colour can be characterised as tasting salty; examples would be pretzels (brown), potato chips (yellow), popcorn (white), olives (green, black) and pickles (green) and, therefore, people have few direct food colour associations with saltiness.

Johnson and Clydesdale[30] investigated the effect of colour and/or flavour on sweetness threshold using unsweetened distilled water as the zero stimulus reference. The method used to determine the stimulus threshold ('Reiz Limen' or 'RL') was a variation of limits or serial exploration which reflects the minimum sucrose concentration at which a sweet taste can be detected. The composition of samples and threshold values obtained are shown in Table 4. The results indicated that both colour and flavour affected the threshold of the group. Although the intensity of the red colour (0.325 ml% in Test C and 1.5 ml% in Test E) made no significant difference, the interaction effect between the subject and colour was significant at the 2% level of confidence (Test A vs. Tests C and E) whereas the interaction effect of flavour on the subjects' sweetness thresholds only approached significance. Overall variation among the subjects was highly significant ($p < 0.001$) which would be expected from a random population of people with different sensitivities to the basic taste components of food systems. The standard errors of the mean ranged from 0.09 to 0.54, indicating little variability of the RL within the group threshold. Nonetheless, the effect of colour and flavour was evident.

The response by the panel to the addition of colour may be explained by the psychological association of the cherry red to the optimal development of sweetness and quality in fruits. However, a comparison of individual thresholds in the darkest solutions showed variation among the responses.

TABLE 4

FORMULATION AND THRESHOLD VALUE OF SAMPLES CONTAINING
DISTILLED WATER, COLOURANT, SUCROSE AND FLAVOUR UTILISED
IN THE THRESHOLD TESTS FOR SWEETNESS PERCEPTION

Test	Medium in which sucrose[e] was dispersed	Group sucrose threshold (M) $n = 13$
A[a]	Distilled water	0·005 4
B[a]	Distilled water 1·4 ml % of 1 % Cherry Flavour[b]	0·003 8
C[a]	0·325 ml % of 1 % Red No. 40[c] 0·12 ml % of 0·02 % Blue No. 1[d]	0·003 8
D[a]	0·325 ml % of Red No. 40 0·12 ml % of Blue No. 1 Cherry Flavour	0·003 7
E[a]	1·5 ml % Red No. 40 0·12 ml % Blue No. 1	0·004 6
F[a]	1·5 ml % Red No. 40 0·12 ml % Blue No. 1 Cherry Flavour	0·004 1

[a] Colourless, unsweetened, unflavoured distilled water was used as the reference.
[b] Flavour-cap imitation Cherry, #30042 (McCormick & Co., Hunt Valley, MD).
[c] FD & C Red No. 40, #7700 (Warner Jenkinson Company, St Louis, MO).
[d] FD & C Blue No. 1, #5601 (Warner Jenkinson Company).
[e] Sucrose concentrations: 0·001, 0·001 5, 0·003 6, 0·007 3, 0·001 1, 0·015 and 0·029 M.
Reprinted from Reference 30. Copyright © by Institute of Food Technologists.

For some the darker colours may 'psychologically' mask the sweet taste thus raising their threshold or it may have been associated with a specific food. Maga,[29] who found that colour often raised the taste threshold, speculated that colour–taste associations with frequently consumed foods have the effect of raising the individual's basic taste threshold, which may in part explain this result.

Johnson[31] also evaluated the effect of strawberry colours and flavour and raspberry colours and flavour on threshold levels of sucrose. In the case of strawberry beverages, the average group threshold in the lighter coloured samples showed an increase over that in the colourless reference sample which was similar to Maga's results.[29] However, there was essentially no change in threshold value with the darker colour. From an analysis of variance the subject–colour interaction effect was significant and the effects of flavour on the group threshold as well as subject variation were highly significant.

The noticeable response to the light strawberry colour may be related to a subjective bias with respect to the colour itself. Kostyla[32] reported that the addition of yellow to red fruit colours lowered the magnitude estimates of perceived sweetness. On the threshold level for sweetness this would be expressed in a need for higher concentrations of sucrose to stimulate sweetness perception in the light, yellow–red strawberry colour. The judges were more sensitive to sweetness in the darker strawberry colours in threshold Test E than to the colour of Test C.

The evaluation of beverages with raspberry colour and flavour introduced some rather interesting results. In colourless distilled water, the addition of flavour tended to raise the threshold instead of lowering it as observed in the other flavoured threshold tests. However, this might be explained by the fact that the observed differences in thresholds due to flavour or colour among the six tests were not significant and variation in threshold responses due to colour effects only approached significance. As well, overall variation among the subjects was highly significant.

From this discussion it is obvious that colour plays a significant role in taste thresholds. However, it is also obvious that this role is not consistent and, therefore, may not be generalised from food to food, colour to colour or flavour to flavour. This does not decrease the significance of its role but simply means that effects, if they exist, will probably be food–flavour–colour specific. Therefore, the dependency of individual taste threshold and perhaps food choices will be a function of the role of colour in a particular food.

6. COLOUR–FLAVOUR INVESTIGATIONS UTILISING QUANTITATIVE COLOUR MEASUREMENT TECHNIQUES

In addition to the studies discussed previously, several other investigations have been concerned with the effect of colour on specific flavours both in foods and in model systems. These studies are of interest because they further delineate the degree of importance and complexity of the role of colour in food acceptance, selection and choice. As noted previously, Maga[29] concluded that colour can alter basic taste thresholds. For instance, green decreased the threshold for sweetness (sucrose) while yellow increased it and red had little effect. Interestingly, these findings seem to be contrary to those of Pangborn[26] and Pangborn and Hansen,[33] but similar to those of Grinker et al.[34] for the red, since they found no difference in the detection of sucrose when a tasteless red vegetable dye was added to the medium. Maga[29] explains the differences between his study and Pangborn's[26] by the fact that Pangborn's study was performed with 5 % sucrose solutions, while his study employed only threshold levels of sucrose. In the Pangborn study[26] it was reported that a green-coloured pear nectar was judged less sweet than other coloured samples. This was explained by Maga as being due to the fact that most people would associate a green-coloured pear nectar as being derived from immature pears, which would not normally be sweet.

In a recommendation for further research in this area, Kostyla and Clydesdale[14] suggested studies which would begin to define, in a quantitative manner, what a quantitative shift in colour would do to flavour, utilising the objective methodology available for not only flavour but for colour as well. They proposed the use of tristimulus colorimetry so that mathematical colour functions could be used and exact distances in colour space measured in order to define differences in colour. This was a departure from most of the colour/flavour research performed up until this time, which utilised only sensory perception of colour and not objective instrumental techniques. On this recommendation Kostyla[32] instituted a study to evaluate not only the relationship between several colours and flavours, but also to evaluate instrumentation and colour scales which might best be utilised in such a study. It was found that both the Gardner and Hunter tristimulus colorimeters were well suited for such a study utilising the modified L^*, a^*, b^* [35] scale to describe the colours. Employing red-coloured beverages of different flavours, it was found that the expression representing total colour difference (ΔE) was the most useful for describing psychophysical relationships between colour and taste in this study.

Cherry-, strawberry-, and raspberry-flavoured beverages, with all ingredients kept constant except for colour, were evaluated for perceived changes in aroma, flavour, sweetness and tartness after the addition of red, blue, green or yellow food colourants.

The general trend obtained from this particular set of panelists was towards an increase in the perceived sweetness as the redness of some fruit-flavoured beverages was increased. It may be remembered that Pangborn[33] did not report such a correlation in aqueous solutions while Maga[29] found green to increase sweet taste threshold sensitivity. Kostyla[32] proposed to explain these discrepancies by pointing out that the studies of Pangborn[33] and Maga[29] were performed on unflavoured sucrose solutions. Unflavoured solutions to which colourants have been added might confuse the panelists. In such preparations there are no specific flavours to identify the samples with and, therefore, they rely on their past experiences. However, relying on memory may also cause confusion because there are foods that are of one general colour but are of conflicting basic tastes. For example, there are sweet yellow bananas and sour yellow lemons. There are sweet green grapes and sour green apples. In addition to this, there are also foods which are consumed in both the immature and the mature stages such as sour green mangoes and sweet yellow mangoes or sour green tomatoes and sweet red tomatoes. The absence of a definite flavour in the samples being tested may also have contributed to the discrepancies.

Thus, when Pangborn[33] employed a pear nectar medium, she detected a decrease in sweetness in green coloured samples since green pears are quickly associated as immature and not sweet, as previously suggested by Maga.[29] Similarly, cherries, strawberries, and raspberries are red (sometimes deep red) when mature, and, at which stage are sweet. Although consumers may not be aware that they are following a psychological association of colours with foods, there is no doubt that they do.

The addition of a blue colourant to a cherry-flavoured and red-coloured beverage to achieve a colour which was still realistically acceptable caused a decrease in both flavour and tartness by as much as 20 %. Similar results were seen in strawberry-flavoured beverages, but a lesser effect was seen in raspberry-flavoured beverages.

The addition of increasing amounts of green was detected by the panelists in cherry-flavoured beverages and, to a lesser degree, in strawberry- and raspberry-flavoured drinks. Green actually deepened the cherry colour to brownish black, almost the shade of root beer, and although the intensity scale was employed for the entire experimentation the panelists revealed a dislike for the changes made in the cherry colour. Qualitatively, green did not enhance the fruit colour.

Unlike the addition of red and blue to the beverages, the addition of green to red-coloured beverages did not produce any consistent psychophysical correlations in this study.[32] Although Pangborn[33] reported that green pear nectar solutions were detected to be least sweet and Maga[29] found just the opposite using unflavoured sucrose solutions, there was no detection of a significant green–sweet correlation in the present study. However, the perceived tartness of the strawberry samples seemed to increase, while that of the raspberry samples decreased by approximately

10 % with an approximate increase of 5 % in perceived flavour. Insufficient correlations restricted any further comparisons with perceived sweetness or aroma. Inconsistencies may be due to the particular colourant added. Kostyla[32] suggests that this is due to the fact that green did not complement the colour of the beverages and created 'unnatural colours' making the panelists unclear and confused as to the sensations being perceived. The fact that the panelists were not able to identify the correct fruit flavours of these unnaturally coloured beverages supports this postulation, since it follows that if the basic fruit flavour was not certain, the panelists might have difficulty in evaluating the specific flavour attributes of the beverage such as sweetness and tartness. Consumers prefer foods which they can identify and are familiar with—either through their own experience or through the experiences of others. They like 'naturally' coloured foods such as red beets or green spinach. Foods which have been unacceptably coloured (or uncoloured) might not be consumed and any efforts which would have contributed to the enhancement of the taste attributes would not be fully realised.

Yellow produced a golden tone in the beverages which consequently tended to decrease the redness of the samples and this was perceived by the panelists as a decrease in the fruit colour, which they liked less. However, this created only slight changes in the perception of sweetness and tartness in the samples. The reduction in sweetness tends to agree with the results obtained previously since the yellow decreased red perception which was found to affect sweetness in other experiments. It is interesting to note that yellow was more acceptable than green when added to these beverages, perhaps because the flavour was more identifiable. However, it was reported[32] that the addition of yellow did affect overall perception of fruit flavour in the beverages.

Kostyla's study[32] attempted to quantify some of the colour/flavour interactions utilising a constant level of sucrose and varying the colour in flavoured beverage solutions. The results obtained were interesting, but it was felt that more information could be obtained by designing experiments with varying levels of sugar as well as colour in both flavoured and unflavoured beverages. In the first of several such studies, Johnson and Clydesdale[30] evaluated the effects of colour on sweetness perception in red-coloured solutions. In this study the five cherry colours utilised were chosen to represent a range about a commercially acceptable sample and were formulated as follows. Each red-coloured solution contained 0·12 ml % of a 0·02 % solution of FD & C Blue No. 1 plus the following amount of a 1·0 %

TABLE 5
CONCENTRATIONS OF SUCROSE UTILISED IN
EACH TEST GROUP FOR EVALUATION IN THE
CHERRY-COLOURED SOLUTIONS AND DISTILLED
WATER

Group	Sucrose concentrations (% w/v)				
I	2·7	3·3	4·0[a]	4·7	5·3
II	3·2	3·6	4·0	4·4	4·8
III	3·4	3·8	4·0	4·2	4·6

[a] Reference concentration.
Reprinted from Reference 31 with permission.

solution of FD & C Red No. 40: 0·25 % Red No. 40 (Colour 1); 0·50 % Red No. 40 (Colour 2); 1·0 % Red No. 40 (Colour 3—reference); 2·0 % Red No. 40 (Colour 4); and 5·0 % Red No. 40 (Colour 5).

Interestingly, the reference chosen for this study was darker in colour than commercial samples since preliminary studies indicated a panel preference for the darker colour. Colour was measured instrumentally using the Gardner XL-23 Colorimeter and the G.E. Recording Spectrophotometer and all values were converted to the CIE 1976 L^*, a^*, b^*[35] by computer programs developed in our laboratory.

Thirteen sucrose concentrations were chosen for the study and divided into three groups (I, II and III) as shown in Table 5. Each sucrose group was evaluated with a single colour (1, 2, 3, 4 or 5) described above. Colour versus sweetness was evaluated utilising the technique of magnitude estimation for each group with each colour over a six-day test period for a total of 18 days. A single panel of 14 subjects evaluated a single sugar group and then a new panel with some small member overlap was chosen to evaluate the next group in order to minimise fatigue. Each sugar group had the same reference concentration of 4 % sucrose, a concentration similar in taste to that of commercial fruit drinks. The concentration of sugar and the cherry red colours evaluated daily were chosen at random so by the end of the six-day period, each red colour had been sweetened with all 5 sucrose concentrations within a sugar group. Only the 4 % sucrose reference remained the same each day. All of the solutions were formulated and sweetened 24 h in advance and were served at room temperature, $24 \pm 1\,°C$.

To quantify the effect of colour on the consumer's perception of

TABLE 6

REGRESSION ANALYSIS OF PERCEIVED SWEETNESS IN RED-COLOURED SOLUTIONS VERSUS
SUCROSE CONCENTRATIONS RANGING FROM 2·7 % TO 5·3 % (GROUP I), 3·2 % TO 4·8 %
(GROUP II), 3·4 to 4·6 % (GROUP III)

Physical variable[a]	Y-Intercept (log)	Slope (log)	Coefficient of determination r^2
Group I			
Colour 1	−0·381	2·20	0·947
Colour 2	−0·543	2·55	0·990
Colour 3	−0·750	2·86	0·976
Colour 4	−0·458	2·39	0·953
Colour 5	−0·606	2·70	0·992
Group II			
Colour 1	−0·113	2·23	0·817
Colour 2	−0·359	2·61	0·956
Colour 3	−0·290	2·53	0·988
Colour 4	−0·340	2·62	0·902
Colour 5	+0·580	1·09	0·956
Group III			
Colour 1	−0·602	3·32	0·906
Colour 2	−0·249	2·79	0·835
Colour 3	+0·223	2·20	0·817
Colour 4	−0·256	2·85	0·899
Colour 5	−1·200	4·41	0·817

[a] Colour 1 = 0·25 % Red 40, Colour 2 = 0·50 % Red 40, Colour 3 = 1·0 % Red 40,
Colour 4 = 2·0 % Red 40, Colour 5 = 5·0 % Red 40.
Reprinted from Reference 30. Copyright © by Institute of Food Technologists.

sweetness, it was felt that different intensities of colour should be evaluated
at various concentrations of sucrose. This test was designed not only to
quantify the colour–sweetness relationship but also to evaluate the
potential of utilising colour to create the same sweetness perception at a
lower concentration of sugar. As previously mentioned, each of the five
colours was sweetened to the five sugar concentrations over the six-day test
period. The colours and sugar levels used daily, except the reference colour
and sugar levels, were chosen at random. The greater the number assigned
to the sample, the sweeter the perceived taste.

The normalised magnitude estimates obtained from the evaluation of
sweetness in each of the five coloured solutions within the three sugar
groups were plotted as log-sweetness against the log-percent sugar (Figs 1,

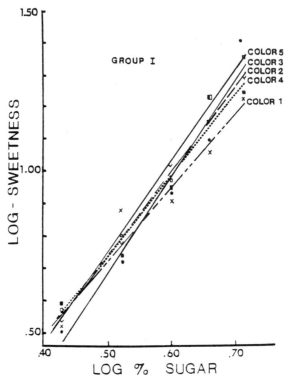

FIG. 1. Perceived sweetness (log-sweetness) in five cherry-coloured solutions containing 2·75%–5·3% sucrose plotted against sugar concentration (log-percent sugar). Colour 1 (×) = 0·25% Red No. 40; Colour 2 (∨) = 0·5% Red No. 40; Colour 3 (●) = 1·0% Red No. 40; Colour 4 (□) = 2·0% Red No. 40; Colour 5 (■) = 5·0% Red No. 40. Reprinted from Reference 30. Copyright © by Institute of Food Technologists.

2, 3) with the results of the regression analysis for each group given in Table 6. The difference in concentration between sugar levels within each sugar group affected the panel's ability to quantify the sweetness perceived. The wider difference between the reference concentration (4% sucrose) and each sugar level within Groups I and II made the panel's task of evaluating the sweetness easier. Many of the panel members evaluating the sugar levels within Group III commented that they had difficulty tasting a difference between some of the samples and, therefore, the magnitude estimates may not reflect the quantity of perceived sweetness. An examination of the coefficients of determination in Table 6 shows a higher correlation between

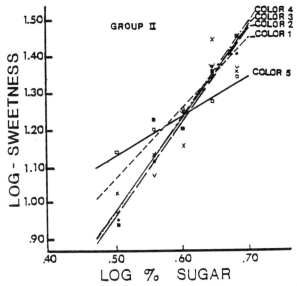

FIG. 2. Perceived sweetness (log-sweetness) in five cherry-coloured solutions containing 3·2%–4·8% sucrose plotted against sugar concentration (log-percent sugar). Colours 1–5 are the same as defined in Fig. 1. Reprinted from Reference 30. Copyright © by Institute of Food Technologists.

the psychological perception of sweetness and sugar concentration within Groups I and II than observed for Group III. The lower values for r^2 within Group III suggest the following:

1. There is a sugar concentration range of ±5% about the reference within which an untrained, consumer panel such as this one is unable to taste any difference in sweetness.

2. The influence of colour intensity on perceived sweetness may compound the difficulty of quantifying sweetness in samples with small differences in concentration.

The values of the power exponent n expressing the rate of change in sweetness perception versus increase in sugar concentration (slope) for sugar Groups I, II and III are shown in Table 6. For Group I these values ranged from 2·2 to 2·86 and are all consistent with those found for the same sugar group in sweetened distilled water (slope = 2·52). Therefore, the addition of colour did not affect the apparent relative relationship between the magnitude estimates for sweetness and sugar concentration. However, from an inspection of the spatial relationship of the lines representing each

F. M. CLYDESDALE

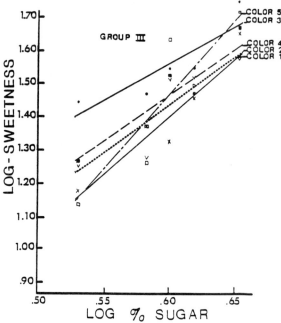

FIG. 3.   Perceived sweetness (log-sweetness) in five cherry-coloured solutions containing 3·4%–4·6% sucrose plotted against sugar concentration (log-percent sugar). Colours 1–5 are the same as defined in Fig. 1. Reprinted from Reference 30. Copyright © by Institute of Food Technologists.

of the red colours in Fig. 1, the differences in the calculated values of the slopes and Y-intercepts may be related to psychological associations between the intensity of fruit colour and sweetness and between the intensity of red colour and pleasantness. At a lower or equal concentration range to the reference (less than log = 0·6) Colours 2, 4 and 5 were assigned higher magnitude estimates, i.e., perceived to be sweeter than the reference colour (4% sucrose) and Colour 1 (2·8–4·0% sucrose), the lightest cherry red colour. Colour 5 (the darkest colour) was consistently reported as sweeter than any of the other samples between a sucrose concentration of 2·8% and 5·3% (log = 0·72). Colour 2 samples containing approximately 3·0%–4·0% sucrose were found somewhat sweeter than the same concentrations containing Colour 4. Pleasantness effects may have contributed to these results because, as shown in Fig. 4, at a sucrose concentration of 4% (log = 0·60) the panel rated the samples containing Colour 2 as more pleasant than those with the darker cherry colour 4.

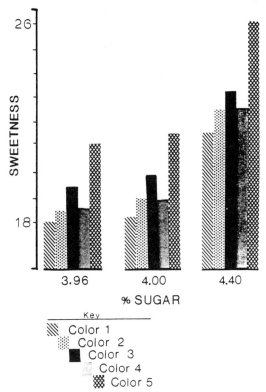

FIG. 4. Sweetness estimates for cherry-coloured and -flavoured solutions containing 3·96%, 4·0% and 4·4% sucrose. Colour 1 = 0·25% Red No. 40, Colour 2 = 0·50% Red No. 40, Colour 3 = 1·0% Red No. 40, Colour 4 = 2·0% Red No. 40 and Colour 5 = 5·0% Red No. 40. Reprinted from Reference 40 with permission.

However, by defining the psychophysical relationship between perceived sweetness and sucrose concentration in coloured solutions (as shown graphically in Fig. 1), it seems that colour accounts for a small percentage of our sweetness perception. For example, from the regression analysis of the normalised grand geometric means, the reference sample (Colour 3 with 4% sucrose) was rated a sweetness value of log 0·972. To maintain this level of sweetness in the darker samples, Colours 4 and 5, the sugar would be reduced 1·5% and 4·5% respectively so Colour 4 would be a 3·94% sucrose solution and Colour 5, a 3·82% sucrose solution. If the sugar content for all three colours were reduced by 1% (to 3·96% sucrose), the increase in perceived sweetness from Colour 3 to Colour 4 would be approximately 2·5 % and from Colour 3 to Colour 5 it would be over 10 %. However, a substitution of Colour 5 for Colour 3 should not be considered as a feasible change without first considering interaction effects of pleasantness and colour acceptability, which can bias the consumer's basic taste responses.

If each judge had been trained to detect small changes in sucrose concentration and to quantify them more precisely, it may have been possible to reduce the personal biases which can complicate the interpretation of the sensory responses from a consumer panel. In Fig. 2, Group II, the slope of the line representing Colour 5 approaches a linear relationship with respect to the increase in sugar. The value of the slope, 1·09, is shown in Table 6 and is inconsistent with both the panel's responses to the other four coloured, sweetened solutions within Group II and with the results obtained from the sweetened distilled water test where the exponent n for Group II was calculated to be 2·63. It is suspected that the panel's responses may have been biased by a response to pleasantness, taste adaptation, regression effects or lack of colour acceptability for a cherry red solution. These same factors may also account for the graphic representation of sweetness in samples containing Colour 1. Pleasantness effects are a problem associated with the method of magnitude estimation[36,37] and will be discussed later in this chapter.

Regression effects, like pleasantness effects, are a problem associated with magnitude estimation. Observers have been found to constrict the range of their numerical values in avoidance of extreme numbers representing sweetness at the lower and higher concentration levels. This results in exponents which are lower than would be expected without the observer's bias. A bias to the colour itself, i.e., its acceptability as a cherry red colour, may lower or raise the values of the power exponents at the extreme colour ranges. Colour 1 was a very pale cherry red and Colour 5 was an intense dark red. If the colours were visually unappealing, the judges may have biased their sweetness estimates by assigning lower than expected numbers.

The rates of increase in perceived sweetness in Colours 2, 3 and 4 were consistent with that obtained in sweetened distilled water, showing an accelerated function between sweetness and concentrations, $n > 2·5$. The intensity of the red colour also had an effect on the magnitude of assigned sweetness estimates as shown in Fig. 2 by the line positions representing Colours 3 and 4 and by the values of their respective slopes of 2·53 and 2·62. Perceived sweetness increased at a faster rate in the darker colour which tells us at the same level of sugar the darker Colour 4 solution would be perceived sweeter than one with Colour 3. The coefficients of determination for Colours 2–5 in Group II and for all 5 colours evaluated in Group 1 indicate that over 90 % of the changes in perceived sweetness are attributed to changes in the sugar concentration.

There was considerably more variation in response to Group III. The slopes, Y-intercepts, and coefficients of determination were less consistent suggesting that:

1. The panel had more difficulty in perceiving and quantifying small changes in sugar concentration.

2. Over a medium range of sugar concentrations as found in Group III, perceived sweetness is influenced by factors other than sugar concentration. Some of these factors may include the effects just discussed above, i.e. pleasantness, regression, taste adaptation and colour acceptability.

Utilising a similar experimental design, Johnson et al.[39,40] continued their investigation using flavoured and coloured beverages with varying amounts of sucrose rather than the more simple unflavoured system just described.

Five different strawberry colours were formulated using increasing volumes of FD & C Red No. 40 and a constant volume of both FD & C Yellow No. 6 and strawberry flavourings.[39] In this study one range of sucrose concentrations was used varying from 3·2 % to 4·8 % as follows: 3·2 %, 3·4 %, 3·6 %, 4·0 %, 4·4 %, 4·6 % and 4·8 % (w/v). It was found that the colour–sweetness function was linear over a narrow colour range and that sweetness perception increased 2–12 % with increasing colour in 4 % sucrose solutions. In general, sweetness was influenced by both pleasantness effects and colour acceptability, with the mid-range coloured sample being perceived as one of the sweetest, most pleasant tasting drinks with the most acceptable colour.

In another study[40] which served to confirm these results, five red colours were formulated to simulate cherry red colours. Increasing volumes of 1 % FD & C Red No. 40 were added to a constant concentration of both 0·02 % FD & C Blue No. 1 and imitation cherry flavour to produce visually perceptible changes in colour. The reference colour was anchored in the middle of the range so responses could be evaluated in lighter and darker solutions. Sucrose was used at the following levels: 3·2 %, 3·4 %, 3·6 %, 4·0 %, 4·4 %, 4·6 %, and 4·8 %, which were also utilised in the strawberry beverage study.[39] The 4 % sucrose reference had a taste similar to a commercial cherry drink. In accord with the previous studies, it was found that over 90 % of the perceived sweetness could be accounted for by the increase in sucrose concentration, as might be expected. This means that in the ranges used in these studies the maximum effect of colour would be 10 %, which is not insignificant. Also, it was noted in this study that the presence of flavour in combination with colour seemed to decrease the magnitude of sweetness differences between samples, thus slowing the rate of increase in sweetness and producing smaller exponents than were found in the unflavoured study.[30] One of the judges said he expected a 'more intense taste' in the darker flavoured drinks because of the intensity of the colour and the familar fruit odour. It will be remembered that Pangborn[26] reported greater sweetness and flavour perception in red- and orange-coloured solutions containing apricot and cherry flavouring, which seems to lend credence to this observation.

A comparison of perceived sweetness at 3·96 %, 4·0 % and 4·4 % sucrose in the coloured, flavoured drinks is shown in Fig. 4. Sweetness increased 3–13 % with increasing colour intensity except with Colour 4 which was approximately as sweet as Colour 2 solution. If Colours 2, 3 and 4 were formulated with 3·96 % sucrose (1 % below the reference concentration) and compared to a 4 % solution of Colour 1, the darker colours would be 1·2 %, 6·7 % and 1·3 % sweeter, respectively. To obtain the same magnitude of sweetness as reported in the Colour 1 solution with 4 % sucrose, Colour 2 solution would contain 1·5 % less sucrose, Colour 3 solution would have approximately 4 % less and Colour 5 solution would have about 7 % less sucrose. Thus colour might be considered for a slight enhancement of sweetness perception.

Although the statistical evaluation of sweetness against colour, expressed as arctan a^*/b^*, produced poor coefficients of determination, it should be noted that the subject–colour interaction effect was highly significant at the 4 % sucrose level and approached significance at the 4·4 % sucrose level.

Deviations at the lowest and highest stimuli concentrations of colour and sucrose may be related to interactions of the dependent variables, colour and sucrose concentration, on the original power law control function, resulting in a new expression. Similar reports have been made previously[36] suggesting that more accurate discrimination of sweetness occurs at lower sucrose concentrations with deviations more likely at the medium and higher concentrations.

From these studies,[39,40] it is apparent that the perception of sweetness in a flavoured and coloured beverage seems to be a highly complicated function of many factors related most highly to sucrose concentration but significantly to the colour of the beverage as well. Obviously the colour would play an important role in the preference and choice of such a food.

7. EFFECT OF COLOUR ON ODOUR

Food choices and food preferences are predicated upon flavour among other things. Flavour in turn is dependent upon both taste and odour. Therefore, in an evaluation of the effect of food colour on preference and choice, it would seem prudent to examine the effect of colour not only upon taste but upon odour as well.

There has been a limited amount of work conducted in this area but due to its potential importance two studies will be mentioned briefly. Kostyla[32] found that for a 10 % change in redness the perceived aroma of a cherry-flavoured beverage was decreased by up to 5 % but this effect was not seen in strawberry- and raspberry-flavoured beverages. In these same beverages the addition of blue caused a random but significant difference in fruit aroma. Green provided insufficient correlation for any conclusions to be drawn about aroma, probably for the same reasons as were discussed previously, and yellow did not affect aroma judgements.

An interesting approach to this problem was offered by Vargo[41] who conducted experiments on the influence of colour on identification, perceived intensity and degree of liking of the odours of micro-encapsulated fragrances (MF) and of the odours and flavours of sweetened, acidified solutions.

In the first part of this study micro-encapsulated food fragrances (vanilla, orange, mint, strawberry, grape, chocolate, anise and diethyl-phthalate blank (DEP)) were each mounted on cards against background colours of creamy white, orange, green, red, purple, brown, black and colourless. Identification was greatest for mint and least for vanilla, grape, and strawberry. More correct identifications were obtained against 'appropriate' colours for orange, mint, grape, anise and the control; however, few odour intensities were colour dependent. The mint aroma was considered to be most intense and the control was the weakest and only the vanilla and orange samples provided hedonic responses greater on the 'appropriate' creamy white and orange background colours, respectively. Mint and orange were liked best and the control was liked least. It seems obvious from this rather unique study that colour has a significant but rather unpredictable effect on odours, at least micro-encapsulated fragrances.

In the second part of the study, 55 subjects smelled MF and smelled and tasted solutions with seven flavours (mint, orange, strawberry, grape, chocolate, anise and the blank), in each of seven colours (green, orange, red, purple, brown, black and colourless). For MF, only orange, grape and chocolate aromas were more easily identified when on 'appropriate' background colours. Mint received the most and strawberry the least number of correct identifications. The MF aromas were most intense on 'appropriate' colours only for orange and the control. There was a greater liking against the 'appropriate' colours only for mint, orange and chocolate. In general, mint and orange were liked most and grape was liked least.

The aromas of the solutions were identified with greater accuracy when in the 'appropriate' colour for all samples except anise. When taken by mouth, more correct flavour identifications were made when solutions had the 'appropriate' colours for all samples except chocolate and anise. For both aroma and flavour, there were more correct identifications for chocolate and least for strawberry.

No significant colour effects were noted for the odour intensity of solutions, however, strawberry had higher scores when red. No significant odour/colour effects were obtained for degree of liking of aroma or of flavour of the solutions, although mint and chocolate were considered more intense and were better liked in their 'appropriate' colours. In general, strawberry and orange were the best liked aromas/flavours and the control was liked least.

Hedonic responses were positively correlated with intensity for smelling MF ($r = 0.36, p > 0.05$), for smelling solutions ($r = 0.78, p > 0.001$) and for tasting solutions ($r = 0.46, p > 0.01$) [47 df]. This study shows a potentially fertile area for more psychophysical research and introduces still another important consideration in assessing the role of colour in food preferences and choice.

8.   EFFECT OF COLOUR ON 'PLEASANTNESS' OF FOOD

The choice of food will in large part be controlled by the consumer's like or dislike of a particular food, which could be called the 'pleasantness' or 'acceptability factor' for that particular food. This concept implies that there is a maximum for colour as well as the other sensory functions and that both below and above that maximum the degree of pleasantness will

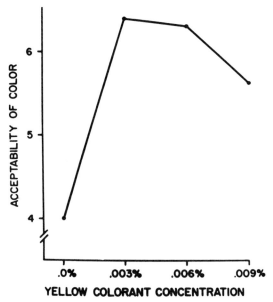

FIG. 5. Ratings of acceptability of colour for samples of lemon cake. Ratings are collapsed across the samples varying in flavour. Mean scores are shown. Colour acceptability scale ranged from 1 (= dislike extremely) to 9 (= like extremely). Reprinted from Reference 23. Copyright © by Institute of Food Technologists.

decrease and in turn affect such factors as flavour, taste, liking, acceptability and therefore food choice.

DuBose et al.,[23] as well as assessing the effect of colour on overall acceptability, also evaluated the effect of colourant concentration on colour acceptability. It may be seen in Fig. 5 that the ratings for acceptability of colour for samples of lemon cake were significantly affected by the colour level. Colour levels of 0·003 % and 0·006 % had approximately maximal and equal acceptability, while acceptability decreased both below and above these maximum values.

Johnson and Clydesdale[30] evaluated unflavoured, sweetened and coloured beverages for pleasantness as well as sweetness versus colour. The sweetness results discussed previously were found to deviate from Stevens' power law[38] and it was suspected that pleasantness effects might account for part of this deviation. Coloured solutions 2–5 (defined in Figs 1 and 6) were utilised and log-pleasantness was plotted versus log-percent sugar (4–5·3 % sucrose) as shown in Figs 6 and 7. Although there were variations among the panel's responses, the interrelationships between pleasantness,

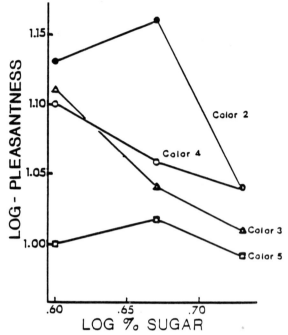

FIG. 6. Perceived sweetness (log-pleasantness) versus sucrose concentration (4·0%, 4·6% and 5·3%) plotted as log-percent sugar in red-coloured solutions: Colour $2 = 0.5\%$ Red No. 40; Colour $3 = 1.0\%$ Red No. 40; Colour $4 = 2.0\%$ Red No. 40; Colour $5 = 5.0\%$ Red No. 40. Reprinted from Reference 30. Copyright © by Institute of Food Technologists.

colour and sucrose are clearly demonstrated. The darker intensity of Colour 5 was consistently given a lower rating suggesting the following:

1. The darker colour may have been perceived as sweeter, therefore, at some sucrose concentration, the sensory stimuli are no longer pleasant to taste.
2. The intensity of colour may not have been associated with the panel's expectations of a desirable red colour.

Moskowitz et al.[37] investigated the psychophysical relationship between perceived sweetness, sucrose concentration and pleasantness and defined the pleasantness function by its own unique mathematical equation:

$$\log P = k_1(\log C)^2 + k_2(\log C) + k_3$$

where k_1, k_2 and k_3 are constants.

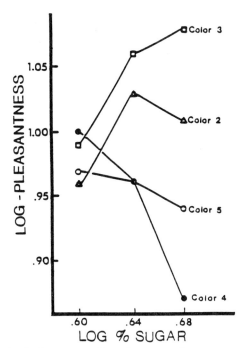

FIG. 7. Perceived pleasantness (log-pleasantness) versus sucrose concentration (4·0%, 4·4% and 4·8%) plotted as log-percent sugar in red-coloured solutions: Colours 2–5 as defined in Fig. 6. Reprinted from Reference 30. Copyright © by Institute of Food Technologists.

Johnson *et al.*[39,40] also utilised the objective colour function $\arctan a^*/b^*$ to assess colour acceptability in sweetened, flavoured and coloured beverages of raspberry, strawberry and cherry. As can be seen in Fig. 8, acceptability increased with increasing redness up to a maximum and then decreased in all cases. The maximum was different for all three beverages, which might be expected since the colour associations for each of these fruits is different. In all cases, there were at least 2 colours close together in acceptability at the maximum, such that either colour could be used without loss of acceptance for that particular flavour. However, it should be remembered that other factors such as sweetness versus sucrose concentration and pleasantness must be considered along with colour in choosing the final product.

It is apparent from these studies that the overall perception and choice of a beverage in a model system consists of a complex relationship between the

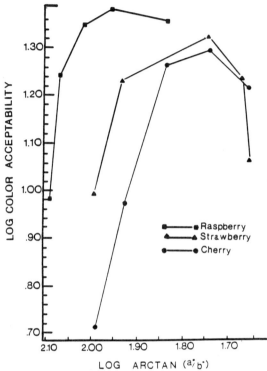

FIG. 8. Evaluation of colour acceptability (log colour acceptability) versus red colour intensity (log arctan (a^*/b^*)) of five cherry (●) colours, five strawberry (▲) and five raspberry (■) colours. Cherry colours are the same as in Fig. 4. Strawberry colours are: Colour $1 = 0.33\%$ Red No. 40, Colour $2 = 0.67\%$ Red No. 40, Colour $3 = 1.0\%$ Red No. 40, Colour $4 = 2.3\%$ Red No. 40 and Colour $5 = 5.56\%$ Red No. 40. Raspberry colours are: Colour $1 = 0.05\%$ Red No. 40, Colour $2 = 0.10\%$ Red No. 40, Colour $3 = 0.20\%$ Red No. 40, Colour $4 = 0.40\%$ Red No. 40 and Colour $5 = 0.60\%$ Red No. 40. Reprinted from Reference 31 with permission.

discriminatory aspects of taste perception, colour, flavourant, sucrose concentration and the effective aspects of taste, pleasantness, and colour associations.

Moskowitz[42] provides some interesting thoughts on this issue of pleasantness and 'liking' and discusses the concept of maximum pleasantness, introduced above, in somewhat different terms. He points out that:

in traditional studies researchers have assessed the relative importance of sensory factors to acceptance by correlating the liking ratings,

TABLE 7
INTERCORRELATION MATRIX OF ATTRIBUTES

	Liking	Sweetness	Sourness	Appearance
Liking	1·00			
Sweetness	0·73	1·00		
Sourness	−0·69	−0·95	1·00	
Liking of appearance	0·50	0·85	−0·75	1·00

Reprinted from Reference 42. Copyright © by Institute of Food Technologists.

separately with the separate sensory ratings, to generate a simple correlation matrix. Table [7] presents the simple correlation matrix for some beverage data. It shows that the perception of sweetness correlates 0·73 with liking, the perception of sourness correlates −0·69, and the perception of acceptable appearance correlates 0·50 with liking.

These simple correlations, however, mislead. Let us consider what the correlation actually implies. When the statistician correlates two variables, he or she assumes that the two variables are linearly related. On the basis of that linearity assumption, the statistician calculates the Pearson correlation coefficient to assess the degree of relatedness. In actual evaluation of products, where the attributes are sensory characteristics (such as sweetness or sourness) we have no reason to conclude that either sensory characteristic is linearly related to or even monotonically related to acceptability. A simple analogy will illustrate this point. An individual who likes sugar in his or her coffee will downrate coffee with very little or no sugar. As one adds sugar, the coffee increases in acceptability, until at some point the sugar is 'just right' and the coffee becomes optimally acceptable to that particular individual. Further increases in sugar level only diminish acceptability, with the too-sweet coffee often rejected on the basis of its overly sweet taste. Similarly, with sourness and sweetness in orange drinks, or in any other product with such *nonevaluative* sensory characteristics. As the orange beverage (of a single type) becomes increasingly sweet, panelists will find the beverage increasingly acceptable until the beverage reaches the optimum sweetness. Any sweetness higher than that optimum or 'bliss point' will diminish acceptability, down from the optimum to a lower level. Hence, the Pearson correlation coefficient relating liking to sweetness will vary. On the ascending portion of the curve, increasing sweetness will show a positive correlation with liking. On the descending portion of the curve, increasing sweetness will show a negative correlation with liking. If by chance, the researcher has included points around the optimal level, equally sampling the higher and lower values around the optimum, the correlation will dramatically decrease, perhaps close to zero.

For these reasons, Moskowitz[42] proposed a nonlinear quadratic function for the analysis of 'relative importance data' with 'relative importance' being defined as the momentary rate of change of overall liking with respect to each separate sensory characteristic. In terms of the differential calculus, this becomes the partial derivative of the liking function at the specific sensory profile level.

9. CONCLUSION

The role of colour in quality of life, total sensory perception and food choices is an unquestionable fact. However, its role is elusive and difficult to quantify. This creates problems in a technologically oriented society that demands numbers in order to believe. Unfortunately, this has led to a situation where colour is often not even recognised as an important sensory parameter, but is taken for granted as a part of our food environment which we might be able to do without.

In recognition of the bounty which colours provide, not only in food but in everyday living, I would like to conclude with the following story told by Athenaeus the Greek[43] about a sybarite who went to Sparta and was invited out to dine. 'As he lay on the wooden benches and ate with them, he remarked that he had always before been astounded to hear of the Spartans' courage; but now ... he did not think they were in any respect superior to other peoples, for the most cowardly man in the world would prefer to die rather than endure living that sort of life.'

REFERENCES

1. Old Testament (King James version), The Book of Esther, Chapter 1, Verses 5, 6 and 7.
2. Coriat, I. H., 'An unusual type of synaesthesia', *Jour. Abnormal Psych.*, 1913, **8**, 109–12.
3. Scott, R., ' "It hurts red": a preliminary study of children's perception of pain', *Perceptual and Motor Skills*, 1978, **47**, 787–91.
4. Francis, F. J. and Clydesdale, F. M., *Food Colorimetry: Theory and Applications*, 1975, AVI Publishing Co., Westport, CT.

5. Hunter, R. S., *The Measurement of Appearance*, 1975, 348 pp., John Wiley and Sons, New York.
6. Wright, W. D., *The Measurement of Color*, 4th Edn, 1971, Van Nostrand Reinhold Co., New York.
7. Billmeyer, F. W., Jr and Saltzman, M., *Principles of Color Technology*, 2nd Edn, 1981, John Wiley and Sons, New York.
8. Boynton, R. M., *Human Color Vision*, 1979, Holt, Rinehart and Winston, New York.
9. Dember, W. N. and Warm, J. S., *Psychology of Perception*, 2nd Edn, 1979, Holt, Rinehart and Winston, New York.
10. Sadalla, E. and Burroughs, J., 'Profiles in eating: sexy vegetarians and other diet-based social stereotypes', *Psychology Today*, 1981, 15(10), 51–7.
11. Hutchings, J. B., 'The importance of visual appearance of foods to the food processor and the consumer', *J. Food Qual.*, 1977, 1, 267–78.
12. Kramer, A. and Szczesniak, A. S., *Texture Measurements of Food*, 1973, D. Reidel Publishing Co., Hingham, MA.
13. Clydesdale, F. M., 'Colorimetry—methodology and applications', *Critical Reviews in Food Science and Nutrition*, 1978, 10, 243–301.
14. Kostyla, A. S. and Clydesdale, F. M., 'The psychophysical relationships between color and flavor', *Critical Reviews in Food Science and Nutrition*, 1978, 10, 303–321.
15. FAO/WHO Joint Expert Committee on Food Additives. *General Principles Governing Food Additives*, 1957, World Health Organisation Technical Report Series No. 129, pp. 7–8.
16. Institute of Food Technologists, 'Food colors', *J. Food Technol.*, 1980, 34(7), 77–84.
17. Rolls, B. J., Rowe, E. A., Rolls, E. T., Kingston, B., Megson, A. and Gunary, R., 'Variety in a meal enhances food intake in man', *Physiol. and Behavior*, 1981, 26, 215–21.
18. Wheatley, J., 'Putting color into marketing', *Marketing*, 1973, October 26–29, 67.
19. Hall, R. L., 'Flavor study approach at McCormick and Co., Inc.,'in *Flavor Research and Food Acceptance*, Ed. A. D. Little, Inc., 1958, Reinhold Publishing Co., New York.
20. Foster, D., *Psychological Aspects of Food Colors from the Consumer's Standpoint*. 1956, US Testing Co., Hoboken, NJ.
21. Schutz, H. G., 'Color in relation to food preference', in *Color in Foods: A Symposium*, Eds K. T. Farrell, J. R. Wagner, M. S. Peterson and G. M. Mackinnery, 1954, US Food and Container Corp., Chicago.
22. Ringo, L., MS Thesis, 1982, Univ. of California, Cavis, CA.
23. DuBose, C. N., Cardello, A. V. and Maller, O., 'Effects of colorants and flavorants on identification, perceived flavor intensity, and hedonic quality of fruit flavored beverages and cake', *J. Food Sci.*, 1980, 45, 1393–9, 1415.
24. Pangborn, R. M.,'Parotid flow stimulated by the sight, feel and odor of lemon', *Perceptual and Motor Skills*, 1968, 27, 1340–2.
25. Pangborn, R. M., 'Effects of light and sound on parotid secretion and taste perception in response to sodium chloride', *Chem. Senses Flavor.*, 1978, 3, 81–91.

26. Pangborn, R. M., 'Influence of color on the discrimination of sweetness', *Amer. J. Psych.*, 1960, **73**, 229–38.
27. Schutte, W. and Zubek, J. P., 'Changes in olfactory and gustatory sensitivity after prolonged visual deprivation', *Can. J. Psych.*, 1967, **21**, 337–45.
28. Gregson, R. A. M., 'Modification of perceived relative intensities of acid tastes by ambient illumination changes', *Australian J. Psych.*, 1964, **16**, 190–9.
29. Maga, J. A., 'Influence of color on taste thresholds', *Chem. Senses Flavor.*, 1974, **1**, 115–19.
30. Johnson, J. and Clydesdale, F. M., 'Perceived sweetness and redness in colored sucrose solutions', *J. Food Sci.*, 1982, **47**, 747–52.
31. Johnson, J., 'Psychophysical relationships between color and sweetness in fruit flavored solutions', PhD Thesis, 1982, Univ. of Mass., Amherst, MA.
32. Kostyla, A. R., 'The psychophysical relationships between color and flavor of some fruit flavored beverages', PhD Thesis, 1978, Univ. of Mass., Amherst, MA.
33. Pangborn, R. M. and Hansen, B., 'The influence of color on discrimination of sweetness and sourness in pear nectar', *Amer. J. Psych.*, 1963, **26**, 315–17.
34. Grinker, J., Hirsch, J. and Smith, D. V., 'Taste sensitivity and susceptibility to external influence in obese and normal weight subjects', *J. Personality Social Psych.*, 1972, **22**, 320–5.
35. Pauli, H., 'Proposed extension of the CIE recommendation on "uniform color spaces, color difference equations, and metric color terms"', *J. Opt. Soc. Am.*, 1976, **66**, 866–7.
36. Moskowitz, H. R., 'The sweetness and pleasantness of sugars', *Amer. J. Psych.*, 1971, **84**, 387–91.
37. Moskowitz, H. R., Kluter, R. A., Westerling, J. and Jacobs, H. L., 'Sugar sweetness and pleasantness: evidence for different psychological laws', *Science*, 1974, **184**, 583–5.
38. Stevens, S. S., 'On the psychophysical law', *Psych. Rev.*, 1957, **64**, 153–81.
39. Johnson, J., Dzendolet, E. and Clydesdale, F. M., 'Psychophysical relationships between sweetness and redness in strawberry flavored drinks', *J. Food Prot.*, 1983, **46**(1), 21–5.
40. Johnson, J., Dzendolet, E., Damon, R., Sawyer, M. and Clydesdale, F. M., 'Psychophysical relationships between perceived sweetness and color in cherry-flavored beverages', *J. Food Prot.*, 1982, **45**, 601–6.
41. Vargo, D., 'Color–odor interactions of microencapsulated fragrance strips and of solutions', MS Thesis, 1982, University of California, Davis, CA.
42. Moskowitz, H. R., 'Relative importance of perceptual factors to consumer acceptance: linear versus quadratic analysis', *J. Food Sci.*, 1981, **46**, 244–8.
43. Tannahill, R., *Food in History*, 1973, p. 82, Stein and Day, New York.

Chapter 4

SYNTHETIC CERTIFIED FOOD COLOURS OF THE USA

R. K. JOHNSON and F. J. LICHTENBERGER

Chemical Division, Hilton-Davis, Cincinnati, Ohio, USA

SUMMARY

This chapter describes the current status of the certified food colours listed in the US, with selected information from the past 30 years which is helpful in relating how the current situation arose. Close cooperation between a small regulated industry and the Food and Drug Administration's (FDA's) Division of Colors and Cosmetics has been the critical factor during this time. The certified colour manufacturers have repeatedly demonstrated that these products, properly used, are both safe and useful, and that they make a unique contribution to the abundant supply of wholesome, nutritious and appetising foods.

1. USA CERTIFIED SYNTHETIC COLOURS

From a group of about 80 food colour additives being used in the US, about one hundred years ago there are available now just nine approved synthetic organic colours. Only two of these nine (FD & C Blue No. 2 and FD & C Red No. 3) were in use in the previous century; the other seven were listed in the years shown. The structures and names of the current colours are:

Name	*Structure*
FD & C Blue No. 1 Brilliant Blue FCF CI 42090 Listed in 1929	
FD & C Blue No. 2 Indigo Carmine (Indigotine) CI 73015 Listed in 1907	
FD & C Green No. 3 Fast Green FCF CI 42053 Listed in 1927	
FD & C Red No. 3 Erythrosine CI 45430 Listed in 1907	
FD & C Red No. 40 Allura Red® CI 16035 Listed in 1971	
FD & C Yellow No. 5 Tartrazine CI 19140 Listed in 1916	

Name	Structure
FD & C Yellow No. 6 Sunset Yellow FCF CI 15985 Listed in 1929	
Citrus Red No. 2 CI 12156 Listed in 1959	
Orange B CI 19235 Listed in 1966	

The reduction in availability by about 70 colourants resulted, in part, from:

1. Advances in the science of toxicology which enable one to assess more subtle effects.
2. Excessively high use levels on the part of a few uninformed users.
3. Unwarranted conclusions sometimes drawn from less than the best toxicology work. Example: FD & C Red No. 4.
4. Toxicology study in another country using a test substance probably not meeting USA certification requirements. Example: FD & C Violet No. 1.
5. Political pressure. Example: FD & C Red No. 2.
6. Lack of market demand. Examples: FD & C Green No. 1 and Green No. 2.

Although today's list is much shorter in the US than it is in some other countries, the safety in use of these products rests today on more firm ground than ever before. This is due to the fact that these synthetic organic colours have been more thoroughly tested than almost all the other, far more numerous, food additives.

2. MARKETED FORMS OF COLOURS

Food colours are available as straight colours, referred to as 'primaries', and blends of two or more straight colours, with or without diluents, referred to as blends, mixtures, 'secondaries' or 'secondary blends'. The blends are standardised in strength by mixing the colours with approved diluents such as sucrose, salt, caramel, flour, etc. Sodium sulphate is not used as a diluent in the USA.

Mixtures of just one straight colour with one or more diluents are also provided on special order for colour users who want other functional food additives blended with their colours. In the USA, the colour regulations do not permit strength reductions of straight (i.e. a single) colour with diluents except when the resulting product is labelled as a blend or mixture. In all cases mixtures must be made only from previously certified straight colours.

Typical forms of certified primary food colours are:

Powder
Ultra-fine powder
Plating grade powder
Granules
Dry blends
Wet–dry blends
Solutions (preserved)
Pastes (preserved)
Dispersions (preserved)

The latter three forms are used infrequently because of the added costs incurred in their preparation.

Prior to 1964 secondary blends were required to be recertified by the FDA prior to use or sale, but since then exclusive control and responsibility for this area of production has resided with the manufacturers. Secondary blends are the forms used for creating a wide variety of shades ready for immediate use in food products, for example: grape, black cherry, raspberry, lime and various chocolates. The processing of secondary blends is dictated by the needs of the customer. Many blends can be combinations of all dry ingredients. Some blends, especially those containing blue or green, must be combined in a wet state, then redried in order to prevent 'flashing' at the time the consumer combines the product with water or milk. The dried products are ground, blended and standardised in strength within carefully controlled limits as required by the product specifications.

The approved lists of diluents include 'GRAS' items (Generally Recognised As Safe for use in foods) plus other diluents which have been listed by the petition method. The latter diluents may be found in the *Color Additive Regulations* at 21 CFR 73.1.

Where water-insoluble colourants are desired, the lakes are useful as insoluble pigments. In the USA these are usually made by precipitation of straight colours as aluminium salts on a substratum of alumina hydrate. The lakes are available as lakes of straight colours and as lake blends. Lakes for use in food must be made from previously certified straight colours. In general, the terminology 'lake' in the food colour industry describes a product that is practically insoluble in water under controlled conditions. The word 'lake' had its origin in the pigment industry. The pigment of choice for magazine and newspaper printing to give a transparent blue shade is very similar to FD & C Blue No. 1 Lake; FD & C Blue No. 1 Lake itself is used to make a printing ink for advertising matter or coupons that might be enclosed in a box of cereal or other dry food.

Another special use of FD & C lakes is in the coating of pills. This is an especially attractive application because the finely ground pigment particles can be distributed over a pill to give a more uniform coating than that normally obtained by using water-soluble dyes. Grinding or mixing an FD & C lake in an oil or a fat achieves a result which, for some applications, is superior to colouring the product with a water-soluble dye. Other lake applications include such products as candy coatings and snack foods. Novelties such as stripes on chewing gum can be achieved by printing with FD & C lakes of the appropriate colours.

Another area of use found in the confectionery and drug field is the colouring of tablets using FD & C lakes in the total blend of ingredients. Properly administered, this gives beautiful colours when the tablets are compressed. Although the FD & C lakes are described as 'water insoluble', they are subject to 'bleeding' in hot water and/or in strongly acid or alkaline conditions. In spite of the fact that per-unit-of-colour the lakes are considerably more expensive than the water-soluble dyes, there are, as noted, some specialty uses where their application is practical.

Typical package sizes in the USA are 25 and 100 lb net weight with some type of moisture barrier built into the package. All containers must be sealed as required by Federal regulations and broken seals must be recognisable upon casual inspection. The straight colour additive and lake labels must bear the name of the colour or lake, the Food and Drug Administration assigned lot (i.e. certification) number, and the percent of pure colour. In addition, all use restrictions described in the colour regulations must be on the label. (Examples: 'Do not use in products used in the area of the eye', 'Do not use for colouring drugs for injection', 'Not for use in surgical sutures' (21 CFR 70.5).) Mixtures are required to list the name of each colour and diluent ingredient without any quantity statement except for the total percent of pure colour. In the retail markets the food colours for home use are usually sold as 3 % preserved solutions.

TABLE 1

QUANTITIES OF SYNTHETIC FOOD COLOURS CERTIFIED IN THE USA IN METRIC TONNES

Fiscal year ending 30 September	FD & C primary colours	FD & C lakes	As is weight percent as lakes	Total
1982	2 300	618	21	2 918
1981	2 500	587	19	3 087
1980	2 270	667	23	2 937
1979	2 662	786	23	3 448
1978	2 333	650	22	2 983
1977	2 068	767	27	2 835
1976	1 740	367	17	2 107
1975	2 390	493	17	2 883

TABLE 2

INDIVIDUAL QUANTITIES OF SYNTHETIC FOOD COLOURS CERTIFIED IN THE USA BY COLOUR IN FISCAL YEAR 1982 (1 OCTOBER 1981 TO 30 SEPTEMBER 1982)

Colourant	FD & C primaries (kg)	FD & C lakes (kg)	As is weight percent as lakes
FD & C Blue No. 1	83 732	38 386	31
FD & C Blue No. 2	38 062	39 925	51
FD & C Green No. 3	2 242	None	0
FD & C Red No. 3	190 907	148 623	44
FD & C Red No. 4[a]	7 467	None	0
FD & C Red No. 40	793 138	48 552	6
FD & C Yellow No. 5	660 459	196 356	23
FD & C Yellow No. 6	523 719	146 194	22
Citrus Red No. 2[b]	303	None	0
Orange B	None		
Total	2 300 029	618 036	21

[a] Not permitted for use in foods.
[b] For colouring orange skins only.

3. PRODUCTION AND USE

The quantities of synthetic food colours certified in the USA are shown in Tables 1 and 2. A recent attempt to estimate typical *per capita* daily intakes of colourings was included as a part of the 1977 Phase III *Survey of Industry on the Use of Food Additives* under the auspices of the National Academy of Sciences.[12] Tables 3 and 4 were derived from the 1972 predecessor of that report.[1]

The National Academy of Sciences/National Research Council (NAS/NRC) report comments on the accuracy of the data as follows:[12]

The intakes of some food colors are overestimated. They are used in a variety of combinations, and each may be used in only a few products in the subcategories reported. Estimated poundage based on intake was compared with measures of actual poundage (e.g. certification figures) whenever the latter were available. Most of the certified colors appear to fall within the *five-fold* limit for overestimation, but some appear to be more severely exaggerated.

This fact can be more readily understood from a consideration of the latest certification data for the fiscal year of 1982:

$$\frac{5\,070\,642 \text{ lb primary colour} + \frac{1}{3}(1\,362\,522)\text{ lb lakes PCE}^*}{232\,000\,000 \text{ USA population}}$$

$$= \frac{5\,524\,816}{232\,000\,000} = 0 \cdot 0238 \text{ lb colour/person/year}$$

This is $0 \cdot 38$ oz/year or $10 \cdot 8$ g/year. If the average person consumes 680 kg (1500 lb) of food per year (food intake per day ranges from about $1 \cdot 1$ kg for young children to about $2 \cdot 1$ kg for adult males) this $10 \cdot 8$ g of colour averages 16 ppm in the total diet. Then, (10 800 mg/year)/(365 days) = $29 \cdot 6$ mg/day and, for a person weighing 70 kg (154 lb),† the average daily intake is $0 \cdot 42$ mg/kg of body weight. Due to differences in age and eating habits one may expect considerable variation both above and below this average daily intake estimate. In any case the consumption of these colours in the USA has been judged to be well below the acceptable daily intake limits established by the FDA.

* PCE is here defined as 'Pure Colour Equivalent' for purposes of estimating the quantity of primary colour equivalent to the quantity of lakes certified in any time period. Assuming that all lakes average 30 % pure colour and that primary colours average 90 % pure colour then the PCE for lakes is 30/90 or 1/3.
† In 1980 the median age of the USA population was 30 years.

TABLE 3

PER CAPITA AVERAGE DAILY INTAKE OF STRAIGHT COLOURS IN MILLIGRAMS

Colourant	Age		
	6–23 Months	6–12 Years	18–44 Years
FD & C Blue No. 1	2·9	4·5	3·6
FD & C Blue No. 2	0·59	1·6	1·0
FD & C Green No. 3	0·68	1·1	0·8
FD & C Red No. 3	5·9	9·9	7·0
FD & C Red No. 40	19·0	31·0	26·0
FD & C Yellow No. 5	9·4	15·0	13·0
FD & C Yellow No. 6	6·8	14·0	11·0
Total	45·3	77·1	62·4

TABLE 4

PER CAPITA AVERAGE DAILY INTAKE OF LAKES IN MILLIGRAMS

Colourant	Age		
	6–23 Months	6–12 Years	18–44 Years
FD & C Blue No. 1 Aluminium Lake	0·52	1·0	0·76
FD & C Blue No. 2 Aluminium Lake	0·35	0·54	0·49
FD & C Green No. 3 Aluminium Lake	None	None	None
FD & C Red No. 3 Aluminium Lake	1·3	2·8	2·1
FD & C Red No. 40 Aluminium Lake	2·2	4·9	3·8
FD & C Red No. 40 Calcium Lake	None	1·8	2·5
FD & C Yellow No. 5 Aluminium Lake	2·2	4·3	3·0
FD & C Yellow No. 5 Calcium Lake	0·09	0·10	0·11
FD & C Yellow No. 6 Aluminium Lake	1·1	2·7	1·7
Total	7·8	18·1	14·5
Total PCE[a]	2·6	6·0	4·8

[a] Added by author; see explanation.

4. MANUFACTURING

At the present time synthetic straight colours, their lakes and their precursors must be manufactured by the processes which were disclosed, on a confidential basis, to the Food and Drug Administration by each of the producers. With the advent of additional 'permanent' listings in 1982, the documents published in the *Federal Register* have contained the following statement (*Federal Register*, **47**, p. 42564, 28 September 1982) about the method of manufacture:

> The agency concludes that it is necessary to include in the listing regulation for . . . . a brief description of the manufacturing process to ensure the safety of the color additives. The agency is concerned that the color additives may contain potentially toxic impurities dependent upon the manufacturing process used to produce the color additives. The agency is not able at this time to set specifications that would control the presence of these impurities. The agency has contracted the National Academy of Sciences/National Research Council (NAS/NRC) to develop appropriate specifications for color additives for use in food as part of the Food Chemicals Codex. Similarly, appropriate specifications for color additives for use in drugs and cosmetics will be developed following the general guidelines used by NAS/NRC in its evaluation of color additives used in food.[8] The agency concludes that specifying, through a general description, the manufacturing process in the regulations for these color additives will provide an adequate assurance of safety until suitable specifications can be developed. Production of the color additive by the specified method will assure qualitatively similar batches and thus adequately assure the absence of unanticipated potentially toxic impurities.

Synthetic colour raw materials are either prepared and tested by the colour producer himself or are purchased from reputable suppliers against well-defined specifications. In addition to the commonly described analytical tests and assays, some form of chromatography is normally used to verify the acceptability of starting materials and the intermediate product steps leading up to the finished colours. Thus, the exceptionally high quality, uniformity and performance characteristics of the synthetic colours are remarkably uniform from lot to lot. Since few of the exempt 'natural' colours are capable of being characterised, or chemically specified as to their total composition, some variability in their performance might be expected from lot to lot.

At the end of the preceding excerpt from the 28 September 1982 *Federal Register* the phrase 'qualitatively similar batches' appears. This is a reference to the pioneer work of the FDA and the certified colour producers with high pressure liquid chromatography (HPLC).[5] Originally investigated as a matter of laboratory economics, these ultra-discriminating analytical processes have delivered exquisite results in the analyses of synthetic colours for starting materials, intermediate products, by-products and subsidiary colours. These results are of the type generally referred to as 'analyses chasing after the ever-elusive zero', as many of the compounds being found are present in vanishingly small amounts and, in fact, often are not found when the same sample is retested in the same laboratory.

Limits for such results are impossible to specify quantitatively in any written specification. In the meantime, the certified food colour manufacturers and the FDA evaluate the spectra from batches submitted for certification by comparison with spectra from reference batches, including the ones that were used for toxicological studies. Thus, the word 'qualitative' is used here and any of the criteria for rejecting certification applications based upon HPLC test results are derived from the requirement that batches 'shall be free from impurities other than those named to the extent that such other impurities may be avoided by Good Manufacturing Practices'. What is the 'extent' which is cited? It is one that continually changes, for the Good Manufacturing Practices (GMP) of today are not necessarily those of yesterday, nor, for that matter, of tomorrow or next year. Innovation is the lifeblood of the chemical industry. Manufacturing advances applied to synthetic colours tend to bring about a constant improvement in their quality. And so, in the USA today, the synthetic organic colours enjoy the highest quality and reputation of any food additives in the world. Manufacturers are not prone to submit borderline batches to the FDA for certification because they lose their fees of 25¢ per lb on batches which fail to meet requirements.

GMP does not connote a fixed framework of acceptable manufacturing practices within a regulated industry but it is a living, ever-changing body of applicable principles, systems, methods, and techniques. All of these are being upgraded almost continually. For this reason, *Current* Good Manufacturing Practices is a more proper term. The certification requirement ensures that the nation's supply of synthetic food colours will continue to be the best available anywhere. The application of HPLC to the examination of certified colour lakes is not as advanced as that for the straight colours, but is being pursued, chiefly by the manufacturers. Other advances in analytical techniques are to be expected in the future.

There are two methods for assaying the total percent of pure colour in straight colours: the spectrophotometric and the chemical (quantitative reduction with titanous chloride (see Chapter 2, Section 2.2.1.1) on all colours except FD & C Red No. 3, which is precipitated with acid, filtered, dried, and weighed (see Chapter 2, Section 2.2.1.3)). The pure colour content of lakes is determined spectrophotometrically.[2]

5. PERFORMANCE OF SYNTHETIC COLOURS

Colour is a major contributor to flavour anticipation and is often perceived before aroma. If a food is not attractive to the eye it may never reach the mouth! Many food processing methods which are highly efficient when used in modern food technology operations affect foodstuffs in a manner which reduces the natural levels of certain nutrients and/or colour. In these products the proper use of food additives and colour additives plays a very important part. Colour is known to play a major role in the acceptability of food products.[4,16] Indeed there are many product types which would be greatly curtailed without the ready availability of safe colourants.[17] For example, just to name a few: soft drinks, puddings, gelatins, reconstituted and imitation fruits, candies, jelly, pastries, ice-cream, syrups, sauces and snacks. Some studies have shown that food does not taste 'right' when it does not have the proper colour. In fact, experimental work with sherbets coloured improperly (by design) resulted in many errors in flavour identification by tasting panels.[18] See Chapter 3 for a fuller account of the influence of colour on food choice.)

The Codex Alimentarius Commission of the World Health Organisation defined food at their November 1966 meeting:

Food means any substance, whether processed, semi-processed or raw, which is intended for human consumption, and includes drink, chewing gum and any substance which has been used in the manufacture, preparation or treatment of food, but does not include cosmetics or tobacco or substances used only as drugs.

This definition is broad enough to include food additives. In the US pet foods are as fully regulated as are foods for humans since the Food, Drug and Cosmetic Act defines food as 'anything consumed by man or animal'.

Since the synthetic colours have high tinctorial power, very small amounts of them are adequate for practically all applications. Use levels customarily needed range from 20 or 30 ppm to about 300 ppm in foods ready for consumption. Chocolate goods and cake icings may have more.

5.1. Advantages of Synthetic Colours

1. Safe
2. Uniform quality
3. Ready availability in adequate quantity
4. Good stability
5. High tinctorial power makes them economically advantageous
6. Good solubility in water and alcohol
7. Tasteless and odourless
8. Available in several forms
9. Freedom from bacteriological problems
10. Compatible in all foods and beverages when used either as straight colours or as lakes
11. Help to hold down the cost of food since the normal appearance of wholesome, colourful foods can be retained or can be restored if colour is lost during processing
12. Promote good health by making nutritious foods attractive to the consumer
13. Synthetics are instrumental in creating party foods
14. Adaptable for use in food containers and graphic art products which contact foods
15. Purity is assured since each batch is retested under rigid specifications and is certified by the FDA if the requirements are met.

5.2. Contrast with Non-certified Colours

The major non-certified colour additives are paprika, turmeric, annatto, the carotenoids (β-carotene, apocarotenal, canthaxanthin), caramel, cochineal and titanium dioxide. The restrictive regulations for these vary from no limit other than good practice to specific levels for particular products. The high cost of the carotenoids and their low strength limits their use to specialised applications.

A major use of caramel is in whisky and carbonated soft drinks such as colas and root beer. Other flavours of soft drinks use caramel in conjunction with certified colours to reduce the azo dye level, which has been shown to be a cause of corrosion in some can linings. Caramel is comparatively inexpensive, but it has several disadvantages. Its tinctorial power is only about one-tenth that of an equivalent food colour mixture. In addition, this property, as well as moisture content, varies from batch to batch. When present as a large proportion of a secondary food colour blend, it can cause lumping, due to its relatively high hygroscopicity.

Some of the other non-certified colours have properties making them specifically useful in unique applications. For example, turmeric in mustard, and paprika oleoresins in salad dressings are included in the standards of identity. Cochineal, or its aluminium lake carmine, is an expensive additive, but it can be used in some protein products which are heated during manufacture. Titanium dioxide as 'anatase' is used as a white colouring in baked goods, cheese and pill coatings. Its use is confined to 1 % of the weight of the consumed product.

6. SPECIFICATIONS

Specifications for certified colour additives may best be visualised as a 'family tree' of requirements (Fig. 1), which includes the aspects required for certification (official requirements) and those required by the users (proprietary requirements). For this reason, customers will find that nominally equivalent colour additives from different sources usually vary in their performance characteristics.

Customarily the specifications for blends and lakes are designed specifically for the system or product(s) to be coloured and, for this reason, it is very advantageous for the colour supplier to know as much as possible (excluding only trade secrets) about the processing and conditions of use to be expected.

Some comments and examples concerning the numbered boxes in Fig. 1 should be given. Under Items 4 and 8, the FDA laboratory regularly determines the pure colour of each batch by two separate methods, usually spectrophotometrically and by reduction with titanous chloride. Under Item 6 only the spectrophotometric method is used. Under Items 9, 10 and 12, the colour manufacturer customarily determines (where appropriate) such properties as plating strength on sugar crystals, particle size distribution, loose and packed density, solubility at high concentrations, freedom from flashing (on wet–dry blends) and other similarly specific tests, both chemical and physical. These are particularly necessary on lakes since they perform as pigments rather than as dyes.

Under Item 11 the colour manufacturer must maintain rigid controls over the distribution of primary colours in each secondary blend and lake. For blends spectrophotometric absorption curve data are used in sets of simultaneous equations to calculate the content of each primary colour. If corrections on blends in process are found necessary the same results may be independently obtained without spectrophotometric testing by making 'titrated' colour matches in white porcelain dishes with standard solutions

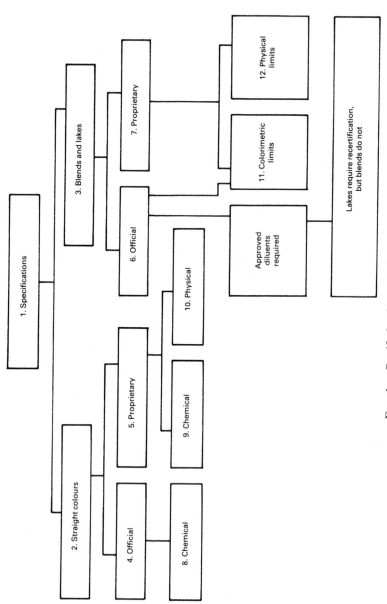

FIG. 1.   Certified colour requirements.

TABLE 5
FD & C COLOURS: CURRENT OFFICIAL SPECIFICATION (FEBRUARY 1983)

FDA identity	Common name	Reference in 21 CFR
FD & C Blue No. 1	Brilliant Blue FCF	74.101
FD & C Blue No. 2	Indigo Carmine	74.102
FD & C Green No. 3	Fast Green FCF	74.203
FD & C Yellow No. 5	Tartrazine	74.705
FD & C Yellow No. 6	Sunset Yellow FCF	82.706[a]
FD & C Red No. 3	Erythrosine	74.303
FD & C Red No. 40	Allura Red AC	74.340
Citrus Red No. 2	Citrus Red No. 2	74.302[b]
Orange B	Orange B	74.250[c]

Full specification details are given in the Code of Federal Regulations (CFR) Vol. 21.
[a] Provisional listing. New specification to be proposed jointly by FDA and CCMA (Certified Color Manufacturers Association) before expiry of provisional listing February 1984.
[b] Limited to colouring skins of oranges at a maximum use level of 2 ppm.
[c] Limited to colouring casings of frankfurters and sausages at a maximum level of 150 ppm.

of the straight colours. In such cases the analyst works with aqueous solutions when the blend is to be used in transparent media and he works with solutions in milk when the blend is to be used in opaque media. Corrections for lakes and lake blends are controlled by using the customary visual or reflectometer methods of the graphic arts industry.

Table 5 gives the current official specification for FD & C colours.

7. SYNTHETIC FOOD COLOUR ANALYSES

For almost 30 years the Certified Color Manufacturers' Association (CCMA) and its predecessor, the Certified Color Industry Committee (CCIC), have had a chemistry subcommittee responsible for colour specifications and analytical methods. The various people who served on the subcommittee have worked closely with the people in the FDA Color Certification Branch more or less continuously since 1953. The FDA colour certification operations in that time period were successively under the direction of Daniel Dahle, G. Robert Clark, Kenneth A. Freeman, Alfred Weissler and Keith Heine. Since 1960 it has been the responsibility of industry to incorporate specifications and test methods in the petitions for listing.

Specifications and their changes have been published in the *Federal Register* and the *Code of Federal Regulations* (CFR). At the present time the FDA has a contract with the *Food Chemicals Codex* (FCC) to have the certifiable colour specifications reviewed and then added to that compendium. Most of the latest material for each synthetic colour specification has been delivered to the FCC staff.

Many of the interesting new analytical methods are presented at the annual meetings of the Association of Official Analytical Chemists (AOAC) and subsequently appear in its journal (*JAOAC*). Some, but not all, of the collaborative studies conducted by industry chemists and by FDA chemists are also reported at the AOAC meetings and are then published. In order to gain official status* in the *Official Methods of Analysis* of the AOAC,[2] collaborative study and voting approval are required by the governing AOAC committee. In spite of these formal arrangements, both industry and Government research have developed 'ad hoc' methods from time to time in order to effect economies in analysis or to take advantage of new developments. If these newly developed methods lead to improvements in accuracy or precision they may be considered for regulatory adoption. In all cases the official methods are controlling.

Some of the analytical techniques used on raw materials, intermediates and finished colours are:

Spectroscopy—visible, ultra-violet, infra-red, atomic, X-ray emission, and mass.

Gravimetric, quantitative reduction and elemental analyses.

Chromatography—paper, thin-layer, ion, vapour phase and high pressure liquid chromatography with gradient elution and various detectors.†

---

* The General Referee for Color Additives is appointed by the AOAC and he, in turn, appoints Associate Referees for appropriate topics. These referees are responsible for conducting collaborative studies on new methods of analysis.
† Advances in the field of analytical chemistry have increased enormously the ability to detect smaller and smaller amounts of constituents. Where once chemical analysis dealt with hundredths of a percent, it now is routinely dealing with parts per billion (10^9) and even parts per trillion (10^{12}). With high pressure liquid chromatographic and electron capture detector methods we are learning of the existence of compounds in foods and in synthetic substances never before suspected, let alone measured. If you took a 16 000 mile trip, the distance equivalent to one billionth of the trip would be just one inch! A part per trillion is equivalent to moving six inches on a journey to the sun or, in terms of time, one second out of 32 000 years!

TABLE 6

RECOMMENDED CONDITIONS FOR ASSAYING FD & C COLOURS ON RECORDING SPECTROPHOTOMETERS AND BECKMAN DU SPECTROPHOTOMETERS IN 1·0 cm CELLS: SOLVENT DISTILLED WATER

	λ_{max}[a] (nm ± 2)	Absorptivity[b] (a ± 2)	Recording concentration (mg/litre)	DU concentration (mg/litre)	Additive
FD & C Yellow No. 5	426	52·2	21–29	6–10	pH 7·0 Buffer[c]
FD & C Yellow No. 6	484	54·5	20–28	6–10	—
FD & C Red No. 3	526	104	10–14	3–5	pH 10·0 Buffer[c]
FD & C Red No. 4	502	53·8	19–26	6–10	pH 4·0 Buffer[c]
FD & C Blue No. 1	630	163	7–9	2–3	—
FD & C Blue No. 2	612	46·8	23–32	7–11	—
FD & C Green No. 3	625	144	7–9	2–3	—
FD & C Red No. 40	502	54·8	19–26	6–10	—

[a] Wavelength of maximum absorbance in nm.

[b] The absorptivity (a) calculated for 100 % pure colour at the wavelength of maximum absorption (λ_{max}) when observations are made under ideal conditions. $a = A/bc$ where A is absorbance, b is path length in cm, and c is concentration in g/litre.

[c] 10 ml Beckman Standard Buffer Solution per 100 ml in final dilution. The three buffers are used to prevent errors resulting from pH effects.

The pure colour content of each certified straight colour is determined by two different methods, one of which is the spectrophotometric. For the highest possible accuracy, an analyst should verify the calibration of his instrument and should also make use of a recently certified reference sample of the straight colour being determined. The other methods for determining the percent of pure colour in straight colours are gravimetric or quantitative reduction with titanous chloride.

Physical tests such as particle size, bulk density, melting point and specific gravity.

Nuclear magnetic resonance.

Some raw materials have specifications and test methods specified in the standards of the American Society for Testing and Materials (ASTM).

Certified colours may be identified using spot tests, absorption spectra, paper and thin-layer chromatography and electrophoresis.[20] Straight colour mixtures are most easily separated by paper chromatography and are quantitated using visible absorption spectra. Lake mixtures are split with an acid treatment before analysis.

Analysis of colours in foods is required for the examination of imports and for other regulatory purposes. If the colour is extractable in water the analysis is speedily done by visible spectrophotometry. Otherwise leaching, adsorption on a substrate, or extraction with a liquid anion exchange resin and subsequent absorption spectroscopy may be used. A liberal use of reference samples is most helpful in all synthetic colour analytical work.

The most frequently used assay procedure for straight colours and for mixtures of straight colours is the spectrophotometric method. Table 6 gives the recommended conditions for a typical recording spectrophotometer and a typical single wavelength instrument, the Beckman DU.

7.1. 'Zero' is Not the Same as 'None Detected'[6]

When the 1960 Color Additive Amendments became law the limits on by-product content in certifiable colours were specified to the nearest tenth of one percent and the limits on undesirable, but ubiquitous, impurities such as lead and arsenic were specified in parts per million. When any test found none of the sought substance the report usually stated 'nil' or 'none detected'. Non-technical people would have said there is 'zero' or 'none'. However, 'zero' is abstract just as is 'infinity'—each can be approached but never reached. Year by year new instruments for chemical analysis, and new methods, yield results closer and closer to the non-existent 'zero'.

8.   THE USA CERTIFICATION PROCESS

The certification process is described in Title 21 of the Code of Federal Regulations. All of the synthetic colours subject to certification in this chapter must be certified by the FDA before they are sold and/or before they are used to make blends or lakes for use in foods.

Each batch of straight colour or lake manufactured for use in food, drugs or cosmetics must be held sealed and under control of the manufacturer, or the person applying for certification, pending certification by the FDA. After testing each new batch versus the certification requirements and having found the batch suitable, the proper representative sample, letter requesting certification, the prescribed fee and weight of the batch are forwarded to the Color Certification Branch of the FDA in Washington, DC. The time required varies from one to three weeks and during this time period the material is held 'in quarantine'. Currently the fee for straight colours and lakes is 25¢ per lb, with a minimum of $160·00 per batch. The certification applicant loses his entire fee if the submitted batch fails to meet the current specifications. In the 12 months ending 30 September 1979, 112 of the 4412 batches submitted for certification were rejected according to the *FDA Consumer*, March 1980, p. 26.

Any person (other than the original manufacturer) who wishes to repackage a certified colour for sale must obtain recertification. Fees for repacks are as follows:

Weight of batch	Fee
100 lb or less	$25·00
Over 100 but not over 1000 lb	$25·00 plus 6¢ per lb over 100 lb
Over 1000 lb	$79·00 plus 2¢ per lb over 1000 lb

Immediately after the manufacturer, or applicant, has received the Government lot number, certificate and test results from the FDA he is required to apply the certified lot number to each container of the batch. He then continues storage in such a manner as to prevent change in composition. If the newly certified colour is scheduled for use in secondaries it may be so used only after being relabelled with its FDA assigned lot number.

Each person to whom a certificate is issued must keep complete records for a minimum of two years showing the disposal of all the colour additive from each batch certified. These records show the amount, date and use of each withdrawal and the name and address of each person to whom shipment, or delivery, is made.

Certification previously granted expires if any of the following occur:

1. If the composition of the batch changes.
2. If closed packages of the batch are opened for any reason other than:
   a) to colour a food, drug or cosmetic
   b) to sample in the course of certifying a repack
   c) to use as a component in a mixture

d) to repackage into other sizes (by anyone other than the manufacturer)

e) to use in the preparation of a lake.

3. If any shipment is not labelled in accordance with 21 CFR 8.32 of the Color Additive Regulations.

4. If any shipment is not sealed.

5. If any seal on a shipment has been broken, intentionally or accidentally, unless such seal has been broken for the purpose of using the colour additive or has been opened by a duly authorised representative of the FDA or Department of Health and Human Services in the performance of his official duties, and he has immediately resealed the package.

Since 1964 the Regulations have exempted mixtures of certified colours from the earlier requirement of being recertified. Mixtures may include permissible diluents. These colourants are handled with the same rigid controls as the straight colours but their records of distribution are kept with respect to the manufacturer's control number rather than an FDA certified lot number. The term 'lot number' means an identifying number or symbol assigned to a batch by the Food and Drug Administration.

8.1. General Restrictions on Use of Colour Additives
Abstracted from the 21 CFR Color Additive Regulations:

1. No listing or certification of a colour additive shall be considered to authorise the use of any such colour additive in any article intended for use in the *area of the eye** unless listing... specifically provides for such use.

2. No listing or certification of a colour additive shall be considered to authorise the use of any such colour additive in any article intended for use in *injections* unless listing... specifically provides for such use.

3. No listing or certification of a colour additive shall be considered to authorise the use of any such colour additive in any article intended for use as a *surgical suture* unless such listing... specifically provides for such use.

* The term 'area of the eye' means the area enclosed within the circumference of the supra-orbital ridge and the infra-orbital ridge, including the eyebrow, the skin below the eyebrow, the eyelids and the eyelashes, and conjunctival sac of the eye, the eyeball and the soft areola tissue that lies within the perimeter of the infra-orbital ridge.

The style of letter used to request certification of a batch of straight colour is:

Date _____

Division of Color Technology,
HFF-430, Bureau of Foods,
Food and Drug Administration,
200C St., SW.,
Washington, D.C. 20204

In accordance with the regulations promulgated under the Federal Food, Drug, and Cosmetic Act, we hereby make application for the certification of a batch of straight color additive.

Name of color _____
                  (As listed in 21 CFR Part 74)

Batch number _____
                  (Manufacturer's number)

Batch weighs _____ pounds

Batch manufactured by _____

at _____ (Name and address of actual manufacturer)
How stored pending certification _____
_____
(State conditions of storage, with kind and size of
   containers, location, etc.)
Certification requested of this color for use in
_____
_____
_____

(State proposed uses)

Required fee, $_____ (drawn to the order of Food and Drug Administration).

The accompanying sample was taken after the batch was mixed in accordance with 21 CFR 80.22 and is accurately representative thereof.

(Signed) _____
     By _____
        _____
        (Title)

The foregoing and all the other requirements of the Food, Drug and Cosmetic Law and the Color Additive Regulations are rigidly enforced.

Any serious failure to comply, or failure to observe Current Good Manufacturing Practices in the manufacture or use of colour additives, can result in the application of sanctions. One such penalty for a colour manufacturer could be the suspension of certification service for a stated period of time.

The penalty for improper use of colourants might include legal sanctions in addition to recall and destruction of product. Users of certified colours are expected to observe all the Current Good Manufacturing Practices of the food industry and to post on their manufacturing records the FDA lot number for each certified colour incorporated into foods. Good practices for users dictate that colours be protected from microbial or metallic contamination and that aqueous solutions be prepared only in distilled or softened water, free from micro-organisms. Any aqueous solutions not used within a short time should be preserved.

A user must bear in mind that some colourants may have specific use limitations. For example, synthetic iron oxide is permitted for use only in externally applied drugs (21 CFR 73.1200) and in dog and cat foods at 0·25% maximum (21 CFR 73.200). FD & C Red No. 4 has not had its name changed even though it is currently permitted only for *externally* applied drugs and cosmetics (21 CFR 82.304). Both users and colour manufacturers are subject to FDA factory inspections, normally at the frequency of at least once in each two-year period. All food products which have been coloured must be labelled with the phrase, 'artificially coloured', or the equivalent. This statement is required whether using a certified or an uncertified colourant. At the present time the only synthetic colour which must be declared by its specific name is FD & C Yellow No. 5. The amount of colour used must be 'within the limits of Good Manufacturing Practice' which is defined to be 'not more than necessary to accomplish the intended effect'. No use of colour which would deceive or mislead consumers is permitted. Imported foods may be coloured only with USA permitted colourants and, if certified colours are used, they must be from lots previously certified by the FDA. Under USA law any food which has been held under insanitary or other improper conditions, is considered to be adulterated and thus subject to sanctions. Sanctions may take the form of injunctions, seizures or destruction orders. Criminal penalties may include fines and imprisonment.

9.   HISTORY OF CERTIFIED COLOURS

In 1886 the colouring of butter was regulated by Federal law and, subsequently in 1896, the colouring of cheese. By 1900 a number of synthetic dyes were being used to colour food. Several were taken from synthetic colours manufactured for textile use. Some of them may have been from batches which were 'off-shade' and therefore unacceptable for their primary use on textiles. Others may have been from batches of variable purity. A trade group, the National Confectioners Association, published a list (in 1899) of colourings considered unfit for use in foods, but this prudent action by industry had no regulatory or enforcement power.

While appropriating funds for the Department of Agriculture in 1900, the Congress provided money for that department's Bureau of Chemistry to study the health aspects of colourants and to establish conditions of use. The Secretary of Agriculture issued a series of Food Inspection Decisions defining and prohibiting adulteration of food with any colour not known to be safe, and requiring that colours, when properly used, be declared in the food labelling. On 1 May 1906 one of these decisions prohibited the importation of macaroni coloured with Martius Yellow.

An extensive survey of the chemistry and physiological effects of hundreds of synthetic colours was then made by the Department of Agriculture, largely under the direction of Dr Bernhard C. Hesse. The results of this massive survey were reflected in the Food and Drug Act of 1906 and Food Inspection Decision No. 76 of July 1907. This new law and the regulatory decision limited the use of food colours to only those of known composition which also showed no unfavourable physiological effects. The first seven permitted were: Amaranth, Erythrosine (now FD & C Red No. 3), Indigotine (now FD & C Blue No. 2), Light Green SF Yellowish, Naphthol Yellow S, Orange I and Ponceau 3R.

The Department set up a voluntary system of certification of synthetic food colours which was immediately accepted by colour manufacturers and the first certification by the Department of Agriculture was issued in April 1908. The food industry found the seven colours permitted were not adequate for their needs and so, after satisfactory physiological testing, ten more were approved by the Department of Agriculture between 1916 and 1929. These ten included four still in use which are now identified as:

Colour	Year added
FD & C Yellow No. 5	1916
FD & C Green No. 3	1927
FD & C Yellow No. 6	1929
FD & C Blue No. 1	1929

The Federal Food, Drug and Cosmetic Act of 1938 extended Federal control to the colouring of drugs and cosmetics, set up the present three-way system of nomenclature (establishing separate categories for FD & C,

D & C, and External D & C colours), made certification of synthetic colours *mandatory* and transferred jurisdiction to the Food and Drug Administration. This was created by the Agricultural Appropriations Act of 1931. It was moved later into the Federal Security Agency and, subsequently in 1953, into the Department of Health, Education, and Welfare (HEW) which is now the Department of Health and Human Services (HHS).

During and after the hearings on this Act the safety of all the permitted colours was reviewed once again and, in 1940, the FDA published its list of permitted colours along with specifications and regulations covering manufacture, sale, labelling, and certification.

Starting in 1950 the FDA began a new programme of 'state of the art' long term feeding studies on animals, including mice, rats and dogs. (This programme continued for about 14 years as some of the studies were started as late as 1957.) The work was supported by FDA's income from the certification fees levied on each batch manufactured. These tests used doses up to 5 % of the animal diets—the highest dose levels employed up to that time. Shortly thereafter there were three incidents of excessive use levels of colours in candy and on popcorn which resulted in a number of cases of diarrhoea in children. One offending candy was later found by the FDA to have been coloured with 2500 ppm of FD & C Orange No. 1 and some popcorn was found to contain from 3000 to 9800 ppm of FD & C Red No. 32. Another colour misused was FD & C Orange No. 2. These three colours eventually yielded unfavourable test results from the new studies using the high dose levels.

On 6 March 1953 Dr G. Robert Clark of the FDA wrote to each of the synthetic colour manufacturers requesting them to attend a meeting to discuss the latest chronic feeding test results and the chemistry of the colours then described as 'certifiable coal-tar colours'.

These tests clearly showed unfavourable results from azo colours containing unsulphonated naphthalene rings. Dr Clark's call to meet was the immediate cause of the formation of an informal group of colour manufacturers' representatives called, later on, the Certified Color Industry Committee (CCIC). Its first company members were:

Allied Chemical and Dye Corp.
American Cyanamid Co.
Bates Chemical Co.
The Dykem Co.
The Hilton-Davis Chemical Co.

H. Kohnstamm and Co.
Warner-Jenkinson Mfg. Co.
Wm. J. Stange Co.
Sterwin Chemicals, Inc.

Later, in 1953, the manufacturers' committee was composed of the following six people representing the indicated companies:

Individual	Representing
Chairman, Dr C. Boyd Shaffer	American Cyanamid Co.
Mr W. H. Kretlow	Wm. J. Stange Co.
Mr J. C. McCormack	The Dykem Co. and Warner-Jenkinson
Dr Wesley Minnis	Allied Chemical and Dye Corp. and The Bates Chemical Co.
Dr R. C. Sherwood	The Hilton-Davis Chemical Co. and Sterwin Chemicals, Inc.
Dr S. Zuckerman	H. Kohnstamm & Co.

In the early years the group was known as the 'Coal Tar Color Industry Committee'. In July 1956 the name was changed to the 'Certified Color Industry Committee' when Arthur T. Schramm of the National Aniline Division, Allied Chemical and Dye became the second chairman.

Beginning in 1954 industry representatives attempted to get the FDA to establish use level limitations for synthetic colours which could be calculated from the toxicological data and which would serve to prevent incidents like those with the candy and popcorn. These requests were always denied, however, because the FDA held that the Government was not authorised by the law to set any quantity limitations. The delistings of FD & C Orange No. 1, Orange No. 2 and Red No. 32 took place early in 1956 when the CCIC was unable to have the hearings on them reopened. In the same time period the National Academy of Sciences was requested to appoint a review committee to evaluate the FDA research programme on certified colours. This committee recommended that maximum use levels be taken into consideration when evaluating the safe use of food colourings whether they be synthetic or those derived from natural sources.

In September 1956 the following people began work as the Technical Subcommittee of the Certified Color Industry Committee: A. T. Schramm of Allied Chemical (Chairman), Dr R. C. Sherwood of Sterwin Chemicals and Dr S. Zuckerman of H. Kohnstamm, with E. A. Chase of Sterling Drug as counsellor. Their assignment was to cooperate with the FDA on all chemical questions concerning the certifiable synthetic colours. In addition, they contacted many of the national food industry trade associations to enlist their help in making a survey of the industrial use levels of the synthetic colours.

In December 1958 the use level arguments were put to rest when the legal battle had worked its way up to the US Supreme Court which ruled that the FDA did not, under the 1938 law, have any authority to establish maximum use level limits. Then in 1959 FD & C Yellows Nos. 1, 2, 3 and 4 were delisted and the efforts to amend the 1938 law were accelerated. Success was achieved in July 1960 when the Color Additive Amendments became effective as a result of the cooperative efforts of the CCIC, the FDA and several interested representatives of the food industry.

The most meaningful aspects of the very important Color Additive Amendments to the Food, Drug, and Cosmetic Act assigned authority to the Secretary of the HEW Department:

1. To list colours for specific uses, to set the conditions of use and to establish limits on use.
2. To allow continuing use of existing colour additives under certain conditions.
3. To list colours whose safety in use has been demonstrated and to list provisionally other colours.
4. To extend the duration of provisional listings when, in his judgement, no harm to the public would result providing there were ongoing toxicological studies at the time of issuing extensions.
5. To determine what colours should be required to be certified and what colours should be exempt from certification. The law provides equal treatment of both these classes.

The new amendments refrained from using the unfortunate term, 'coal-tar colour', and the obscure term, 'natural colour'. Instead the colours are established as 'certified' or 'exempt' and 'listed' or 'provisionally listed'. The amendments include a cancer clause similar to the Delaney Clause and authorise the appointment of a committee, advisory to the Secretary, to gather facts and make recommendations.

Finally the new law had the effect of transferring the responsibility for establishing safety in use from the Government to the manufacturers. They, or any 'interested person', must submit petitions for the 'permanent' listing of all proposed food, drug and cosmetic colourants. The regulations promulgated by the Secretary and published in the Code of Federal Regulations (CFR) prescribe the requirements for petitions.

By February 1965 adequate data were in hand for the CCIC to submit the first food colour petition (FD & C Yellow No. 5) and it, plus FD & C Blue No. 1 and FD & C Red No. 3, were listed for use in food and ingested drugs in July 1969.* Use levels are limited only by Good Manufacturing Practice. In the 1970s the FDA failed to respond to the other petitions filed by the CCIC because of the need for teratology and reproduction studies. In this decade FD & C Red No. 40 was listed (1971) and FD & C Violet No. 1 and FD & C Red No. 2 were removed from listing in 1973 and 1976 respectively. The violet colour was delisted because of some toxicology work in Japan at a time when American and Canadian tests were still being evaluated. The political demise of FD & C Red No. 2 is well known and its story is too long to recount here. FD & C Red No. 4 is still listed but its use was limited (1976) to externally applied drugs and cosmetics (21 CFR 82.304).

In January 1972 the CCIC was reorganised and incorporated as the Certified Color Manufacturers' Association (CCMA). Currently its directors represent Colorcon, Inc., Hilton-Davis Chemical Co. Div., H. Kohnstamm & Co., Inc., Stange Co. and Warner-Jenkinson Co. For the past eleven years this organisation, as did its predecessor the CCIC, has worked diligently to do everything within its power to keep certifiable synthetic colours available for use by the food, drug and cosmetic industries.

10. APPLICATION OF THE LAW AND REGULATIONS

Between September 1976 and February 1977 the FDA, recognising current method advances in conducting and evaluating chronic toxicity studies, ordered that all the then-listed colours, except FD & C Red No. 40, be retested. This massive new requirement fell upon the three trade associations who are the colour petitioners,† and it required that all of the provisional listing date expirations be advanced about four years. Semi-annual progress reports on all studies were required by the FDA. At the same time, the FDA stated it did not consider any of the several completed

---

* All 'permanent' listings for cosmetic and topical drug uses have been delayed, first by a dispute between industry and the government on pre-market product clearance and second, by the 1976 FDA requirement for a new round of toxicology studies.
† Food colours—the Certified Color Manufacturers' Association (CCMA), drug colours—the Pharmaceutical Manufacturers' Association (PMA) and cosmetic colours—the Cosmetic, Toiletry and Fragrance Association (CTFA).

toxicity tests on each colour to be adequate for the provisional listings (listings which traced their origin back to the Color Additives Amendment of 1960). The agency explained (41 *Federal Register*, p. 41860, 23 September, 1976) that all of the studies were deficient in the following respects:

1. Many of the studies were conducted using groups of animals, i.e., control and those fed the color additive, that were too small to permit conclusions to be drawn today on the chronic toxicity or carcinogenic potential of the color additives tested. The small number of animals used does not in and of itself cause this result, but when considered together with the other deficiencies described in this document, does do so. By and large, the studies used 25 animals in each group; today FDA recommends using at least 50 animals per group.

2. In a number of the studies, the number of animals surviving to a meaningful age was inadequate to permit conclusions to be drawn today on the chronic toxicity or carcinogenic potential of the color additives tested.

3. In a number of the studies, an insufficient number of animals was reviewed histologically.

4. In a number of the studies, an insufficient number of tissues was examined in those animals selected for pathology.

5. In a number of the studies, lesions or tumors detected under gross examination were not examined microscopically.

Shortly thereafter, the Health Research Group and Public Citizen, another activist group, petitioned a US District Court seeking an injunction to direct the Secretary of HEW to withdraw his 1977 extension of the provisional listing dates. Upon request, the court permitted the CCMA and the CTFA to intervene by joining the Secretary and the FDA as defendants. In October the judge upheld the FDA position and its actions. In the following year 23 colours were in new chronic toxicity studies set up by the three trade associations at four independent toxicology laboratories.

The 1977 provisional listing extensions were set to expire on 31 January 1981 when many of the new studies were nearing completion. A further time extension was held up by President Reagan's freeze on Government regulations. The activists seized the occasion to file another suit (Wende McIlwain *et al.* vs. the Commissioner, the FDA *et al.*, 9 March 1981) in the DC District Court seeking a judicial order to force the FDA to cancel all provisional listings. Once again, to assist the FDA, the CCMA and the

CTFA obtained court permission to be joined as defendants. In extensive briefs filed in the case, the FDA was assisted in ensuring that all the pertinent facts were provided to the court. After the plaintiffs lost this action, it was appealed and the decision in favour of the FDA was upheld on 19 October 1982 by the US Court of Appeals on a vote of two to one.[22]

In the meantime, on 28 September 1982, the FDA released its first *Federal Register* publication resulting from the lengthy retesting requirements which had been promulgated more than five years previously for all the synthetic colours. This action 'permanently' listed FD & C Blue No. 1 for cosmetic uses—a colour which had been so listed for use in foods and ingested drugs on 8 May 1969! At that time, the FDA withheld all 'permanent' listings for cosmetic uses because it felt new dermal toxicity studies were necessary. In addition, it was said that the certified colours' permanent listings were 'being held hostage' by the FDA because they wanted the cosmetic industry to furnish the FDA with their cosmetic raw material lists. Now FD & C Blue No. 1 is 'permanently' listed for all uses, including cosmetics, based upon the recently completed new chronic toxicity studies carried out by the CCMA on Charles River albino rats and Charles River CD-1 mice and the new dermal studies carried out by the CTFA. The effective date of 29 October 1982 was confirmed in 47 *Federal Register* p. 54429 on 3 December 1982.

Thus, one might expect that the requirements laid down by the Congress in 1960 have finally been judged by the FDA to have been satisfied for FD & C Blue No. 1. But not completely! All the food colour lakes have been left on the provisional list appearing in 21 CFR 81.1(a). Lakes of some certified colours have been used since 1939 but were not subjected to separate certification until 1959. The FDA announced (44 *Federal Register*, p. 36411, 22 June 1979 and 44 *Federal Register*, p. 48986, 21 August 1979) that in 1979 all the lakes would be treated separately, and by this announcement it terminated a 'permanent' listing proposal for lakes which it had made in 1965! (30 *Federal Register*, p. 6190, 11 May 1965.)

The reasons given by the FDA were that inadequate information was available to support 'permanent' listing of the lakes. In particular, more information was said to be needed on lake definitions, nomenclature, safety, specifications and analytical methods, including those for percent pure colour, subsidiary colour content and residual intermediates.

Since lakes were being made by various processes and may include various diluents (not necessarily present in straight colour mixtures) it is appropriate that the manufacturers collaborate with the FDA in addressing the need for further information on lakes. However, general opinion on the 'safety' of lakes holds that they are every bit as safe as straight colours and far more safe than many other of the less-tested food additives. This principle has been supported by the very fact that the repeated toxicity studies of the straight colours have always been accepted as sufficient evidence to support the safe use of the lakes as well.

Throughout all the years lakes have been certified the regulations have required a second certification for food colour lakes. That is, a food colour lake must be made from previously certified straight colour(s) and the lake itself must then be certified before it may be used in food or sold. Lakes for drug and cosmetics, however, may be made from either certified or uncertified straight colours and only need be certified after the lakes have been made. The lakes of all the food colours except FD & C Red No. 40 have been left provisionally listed under the general entry for FD & C lakes in 21 CFR 81.1(a).

The current Food, Drug and Cosmetic Law, which took effect in 1938, has been amended a number of times since. As cited elsewhere, the amendments with the greatest effect on food colourings were the Color Additive Amendments of 1960. The law makes no safety distinction in the listing requirements between colours which are synthetically prepared and those which are isolated, extracted from or manufactured from vegetable or mineral substances found in nature. In 1977, when extending the provisional listings, the Commissioner responded to comments favouring 'natural' colours by saying (42 *Federal Register*, p. 6992, 4 February 1977):

... the Commissioner advises that 'natural' foods and food ingredients are not necessarily safer than artificial ones. Many natural foods are harmful if ingested in sufficiently large quantities. Additionally, many synthesized ingredients are identical to substances that occur naturally. In short, the notion that all natural foods are safer than all artificial foods is not supported by available scientific data.

Nevertheless, it has been the practice of the FDA to require fewer toxicological data for colours 'derived from natural substances'. Some of the apparent reasons have been that these usually have limited uses and generally are available in smaller quantities, and there seems to be a tendency, even within the FDA, to presume they are safe. On these petitions, the FDA has exercised its discretion over the extent of its toxicology requirements. There were no guidelines available for use so the various sponsors have had to approach the FDA to ask their specific requirements on toxicology for each individual petition. In 1983 we have under review, and open for comment, the *Toxicological Principles for the*

Safety Assessment of Direct Food Additives and Color Additives Used in Food,[15] the so-called 'Redbook', which the FDA made available to the public on 15 October 1982. The CCMA sent its comments on this to the FDA in January 1983. A similar publication is *A Proposed Food Safety Evaluation Process* by the Food Safety Council (June 1982).[7] Comments on these appear later.

From time to time the FDA faces new, unexpected and/or unusual observations in petitioners' periodically submitted toxicology reports or in special incident reports. This is not unusual because the science of toxicology has been advancing quite rapidly and test animals are being kept alive for longer and longer times. The almost completed set of chronic *in utero* studies of the food colours represents years of work with hundreds of rodents and will culminate in millions of biological observations. The histology work carried out far exceeds the amount that was customary prior to 1977 and, naturally, an extra amount of evaluation is done on the control animals as well as the treated. Because of this the data banks on various species and strains of animals are accumulating an extensive amount of information not known previously. Statistical analyses of data groups bridging different time periods are not valid when the data were gathered under disparate conditions. Furthermore, tests of significance conducted by mathematicians require thorough assessment and interpretation in the light of biological factors.[21]

FD & C Blue No. 2 is a recent toxicology example in which unusual observations were made of astrocytomas, a rare type of tumour in the aged male rat brain, and certain other observations which later were determined by the FDA to be anomalous. The anomalous observations were found later to have been reported erroneously. Any such surprising observation immediately precipitates a series of actions which may include any or all of these:

1. Verify the observation(s).
2. Examine more animals.
3. Prepare more tissue slides taken in a random fashion and code them.
4. Have additional pathology work done, normally 'blind'.
5. Examine the data bank on control animals at the conducting laboratory and other laboratories.
6. Engage consultants expert in the matter at hand.
7. Conduct consultations with the FDA.
8. Provide supplementary reports.

9. Provide supplementary tissue samples and exhibits.
10. Arrange for an independent verification of the additional pathology.
11. Obtain the latest evaluation of all the results from the FDA.
12. Study the peer review report if the FDA chooses to submit the question to an advisory committee.*
13. Prepare an evaluation and review document citing independent qualified experts and appropriate references if one appears to be helpful for proper interpretation by the FDA.

All of the above were done in the case of FD & C Blue No. 2 over a period of about 15 months. During this interval the FDA arranged for an advisory committee review by a special National Toxicology Program group which held a public hearing on 11 August 1982. Later, this group, after reviewing all the evidence, concluded that the number of rare brain tumours (6 of 71 animals) observed in one site, in one sex and in one species was, at the most, equivocal in bearing any relationship to the treatment with FD & C Blue No. 2.

The CCMA delivered a document as described in No. 13 above to the FDA on 7 October 1982. On 2 November 1982, the FDA announced that this colour would be 'permanently' listed and, in the meantime, the provisional listing has been extended three times. (47 *Federal Register*, p. 49637, 2 November 1982; 48 *Federal Register*, p. 5261, 4 February 1983; 48 *Federal Register*, p. 19364, 29 April 1983; 48 *Federal Register*, p. 30358, 1 July 1983.) The last two extensions were provided by the FDA to allow more time for their preparation of a reply to the listing objections which they received on 7 March 1983.

11. PROSPECTS FOR AMENDMENT OF THE LAW

In April 1982 the FDA introduced new regulatory proposals (one of which was called the 'constituents' policy) for a method of handling food and colour additives which 'might' or 'could' contain traces of carcinogenic

---

* 'Disputes such as . . . should be decided by the Commissioner on the basis of the best advice he can get from the world's experts on the subject. The best mechanism for securing such advice is clearly FDA's advisory committee structure, which ought to be strengthened; the committees are clearly cost-beneficial in the long run. . . .' Alexander M. Schmidt MD, a former Commissioner of the FDA, in a Guest Editorial, *Pharmaceutical Technology*, 7(1), 1983, p. 15.

chemicals (47 *Federal Register*, pp. 14464–70, 2 April 1982). Two alternative proposals were described as the '*de minimus* migration' and 'sensitivity of the method' approaches. These proposals may help to prevent additional delistings such as the previous FDA actions removing food grade Carbon Black, External D & C Yellow No. 1 and D & C Red Nos. 10, 11, 12 and 13. These were all delisted *not* because of toxicity test results but merely because of the *possibility* that they might contain traces of carcinogenic substances. In effect, the FDA has now recognised that in the past it was over zealous in some product removals, removing them from the market in spite of the fact that the Delaney Clause prohibits the use of additives which are carcinogenic, *not* additives which *may* contain incidental traces of substances which may be carcinogenic for man.

The FDA moved ahead with these proposals because of the lack of progress on various food safety amendments which are attempting to address this problem, among others. Up to the date of writing some of the D & C colours* have been 'permanently' listed by the FDA with a reference to the 'constituents' policy because industry's new chronic toxicity studies have demonstrated that they are safe even when fed at high doses. This process can be controlled by suitable risk-assessment procedures which are capable of assuring that no harm will result from the proposed uses of the petitioned substances.

New food safety bills proposed by various legislators in 1981, and again in 1982, have generated a great amount of heat, and, we hope, some light in the meantime. Prominent proposals were Senator Hatch's 1981 Bill (S 1442) and Congressman Gore's 1982 Bill (HR 5491). In addition, there have been committee mark ups and other proposals made by a White House sub-cabinet panel which includes Dr Arthur H. Hayes, Jr, the FDA Commissioner. These proposals would normally proceed to the President's Cabinet Committee on Human Resources before being sent to the Congress. Also, many suggestions and comments have emerged from trade associations and academe (particularly *A Proposed Food Safety Evaluation Process*, Food Safety Council, June, 1982[7]). Three main recommendations are to update the Delaney Clause, to make a legal framework for a broad use of risk analysis, and to increase the use of peer review in safety assessments. All Bills died with the adjournment of the extra (third) session of the 97th Congress at the end of 1982. To date, we have not seen the 1983 replacement Bill(s). These types of Bills move very slowly through the legislative process and it should be noted the nation has had more than two

* Green Nos. 5 and 6 and Red No. 30. In January 1983 Glenn M. W. Scott filed suit in the US Court of Appeals challenging the FDA listing of D & C Green No. 5.

years' worth of discussion even though not one Congressional Committee hearing has been conducted. According to the *Food Chemical News* (pp. 12–14, 22 November 1982), the Grocery Manufacturers' Association (GMA) president, George Koch, has written to the Secretary of Agriculture to say that the GMA endorses Mr Hatch's Bill, S 1442, but not all of the aspects of the sub-cabinet panel recommendations. There is a great deal of concern that the panel may suggest deleting the risk reference, 'under the intended conditions of use of a substance'.

One proposal of the sub-cabinet panel would provide that future testing requirements for food additives 'shall vary according to the extent of exposure to and probable biological activity of the substance to be evaluated . . .'. This is interesting because it would 'make legal' the disparate treatment the FDA has already given to synthetic colour additives versus those manufactured from vegetable and mineral raw materials.

At the annual meeting of the American Industrial Health Council on 30 November 1982, in Washington (quoted in *Food Chemical News*, p. 22, 6 December 1982) former FDA Commissioner Dr Hayes endorsed broad use of peer review by scientists, but he believes that the Secretary should be authorised to decide, on a case by case basis, when peer review would be used. Further, he said: 'Good science depends at least partly on the closer cooperation between the various sectors of society . . . on the understanding that government cannot know and learn everything, that knowledge and experience exist in the private sector to solve many of the problems government is trying to address.' The CCMA will continue to monitor these developments and will send all needed comments on behalf of food colourings to the appropriate legislative committee when the time for hearings approaches.

12.   RECOMMENDATIONS FOR USERS

The concentration and uniform distribution of a colour additive in food is of primary importance.[9,10] Obviously it must be used at a level to please the eye and give elegance to the product. It must, at the same time, not be deceiving to the public nor have unwanted effects such as staining of the lips. Food colours are not permitted in standardised foods unless the standard permits their use.

Colours must be stable and not affect the taste or flavour of the product in any way. Finally, the use level must be no higher than that required to accomplish the intended effect within the bounds of generally accepted

Good Manufacturing Practice. Permanent listings of three FD & C Colours which were published in the *Federal Register* by the FDA in 1969 and since, have recognised the integrity and usefulness of the 'Guidelines in good manufacturing practice: use of certified FD & C colors in food' presented by the CCIC[3] and so do not restrict use levels to other than 'Good Manufacturing Practice' as so described.

Fortunately, there is no problem in the area of taste as synthetic colours have no taste at the levels which represent 'Good Manufacturing Practice'. Neither have any body staining or elimination problems arisen in humans at these levels. However, in at least one dog-food application it has been found necessary to substitute FD & C Blue No. 2 for FD & C Blue No. 1 because of the unwanted stability of FD & C Blue No. 1 in the dog's digestive system.

Use concentrations of colours should normally be quoted as they exist in food which is ready to eat. A typical gelatin dessert may show 300–400 ppm in the package, but only 55–75 ppm in the finished dessert as presented for consumption.

12.1. Stability and Compatibility

Food colour additives must be both stable and compatible with the medium being coloured. These properties are required during the processing of the foodstuff on a commercial scale as well as throughout its shelf-life, final preparation, use and storage of 'left-overs' by the consumer. When compared to the vast spectrum of synthetic dyes developed in the past 50 years, those approved for general use as food colours are a comparative few: 2 reds, 2 yellows, 2 blues and a green. A total of seven colours comprise the acceptable list. From these seven the food technologist can create any of a myriad of colours. However, ingenuity and experience are required to adapt these colour additives to the many types of food products in which they are used. Many problems may arise because of the varied substances introduced to flavour, enrich, odorise, thicken, thin or reduce, and even to eliminate preparation time, in today's prepared foods. As these products are evolved it is imperative to use the concept of 'Complete Evaluation' before introducing new products to the marketplace. This concept requires development studies of stability, either long-term or accelerated, and of compatibility in the end product as prepared and used by the consumer.

The dry food colour powders have remarkable stability in closed containers. No change in properties has been noticed after a 15-year holding period except a slight loss of dye strength due to absorption of moisture. Synthetic colour solutions should be prepared in either distilled or deionised water, since many public water supplies have appreciable concentrations of metallic ions. Aqueous solutions of most food colours show quite good stability to light. The exceptions are FD & C Red No. 3 and FD & C Blue No. 2. However, it must be noted that preservatives (e.g. acidified sodium benzoate or propylene glycol) must be introduced to prevent the growth of mould and/or bacteria in aqueous solutions not for immediate use. The sale of colours in solution is not popular because of economics, but standard solutions in the laboratory are good tools for matching shade in products.

Protein containing foodstuffs must be carefully tested for food colour application. Heated products will result in fading of most food colours except FD & C Red No. 3 and FD & C Yellow No. 6. Even without heating, the shelf-life of the other food colours in protein products requires study. Iron oxide is approved in the USA for use in dog and cat food only. It is used because of its stability to heat in the presence of protein and its concentration is restricted to 0·25% of the weight of the consumed pet food.

Ascorbic acid is used as a vitamin source and antioxidant, but unfortunately is a reducing agent which can decolorise the azo and triphenyl methane food colours if solutions are exposed to light. A stability study should be run before these ingredients are combined in production. Other reducing agents such as metallic ions and sulphur dioxide must be eliminated or kept at low concentrations, i.e. below 100 ppm, to prevent loss of colour. Bacteria can also cause colours to fade. This may serve as a warning of such contamination when other fading causes have been eliminated.

Food colours must be dispersed thoroughly or dissolved in the coloured product to be effective. Solubilising initially or during processing is the accepted way to do this. Water is the normal solvent, although alcohols such as propylene glycol or glycerine can also be employed. Good agitation is necessary in dry formulations. In some cases a pre-mix of all the food colour with a portion of the media will reduce blending times.

Food colours are available in several forms as stated previously. Primaries are available in powder and granular forms and the powder form can be further refined to a plating grade. Secondaries are available as wet or dry blends, both as powders. These forms have been developed to solve specific needs of application in the food industry. The powder blends are by far the most popular as they are designed to match a particular shade. The wet–dry blends are used primarily in puddings and other applications where flashing of the primary colours must be prevented. In beverages, gelatin and powdered drink, use of the dry blends is normally satisfactory. Granular primaries may be employed when dust cannot be tolerated in an operating area. Plating grade food colours are used to colour the dry media in which the colouring is incorporated, such as sugar in drink powders. Recent processing developments have reduced the need for this type. Food colour lakes have been employed to deepen the shade in the dry state, but they are insoluble in water solutions which may be used by the consumer in the preparation of the product.

13. TOXICOLOGY

Toxicologists grant that substances are not toxic *per se*, but all substances have a toxic dose which, if exceeded, can be harmful to man. Even some essential elements such as zinc are toxic above a certain level. Essential nutrients, such as vitamins A and D, iron and selenium, are toxic at levels less than ten times the recommended dose for good nutrition.[11] The burden of demonstrating that food colours (in each of their petitions for listing) are safe under the intended conditions of use falls upon industry (in FDA parlance 'any interested person'). The judge of safety is the Commissioner of the FDA, who is delegated this power from the Secretary of the Health and Human Services Department (HHS), formerly the Department of Health, Education and Welfare. During the first half of the Reagan administration, there was some departure from this full delegation principle as the Secretary of the Department of HHS exercised his legal authority to review and accept, reject or modify some proposed actions which had been delegated to the Commissioner of the FDA. Due to the resignation of Secretary Richard Schweiker in January 1983 this situation may change. The Commissioner of the FDA determines acceptable daily intakes as described in 21 CFR 70.40.

Some of the general public do not realise that a number of foods that have been eaten by people for hundreds of years contain 'toxic' substances.[19] For example: potatoes may contain solanine, a toxic alkaloid; cabbage contains glucosinolates which cause goitre; overdoses of vitamin A have a variety of toxic responses; lima beans and cashew nuts contain traces of cyanide; sassafras contains safrole; honey may be contaminated with toxic components gathered by bees, etc.

It is possible that, if such foods were tested in the doses used in the

TABLE 7

TOP DOSE FEEDING LEVELS USED IN LATEST CHRONIC TOXICITY TESTS

	Mice		Rats		
	Percent of food	Approximate daily intake in mg/kg of body weight	Percent of food	Approximate daily intake in mg/kg of body weight	
				Male	Female
FD & C Blue No. 1	5·0	7 200	2·0	600	1 000
FD & C Blue No. 2	5·0	7 200	2·0	600	1 000
FD & C Green No. 3	5·0	7 200	5·0	1 470	2 570
FD & C Red No. 3	3·0	4 300	4·0	1 200	2 000
FD & C Red No. 40	5·19	7 500	5·19	1 520	2 650
FD & C Yellow No. 5	5·0	7 200	5·0	1 470	2 570
FD & C Yellow No. 6	5·0	7 200	5·0	1 470	2 570

Note: The daily intakes of male and female rats in Table 7 were estimated from the data in Table 8.

synthetic colours, they too would be found to be 'toxic'! (See Table 7.) This, however, does not mean that the foods are necessarily *hazardous* when consumed daily in a *balanced* diet by healthy individuals. The foods are not hazardous because the concentrations of 'toxics' are very low, the many different 'toxics' in the diet do not have additive effects, and the human body has a marvellous ability to handle the thousands of chemicals to which it is exposed every day.

Food additives outnumber food colour additives more than 200 to 1. Yet very few of the food additives have ever been subjected to the repeated and rigorously extensive toxicological testing required of all the synthetic colours. (Sweeteners are one of the exceptions.) The colours, in fact, have

TABLE 8

RODENT BODY WEIGHT AND FOOD INTAKE

	Typical adult weight (g)		Typical ad libitum daily food intake (g)	
	Male	Female	Male	Female
Charles River albino rat	750	350	22	18
Charles River CD-1 mouse	38	38	5·5	5·5

more than once been some of the first substances to undergo brand new 'state of the art' test protocols.

In 1971 the CCMA committed itself to underwrite the expense of teratology and reproduction studies on the ten (then) listed FD & C Colours (exclusive of FD & C Red No. 40). By 1973 the teratology reports were finished and accepted and by 1974 the balance of the work was concluded. In 1976 the CCMA once again assumed the responsibility and the expense of conducting further toxicology work—this time to repeat lifetime studies in all the general use food colours, except FD & C Red No. 40, in two species as required by reason of advancements in the science of toxicology (41 *Federal Register*, p. 41860, 23 September 1976). After the protocols were established and approved by the FDA,* bids were obtained, laboratories were inspected, and two were selected for the work. The total expense for this round of work was originally estimated to be about three million dollars. As the programme is winding down (1983), the actual costs have exceeded five and a half million dollars already. This is a large expense factor and, even if it is spread evenly over the national production of the intervening six years, it amounts to 37¢/kg of each batch of certified straight colour or lake.† It exceeds the cost of the certification fee which was 33¢/kg until it was increased in August 1982.

Why have some of the current toxicology studies posed new problems in evaluation? Possibly because:

1. *In utero* exposure of animals was a new technique.

2. The required continuation of the studies until 80% of the animals died of old age has generated many observations of phenomena absent in previous studies.

3. The maximum tolerated dose in acute studies may be too much for realistic chronic studies.

4. More thorough and minutely-done pathology evaluations generate more detail than that contained in the historical records of the test animals being used.

5. Disagreements among qualified experts about the significance of benign tumours and questions of whether some may be 'pre-cancerous'. (If an animal dying of old age has a benign tumour is it important to determine whether the tumour was pre-cancerous or not?)

* Modified later by the FDA requirement to move to higher dose levels after the tests were already underway.
† In these six years about 15 000 000 kilograms of the colours being retested were certified by the FDA.

6. There may have been a tendency to disregard the results of the many older studies.
7. Disagreements among qualified experts about interpreting 'statistical significance' in the light of 'biological significance'.
8. The historical tendency of the species and strains chosen to have high, and variable, incidences of spontaneous tumours. Are these animals the best surrogate for man?
9. Allowing rodents to consume food *ad libitum* may lead to abnormal results.

13.1. Newer Guiding Principles

The CCMA has filed comments with the FDA on its *Toxicological Principles for the Safety Assessment of Direct Food Additives and Colour Additives Used in Food* (the Redbook)[15] which was released in 1982 (47 *Federal Register*, pp. 46141–2, 15 October 1982). The CCMA agrees that this clear statement of the FDA scientific decision making process for evaluating additives should, as expected, stimulate comment and scientific discussion. The definition of 'safety' in this context is the one in the Code of Federal Regulations (21 CFR 170.3): 'a reasonable certainty that a substance is not harmful under the intended conditions of use'. Key points in this document are:

1. Proper use of exposure information and molecular structure information.
2. The proper role of short-term tests for carcinogenicity potential.
3. Construction of a tiered system for information development.
4. Use of data from previously performed toxicity studies.
5. The use of priority-setting in managing risks from all additives. Risk estimations should be made from hazard evaluations plus exposure data.

The CCMA believes that some clarification is required on the use of gavage studies. Because gavage places an undue stress on the animal and results in the additive undergoing different kinetics from those of an ingested additive, the Redbook should state a clear preference for feeding studies. Gavage should only be used as the route of last resort where it is impracticable to introduce the additive through the feed or for certain special studies such as one where the pharmacokinetics of the fed additive are compared to those of the additive when administered by gavage.

While the Redbook points out (Appendix II, p. 69 of Reference 15) that care must be taken to avoid strains and species of animals with a marked propensity for spontaneous tumours, it may not adequately stress the importance of consideration of reliable historical data on such tumours to put any observed tumours in proper perspective. It is especially important to give appropriate weight to historical data where test results appear to be aberrant.

Some elaboration is necessary regarding the Redbook's apparent requirement for 'three satellite treatment groups of 10 animals per sex (ibid, pp. 25–26). The exact purpose for this requirement is unclear. The FDA may intend such groups to be a means of identifying target organs for histopathologic examination of the other animals at the termination of the study. Such groups may also be intended to evaluate the reversibility of an effect by removing animals from the test diet, sacrificing some of them, and then resuming the diet. The FDA is expected to clarify its intent in this regard.

The Redbook recommends test doses of up to 5% of the diet. The recognition implicit in this recommendation that proper dose selection is a matter of scientific judgement is laudable. However, the CCMA believes that a 5% dose will not often be satisfactory since the test animals' systems may be overwhelmed or essential nutrients may be displaced from the diet by the test compound.

Finally, the CCMA believes that the principles should recommend raising the level of concern one level for any additive whose exact chemical composition is unknown. Unless the composition is well known, the information obtained about the effects of the additive on the various biological systems cannot be relied upon to justify a low level of concern.

The foregoing document should be considered in comparison with the *Proposed System for Food Safety Assessment*[13] and the recommendations in *A Proposed Food Safety Evaluation Process*,[7] both of which were sponsored by the Food Safety Council. The latter publication (June 1982) was the product of six years of work by the Council's board, staff, and outside consultants and advisors. It is a work of wide scope and input which addresses current laws as well as regulations. The former publication (June, 1980) has already been commended by its considerable use throughout the world.

14. FUTURE OUTLOOK

The expectation of adding other synthetic colours to the USA group now available (Table 9) is centred currently on two products: D & C Yellow

TABLE 9
CURRENT STATUS OF LISTINGS FOR FOOD USES

	Year 'permanently' listed	Provisional listing closing date
FD & C Blue No. 1	1969	
FD & C Blue No. 2		2 December 1983
FD & C Green No. 3	1982	
FD & C Yellow No. 5	1969	
FD & C Yellow No. 6		28 February 1984[a]
FD & C Red No. 3	1969	
FD & C Red No. 40	1971[b]	
Citrus Red No. 2	1959	
Orange B	1966	

[a] This advanced date was a result of the FDA mandate to add another (higher) dose level to the chronic rat and mouse studies after the studies were already in progress.
[b] Lakes of FD & C Red No. 40 are the only lakes for food use which have been listed 'permanently' to date.

No. 10 (Quinoline Yellow, CI 47005) and carmoisine (azorubine, CI 14720). The presently listed D & C Yellow No. 10 of the USA is erroneously described as the disodium salt of the disulphonic acid in 21 CFR 82.1710. Batches being certified contain this moiety but are predominantly the monosulpho-monosodium salt. The Quinoline Yellow of Europe (EEC No. E104) is also described as principally the disodium salt in proposed EEC Specifications 111/809/82. The American error in the chemical description being used by the FDA will be cleared up later when the colour becomes 'permanently' listed, possibly by renaming it FD & C Yellow No. 12 if accepted for food use, or possibly by renaming it D & C Yellow No. 12 if it continues to be listed for drugs and cosmetics only.

The recently completed lifetime *in utero* toxicity studies of this colour were supported by the PMA and the CCMA. These tests were started in August 1977 and the final reports were submitted to the FDA in June 1982. Feeding levels were $0 \cdot 0 \%$, $0 \cdot 5 \%$, $2 \cdot 0 \%$ and $5 \cdot 0 \%$ in rats, and $0 \cdot 0 \%$, $0 \cdot 1 \%$, $1 \cdot 0 \%$ and $5 \cdot 0 \%$ in mice. At the time of writing, the CCMA has not yet finished its petition for food uses. The provisional listing for drug and cosmetic uses is to expire on 1 November 1983. (See Table 10.)

After completing the petition work on D & C Yellow No. 10 the CCMA will be considering a petition for carmoisine which was previously tested in a reproduction study in the USA. This petition should contain the results of

TABLE 10
CURRENT STATUS OF LISTINGS FOR DRUG AND COSMETIC USES

	Date 'permanently' listed	Provisional listing closing date
FD & C Blue No. 1	1982	
FD & C Blue No. 2[a]		2 December 1983
FD & C Green No. 3	1982	
FD & C Yellow No. 5		7 October 1983
FD & C Yellow No. 6		28 February 1984
FD & C Red No. 3		2 October 1983
FD & C Red No. 40	1971	
D & C Yellow No. 10		1 November 1983

[a] Not listed for use in cosmetics.

the toxicology work done on carmoisine in the British Industrial Biological Research Association (BIBRA) programme, especially if an *in utero* stage was included.

There is little, if any, interest in the USA for listing Ponceau 4R (E124, CI 16255) for food, drug or cosmetic uses. In the past there had been some interest in adding another blue to the available USA colours, but concurrently with the 'permanent' listing of FD & C Blue No. 1 (CI 42090) for cosmetic uses in 1982 and the imminent 'permanent' listing of FD & C Blue No. 2 (E132, CI 73015) for food uses, this interest has subsided.

In view of the performance capabilities of the present synthetic colours, and the large expenditures of time and money incurred since 1977 to update their safety evaluations, there is little likelihood that any more than two colours will be added to the present list. Certainly a single manufacturer could not afford toxicology testing costs of five years' time and more than a million dollars for a new colour unless patent protection was available. New patents on methods of use are more probable than new patents on composition of matter.

What other situations may face food, drug and cosmetic colours in the future? Possibly better opportunities to share the results of safety studies run in various countries. And possibly another round of toxicity studies using the latest methods of the 1990s? By that time will we have available a test animal more like man than the rodents?

In the meantime synthetic colour users, and the public, may rest assured that these products are among the most thoroughly tested of all food additives.

156   R. K. JOHNSON AND F. J. LICHTENBERGER

REFERENCES

 1. Agriculture Research Service, *Food and Nutrient Intake of Individuals in the United States*, 1972, US Department of Agriculture, Washington, DC.
 2. Association of Official Analytical Chemists, *Official Methods of Analysis*, 13th Edn, 1980, AOAC, Arlington, VA.
 3. Certified Color Industry Committee, 'Guidelines for good manufacturing practice: use of certified FD & C colors in food', *Food Technology*, 1968, **22**, 946–9.
 4. Damon, G. E. and Janssen, W. F., 'Additives for eye appeal', *FDA Consumer*, July 1973, 15–21.
 5. Debesis, E., Boehlert, J. P., Givand, T. E. and Sheridan, J. C., 'Submitting HPLC methods to the compendia and regulatory agencies', *Pharmaceutical Technology*, **6**(9), 1982, 120–37.
 6. Dinman, B. D., '"Non-concept" of "no-threshold" chemicals in the environment', *Science*, **175**, 1972, 495–7.
 7. Board of Trustees, Food Safety Council, *A Proposed Food Safety Evaluation Process*, 1982, The Nutrition Foundation, Inc., Washington, DC.
 8. Committee on Food Protection, *Principles and Procedures for Evaluating the Safety of Food Additives*, 1959, NAS–NRC Publ. No. 750, Washington, DC.
 9. Committee on Food Protection, *The Use of Chemicals in Food Production, Processing, Storage and Distribution*, 1961, NAS–NRC Publ. No. 887, Washington, DC.
10. Committee on Food Protection, *Food Colors*, 1971, National Research Council, National Academy of Sciences, Washington, DC.
11. Committee on Food Protection, *Toxicants Occurring Naturally in Foods*, 2nd Edn, 1973, National Research Council, National Academy of Sciences, Washington, DC.
12. Committee on GRAS List Survey—Phase III, *The 1977 Survey of Industry on the Use of Food Additives, Vol. 3, Estimates of Daily Intake*, 1979, National Research Council, National Academy of Sciences, Washington, DC.
13. Scientific Committee, Food Safety Council, *Proposed System for Food Safety Assessment*, 1980, The Nutrition Foundation, Inc., Washington, DC.
14. Food and Nutrition Board, National Research Council, *Assessing Changing Food Consumption Patterns*, 1981, National Academy of Sciences, Washington, DC.
15. Food and Drug Administration, *Toxicological Principles for the Safety Assessment of Direct Food Additives and Color Additives Used in Food*, 1982, Washington, DC ('The Redbook').
16. Hutchings, J. B., 'The importance of visual appearance of foods to the food processor and the consumer', *J. Food Quality*, 1978, **1**(3), 245.
17. IFT Expert Panel on Food Safety and Nutrition, *Food Colors, A Scientific Status Summary*, 1980, Institute of Food Technologists, Chicago, IL, 8 pp.
18. Kare, M. R., 'Some functions of the sense of taste', *Journal of Agriculture and Food Chemistry*, 1969, **17**(4), 677.
19. Larkin, T., 'Natural poisons in food', *FDA Consumer*, October 1975, 5–7.
20. Marmion, D., *Handbook of US Colorants for Foods, Drugs, and Cosmetics*, 1979, John Wiley & Sons, Inc., New York.

21. Task Force of Past Presidents, Society of Toxicology, 'Animal data in hazard evaluation: paths and pitfalls', *Fundamental and Applied Toxicology*, 1982, **2**, 101–7.
22. US Court of Appeals, DC Circuit, Civil Action No. 81-00555, 19 October 1982.

FURTHER READING

Association of Official Analytical Chemists, *Journal of the AOAC*, bimonthly, the Mack Printing Co., Easton, PA, 18042.

Burnham, R. W., Hanes, R. M. and Bartleson, C. J., *Color: A Guide to Basic Facts and Concepts*, 1963, John Wiley, New York, London.

Color Research and Application (quarterly), John Wiley & Sons, New York, NY 10158.

Food and Chemical Toxicology, bimonthly, Pergamon Press Ltd, Oxford, England and Fairview Park, Elmsford, NY 10523.

National Research Council, *Food Chemicals Codex*, Third Edn, 1981, National Academy Press, Washington, DC.

FDA Consumer, Superintendent of Documents, Government Printing Office, Washington, DC 20402, Popular Periodical.

Furia, T. E. (Ed.), *CRC Handbook of Food Additives*, Second Edn, Vol. II, 1980, CRC Press, Boca Raton, FL.

General Foods Corp., *Today's Food and Additives*, 1976, White Plains, NY, 10625.

Hunter, R. S., *The Measurement of Appearance*, 1975, John Wiley, New York.

Judd, D. B. and Wyszecki, G., *Color in Business, Science and Industry*, 1975, John Wiley & Sons, New York.

Lowrance, W. W., *Of Acceptable Risk*, 1976, William Kaufmann, Inc., Los Altos, CA 94022.

Mackinney, G. and Little, A. C., *Color of Foods*, 1962, AVI Publishing Co. Inc., Westport, Connecticut.

Monsanto Company, *The Chemical Facts of Life*, 1977, St Louis, MO 63166.

Whelan, E. M. and Stare, F. J., *Panic in the Pantry*, 1975, Atheneum, New York.

Chapter 5

NATURAL COLOURS IN FOOD

A. J. TAYLOR

School of Agriculture, University of Nottingham, UK

SUMMARY

Although the colouring of food with natural compounds is considered to be desirable for various reasons, their use is limited at present. A few substances, notably the carotenoids, have been successfully incorporated into specific products, but natural colourants offer neither the range of colour nor the stability of synthetic dyes. Attempts to improve the situation have taken various forms. There has been an extensive search of the microbial, plant and animal kingdoms for pigments that possess both high tinctorial power and stability but so far no exceptional candidates have emerged. The instability of the common natural colourants in food has been studied to seek means of stabilisation and the environment in which the pigments exist in nature has been investigated for the same reason. Recent work on these approaches is reviewed, but any solution to the problem must be reconciled with the legislative and economic constraints governing the use of colourants in food.

1. INTRODUCTION

1.1. Aim of Chapter

In the previous volume in this series, natural colours were discussed in chapters on anthocyanins, synthetic carotenoids and other naturally occurring colouring materials. The chemistry of the pigments, methods for their extraction and their use in food were described. Currently the use of natural colourants is limited due to their instability, low tinctorial power or price disadvantage and the aim of this chapter is to examine the various ways by which natural colours may be improved and thus made more attractive to the food manufacturer. The various attempts to achieve this aim are outlined in the following pages. For each approach, a table of references is presented and a brief description of each is included in the text. Those ideas which, in the author's view, have particular merit, are then selected for further discussion. There will be a little overlap with work reported in the previous volume but most material mentioned is post-1979 (see Appendix for literature searched). Since many of the references are obscure, both primary source reference (e.g. a Japanese Patent) and a secondary reference (e.g. an abstracting journal) are given for convenience.

1.2. Natural Colourants

The trend towards natural ingredients in foodstuffs is continuing and this is evidenced by consumer acceptance of 'natural' foods and the various national regulations which completely or selectively ban artificial colours from food. Currently, the degree of safety testing required of a synthetic compound designed for food use is prohibitively expensive and the less stringent testing designated for natural compounds has obvious attractions. Whether the situation will become more or less restrictive is difficult to say. In the first volume of this series, Walford[1] suggested that a world-wide list of permitted colours be established to ease the export of processed foods. This ideal has still to be achieved but the permitted lists of each country and the associated labelling regulations generally favour the use of natural colours. It should be emphasised that the current appeal of natural colourants is based solely on their consumer acceptance and the peculiar regulation that allows a natural colour to be listed with perfunctory testing while a pure, synthetic compound is subject to practically every toxicological test ever devised. A change in legislation could alter the situation dramatically as some of the natural colourants would undoubtedly fail the full toxicological testing. Despite the current acceptance of natural colours, their effect on human metabolism should not be ignored. Pharmacological properties have been ascribed to some of the phenolic natural colourants[2,3] and toxicological data have also been published on some.[4,5,6] While mutagenic properties have been ascribed to quercetin[7] (when tested against *Salmonella*) the beneficial effects of flavonols and other polyphenolics have also been illustrated.[8] Besides the pigments themselves, the effect of metabolites or degradation products of the natural colourants on the human system should also be considered.[9]

1.3. Natural Colours Presently Used in Food

At present the use of natural colourants in food is limited, due to their instability, poor tinctorial power and the limited range of colours available.

Natural colourants produced for use in an analogous way to the coal-tar dyes are crude extracts of pigments which are basically unstable. The apparent stability of some food products owes more to the *amount* of pigment present than to the tinctorial power of the pigment itself. For example beetroot, even after prolonged cooking, retains an attractive deep red colour, but the extracted pigment is unstable. Anthocyanin preparations have found use in some products, but their colour variation with pH has restricted their use, mainly to acidic products. However, in nature, the flavonoids produce colours from white through, yellow, red and blue to black at the pH of cell sap. The potential colouring power of flavonoids is therefore great.

Carotenoids are relatively stable and there is sufficient demand to make complex chemical syntheses of 'nature-identical' carotenoids worthwhile. Their colour range is limited to yellow/orange/red and they are naturally oil soluble although water-soluble forms are available.

Chlorophylls are used as colourants in a range of foodstuffs and both natural chlorophyll (containing magnesium as the central metal ion) and 'copper chlorophylls' (copper substituted for magnesium) are available. Both chlorophyll and copper chlorophyll are manufactured in oil-soluble and water-soluble forms by selective retention or hydrolysis of the phytol side-chain.

Apart from these three plant pigments, there are others such as red beet extract (betanin), cochineal, turmeric extract, etc. which have found use in food.[10]

1.4. Methods of Improving Natural Colourants

Granted that many of the natural pigments presently available are unsatisfactory for one reason or another, attempts have been made to improve the situation by various means. One approach has been to search the plant, animal and microbial kingdoms for pigments which are stable under conditions prevailing in foods (pH 2–8, temperature −20 to 120 °C, presence of oxygen, sulphur dioxide etc.). Reports of colourants from novel sources are listed and discussed in Section 2. A second approach has been the prevention of colour loss from foods. After all, it is the destruction of the original colour that necessitates addition of extra colour and, if the loss can be kept to an acceptable level, colouring is unnecessary. Both chemical and physical methods have been used to prevent destruction of natural colours in foodstuffs and they are presented in Section 3. However, this applies only to foods which naturally contain colour. Some foods that are formulated from essentially colourless ingredients (e.g. biscuits) will still require colour addition.

The stability of some natural colourants *in vivo* has initiated a third approach. For instance, stable coloured complexes have been isolated from several sources (e.g. blueberries[11]) and shown to consist of an intimate mixture of polysaccharide, anthocyanin and metal ions. In a similar way, chlorophyll degradation in whole tissue is slow when chlorophyll is in its natural state; bound to protein. Only above the denaturation temperature of the protein is chlorophyll breakdown substantially accelerated. A greater awareness of the form in which natural colourants exist in nature might lead to more stable forms (Section 4). At present the pigments are available as crude extracts which produce coloration very different from that found in the original material. Thus black grape skins yield an anthocyanin which is bright red below pH 2 but colourless or yellow at grape pH. Few attempts have been made to upgrade the extracts apart from the addition of carriers to improve solubilisation and preservatives to stop oxidation or microbial infestation. Attempts to stabilise isolated natural colourants are described in Section 5.

A different approach to the improvement of food colour has been taken by some plant breeders who have attempted to breed strains with increased pigmentation. The philosophy behind this is that the increased amount of pigment will allow an acceptable colour to be achieved even allowing for losses during processing. This approach lies outside the scope of this chapter but, for example, strawberries which have uniform coloration throughout the fruit have been bred and used in canned packs.[12] Similarly Barritt and Torree have described cultivars with increased pigmentation.[13,14]

A common feature of all approaches is that, to remain natural, a natural colourant must be stabilised in a natural way. The legislative definition of 'natural way' has not yet been tested but it would seem that treatments such as heating, extraction with permitted solvents, reaction with enzymes or permitted food additives would be within the spirit of the 'natural' definition. Apart from the legal shackles which hinder the chemist's search for an acceptable stable natural colourant, the cost of the finished product must also be considered. Unless an expensive process confers a vast benefit on the product, it must be considered uneconomic. The economic effects of using natural colourants have been calculated by McClelland[15] who derived a Cost in Use Disadvantage (CIUD) index to compare the costs of natural and synthetic colourants. Natural colourants were significantly more costly than the synthetics but, in McClelland's view, the increase was not prohibitive. Ultimately the consumer will settle the issue by buying or rejecting the more expensive naturally-coloured products.

In this context it is interesting to note the economics of biotechnological processes, as production of natural colours by these means has been suggested. In the report *Application of Biotechnology to the Food Industry—An Appraisal*[16] the authors state that '...the cost of raw material production based on biomass is greater than £2000 tonne^{-1} (1980 prices). For low volume metabolic products produced by plant cell culture, the critical cost is in the order of £100 000 tonne^{-1}'. These latter costs may be acceptable to the pharmaceutical industry but they limit the production of natural food colourants by plant cell culture. Colourants presently available sell for £5000–£150 000 tonne^{-1}, depending largely on their tinctorial power, so production by microbial means may be feasible.

Thus the already onerous task of improving natural colourants is additionally complicated by the financial and legislative constraints. The following sections tackle the various approaches taken to improve natural colourants by listing the relevant literature and discussing the merits and feasibility of each.

2. NOVEL SOURCES OF NATURAL COLOURANTS

In the search for a colourant that has the properties desired for food use practically every part of the biosphere has been investigated. The following sections describe recent discoveries cited in patents and journals and listed here in sections on microbial, animal and plant sources. In addition, some earlier work which falls outside the period of review but which is considered important has also been incorporated.

2.1. Microbial Sources
Production of materials by the culture of micro-organisms has several advantages. The rapid growth of microbes cuts production time to a matter of days and the process lends itself to continuous operation. Compared to plant or animal sources, the production is flexible and can easily be controlled. Microbes produce a variety of colourants such as chlorophyll and carotenoids as well as some unique pigments. By incorporating suitable genetic material into selected microbes, it may be possible in the

TABLE 1
MICROBIAL SOURCES OF NATURAL COLOURANTS

Organism	Description	Reference
Monascus anka	Production and extraction of red pigment	17
Monascus anka	Hyperpigment productive mutant	18
Monascus anka	Structure of ankaflavin	19
Monascus purpureus	Antibiotic production	20
Monascas purpureus	Incorporation into petfood	21
Monascus spp.	Wheat, starch, corn meal substrate	22
Monascus spp.	Combination with amino groups	23
Monascus spp.	Effect of combination on colour	24
Monascus spp.	Controlled culture gives major pigment	25
Monascus spp.	Water soluble pigment with protein	26, 27
Monascus spp.	Yellow pigment from *Monascus*	28
Monascus spp.	Quantity and quality of pigments	29
Monascus spp.	Edible natural red dyestuff	30
Monascus spp.	Pigment in sausages	31
Chlorella	Red carotenoid pigments	32
Yeast	Heated autolysate gives colour	33
Blue-green alga	Blue phycocyanin pigment	34
Nocardia	Red pigment colours fish paste	35

future to produce other pigments not normally associated with micro-organisms, e.g. anthocyanins.

Most of the reports of food colourants from microbial sources involve *Monascus* species (Table 1). Traditionally, micro-organisms of this genus have been grown on rice until the whole mass becomes coloured by the red mycelia. The mass is then dried and powdered to produce a colourant long used in foods of oriental origin. Alternatively, the whole mass (called ang-kak by the Chinese) is consumed as food. The structures of the colourants have been reported[19] and are shown in Fig. 1. In this form, the pigment is orange in colour but it readily reacts with molecules containing amino groups to form red compounds[24] with the typical structure shown in Fig. 2.

A wide range of naturally occurring compounds containing amino groups have been suggested as substituents and they also confer a degree of water solubility on the molecule[26,27] which, without substitution, is normally fat soluble. Thus Moll and Farr[23] produced red colourants substituted with chitosan, ethanolamine or hexosamines. It was suggested that the use of chitosan as the adjunct was beneficial as chitosan is readily available from the insect kingdom and is not digested by humans which means it has a minimal effect on the human organism.

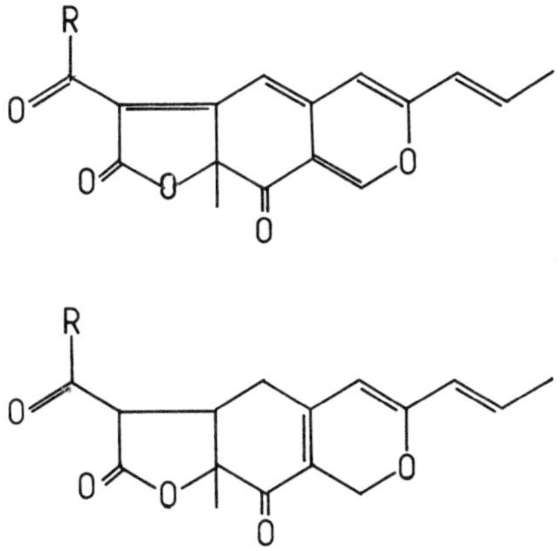

FIG. 1. Structure of pigments from *Monascus*[19] (above) R = nC_5H_{11}, monascin; R = nC_7H_{15}, ankaflavin (below) R = nC_5H_{11}, rubropunctatin; R = nC_7H_{15}, monascorubrin.

Instead of extracting the pigment from *Monascus*, some workers have added the whole coloured substrate to foods for colouring purposes. Corn or rice was used and incorporated into a pet food[21] at a level of 1–5 % to impart a red colour. Successful semi-moist pet foods were also formulated using extracted pigments dissolved in various glycols.

Careful control of the culture conditions selectively improves the yield of the various pigments. Thus under appropriate conditions, the orange pigment can be produced as the major coloured pigment.[25] The production of a single pigment instead of a mixture prevents colour variation between batches due to changes in pigment composition. Culture of *Monascus* on powdered bread is reported to produce yellow pigments[28] while solid culture of a *M. anka* strain gave 'hyperpigment production'.[18]

Other micro-organisms have been cultured and their pigments extracted for use as food colourants. An extract of *Chlorella* yielded 'pure carotene

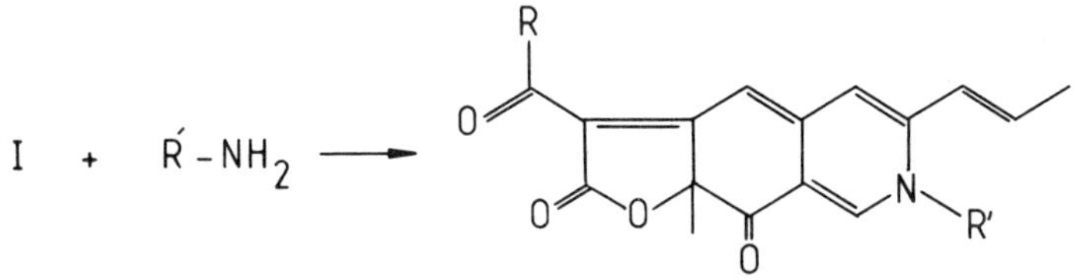

FIG. 2. Structure of substituted pigments from *Monascus*.[23] R = aliphatic radical, R' = radical from R'—NH_2.

TABLE 2
ESTIMATED COSTS FOR PIGMENT PRODUCTION FROM *Monascus*

Substrate	% Solids	Raw material costs[a] £ per tonne (dry wt)	Pigment cost[b] £ per tonne
Corn or rice[c]	50[d]	350	7 000
Molasses	50	300	6 000
Solid substrate[e] (Agar)	7	10 985	215 714
Aqueous media[e]	5·5	3 054	61 090

[a] Including £200 per tonne (dry wt) processing cost.[36]
[b] Assuming 5 % yield.[25]
[c] Reference 21.
[b] Author's estimate.

and a red pigment' claimed to be suitable for food use[32] as was phycocyanin extracted from a blue-green alga[34] and a red pigment from *Nocardia*.[35]

A novel colour claimed to be suitable for food use was produced by heating a 10 % yeast autolysate with sugar at 150 °C, then adding 1 % food grade soda and after 30–40 min adding 0·05 % ammonium chloride.[33] Even though the ingredients may have been of food grade, it seems unlikely that the method of production would be considered 'natural'.

Although cultivation of micro-organisms for the production of food colourants has attractions, these must be measured against the financial, legislative and user constraints. Table 2 summarises the costs of colourant production from *Monascus* under the headings raw material cost (based on laboratory SLR reagents and the quoted papers), processing cost[36] and the cost of a tonne of pigment based on a 5 % yield (a generous estimate from the quoted yield of Shepherd and Carels[25]). No allowance has been made for extraction of the pigment and related solvent and solvent recovery processes.

Although these figures are extremely approximate due to the scarcity of information, they do show that production of *Monascus* pigment using a solid agar substrate as described by Shepherd and Carels[25] is extremely expensive. The simpler substrates such as molasses or corn[22] bring the production cost more into line with the approximate cost of the cheaper colourants whose current prices are given in Table 3. Without more details of the tinctorial power of *Monascus* pigments it is impossible to say whether the estimated prices in Table 2 would be acceptable.

The attitude of regulatory authorities to microbially produced colourants is impossible to anticipate, but no doubt the strains would have

TABLE 3
APPROXIMATE 1982 PRICES OF FOOD COLOURANTS

Colourant	Price £/tonne
Yellow/orange azo dyes	5 000
Erythrosine	25 000
Brilliant Blue FCF	15 000
Cochineal	150 000

(Walford, personal communication.)

to be proved pathogen free and free of any toxic components. The precedent established by the FDA which limits the production of enzymes for food use to just three organisms (*Aspergillus niger*, *Aspergillus oryzae* and *Bacillus subtilis*) might count against *Monascus* produced pigments. Also the fact that *Monascus purpureus* has been reported to produce antibiotics simultaneously with pigments will require close attention.[20]

There is still no substantial evidence to suggest that the pigments from *Monascus* are superior to other natural colourants. Potentially their orange or red colour is suitable for food use, their long usage in Oriental foods is also in their favour and the property of reacting with amino-containing compounds suggests that they could easily be incorporated into food systems. They appear to be stable in the pH range 2–10 although below pH 2 precipitation occurs on standing.[29] Autoclaving of pigment–protein complexes resulted in cloudy solutions presumably due to precipitation of the protein, but methanolic extracts of the native pigments survived 3 h refluxing at 66 °C.[29]

When used in a sausage formulation, monascorubine was well absorbed by meat and non-meat proteins giving them a pink colour of cooked sausage.[31] The pigment was stable to the heat treatment received during cooking and was not released into the meat juice nor did it colour the fat portion of the sausage.

2.2. Animal Sources
The most common animal pigments of use as food colourants are those based on the haem structure. In nature, haem is combined with proteins and occurs mainly as haemoglobin and myoglobin. Although the appearance of these two components is attractive when they are oxygenated (bright red) the colour produced on heating is typically brown (e.g. cooked meat) and removal of oxygen in the native state gives rise to the blue/purplish colour of venous blood. The colour changes are due to the

TABLE 4
NOVEL ANIMAL SOURCES OF NATURAL COLOURANTS

Description	Reference
Haem–imidazole compound preparation and stability	37
Modified preparation and stability	38
Haem pigments stabilised with carbon monoxide	39
Haem pigments stabilised with carbon monoxide (in a semi-moist petfood)	40
Cobalt complex of haematoporphyrin	41
Extraction of cobalt complex of haematoporphyrin	42
Haem and haem/nitrite pigment for fibre coloration	43
Nitrosylhaemoglobin in fibre spinning	44
S-nitrosocysteine coloration of haem pigments	45
Ferrihaemochrome in fish-sausage	46
Oil soluble pigment from Euphasia crustacean	47

oxidation state of the central iron atom in the haem portion of the molecule and the nature of the ligands surrounding the iron atom. The bright red colour of freshly cut meat or arterial blood is due to oxygen binding as a ligand to the iron atom which is in the ferrous state. However oxygen does not bind very strongly (it is easily given up to tissues from blood) and it is known that other ligands bind more strongly, stabilising the molecule and preserving the red colour. Thus one method of producing stable colourants is to find a suitable ligand to stabilise the natural haem pigments. Cyanide is an excellent agent for this purpose but is obviously unsuitable for food use. Nitrite is also a ligand and it is presently used in food products although there is some controversy over its use as an additive.

Ligands suggested for stabilisation of haem pigments are imidazole (and its derivatives), S-nitrosocysteine, carbon monoxide and nitrite (Table 4). The imidazole derivative is prepared by reacting blood at pH 7·0 with an amount of imidazole equivalent to 1–3 times the amount of haemoglobin in the blood.[37] The blood is then heated at 70 °C for 60 min and extracted with alcohol/water to yield the pigment, which is obtained in a powder form by freeze-drying. The properties of the haemoglobin–imidazole compound were investigated. It is poorly soluble in water at pH 7 but soluble in 70 % alcohol and shows a yellow colour at pH 3–4, orange at pH 5 and red at pH 6–8. Storage in the dark caused little pigment loss, but under illumination at pH 3–5 practically all the pigment was destroyed. However, the compound appeared relatively heat stable as 90 % survived a 2 h process at 100 °C. A subsequent paper by the same group describes modifications to the extraction and preparation procedures and further tests to determine the stability of the pigment.[38] The findings are substantially those reported in the earlier publication.[37]

While searching for alternatives to nitrite in the preparation of fish sausages, imidazole, 5(4)-aminoimidazole-4(5)-carboxamide (AICA) and various amino acid derivatives were used and found to impart colour to the finished product.[46] Imidazole gave a red/pink colour with an orange tint which faded on the surface of the produce unless antioxidant was present. A red colour was formed with AICA and this was attributed to the formation of ferrihaemochromes.

Similarly S-nitrosocysteine was used in comminuted turkey meat as a replacement for nitrite.[45] Its anticlostridial power was less than that of nitrite and it formed more nitrosamines although the colour it formed was comparable with that formed by nitrite.

Carbon monoxide is another ligand which produces a red coloration in haem and imparts a cherry-red coloration to the blood of those poisoned by 'town gas'. Attempts to improve the colour of meat by flushing with carbon monoxide gas have not been successful but it is possible to form a stable haem derivative by the following process. Citrated blood is agitated in the presence of carbon monoxide to saturate the haem with carbon monoxide and then treated at 120 °C for 1 h.[39] On cooling, the cooked blood is 'as bright as recently processed blood'. Addition of ascorbic acid to the blood prior to saturation with carbon monoxide gives a final cooked product with a redder hue. Presumably conversion of ferric to ferrous ions in the haemoglobin produces more of the haem(II)–carbon monoxide complex, which is bright red. The process can easily be applied to products containing meat and is claimed to be of use in semi-moist petfoods.[40]

The colouring of spun fibres intended as meat analogues was investigated by Roberts and Lecluse.[43] Inclusion of blood in the protein solution which is spun into fibres coloured the product and, on cooking, gave the fibres the appearance of cooked poultry. When nitrite was included in the protein solution or in the coagulating bath the fibres had typical meat colours and were successfully incorporated into meat products such as ham, luncheon meat and hamburgers. Essentially the same results were reported when solutions containing blood and protein from plant sources were spun into fibres in the presence of nitrite.[44] The fibres resembled cooked meat or ham depending on the concentration of haemoglobin and nitrite.

The methods quoted so far have attempted to stabilise haem pigments by forming stable ligands with iron as the central metal atom. Alternatively the iron atom may be replaced by another metal ion. It is well documented that in porphyrins a series of derivatives containing different metal ions can be prepared, some of which are exceptionally stable (see for example Dolphin[48]). The order of stability of metal derivatives in the tetrapyrrole series has been investigated[49] and the possible use of this method of stabilisation is discussed later (Section 5).

Two reports from Russian authors cite the preparation and use of a cobalt complex of haematoporphyrin.[41,42] Reaction of haemin with cobalt acetate in a mixture of acetic and hydrobromic acids gave the water-soluble cobalt complex of haematoporphyrin. Tests in which sausages were coloured with haematoporphyrin (30–50 ppm) and sodium ascorbinate (500 ppm) were successful in that no adverse taste reaction was noted and the colour was described as intense pink. Preliminary animal experiments showed no toxicity.

Included in this section on animal sources is a red colourant derived from a Euphausia crustacean. A Japanese patent[47] describes the extraction of an oil-soluble pigment (presumably a carotenoid) from the crustacean, but no further details are available from the secondary literature source.

Animals appear to be a poor source of colourants. Haemoglobin, and possibly myoglobin, are available but, without some stabilising treatment, their colour degradation on heating or during storage severely limits their use in food except in those products that require a cooked meat colour.

2.3. Plant Sources

Table 5 lists references cited between 1979–82 which refer to novel plant sources of food colourants. The larger number of references and the diversity of the colours extracted is in stark contrast to the preceding section on animal sources. There are several general reviews on the colours available from plants but only two are readily available;[50,51] the rest are of Russian or Indian origin and most are written in those languages. Although there is a multitude of colours in the plant kingdom, their extraction and use in food systems is not an easy task. Logically, an investigation into the suitability of a particular source for producing colourant should start with the isolation of the coloured component. Following identification of the colour, the yield of colourant from the source should be determined. Stability studies should then be carried out to assess the suitability of the colourant for use in foods. From these laboratory investigations it will be obvious whether further studies are necessary. Unless the colourants have some outstanding advantage, e.g. good stability in food or very high tinctorial power, it is generally not worth continuing. Assuming that the source provides a colourant with exceptional properties, further considerations need to be taken into account. A major problem with plant sources is their availability, as most plants are seasonal. Is it economic to set up a process for part of the year and is there sufficient raw material for the process? To overcome this problem of availability (in quantity terms) some by-products have been studied as colourant sources (Table 5). Many of the sources listed under 'Other Sources' would require major planting programmes to provide sufficient material for production purposes. Another consideration is the cost of extraction and processing, which is obviously minimal for an aqueous extraction but will be greater if organic solvents are used and subsequently recovered.

This logical approach to novel sources is rarely presented in literature on the subject. The patent literature is concerned with the framing of an invention rather than detailed consideration of all the potential problems. Conversely, the scientific literature reports straight scientific facts and does not concern itself with financial or legislative aspects. Thus it is left to the individual (or the reviewer!) to pick out which ideas are viable. A resumé of the sources mentioned in Table 5 is now presented, section by section.

2.3.1. General Reviews

Henry[50] divides natural food colourants from plant sources into five types, namely anthocyanins, betalaines, carotenoids, chlorophylls and curcurmin. The sources, pigment structures and some stability problems are then presented. It is suggested that a combination of various techniques (reduction of colour degradation during harvesting and processing; increased pigmentation through breeding; intensification of natural colours) might improve the acceptability of natural colourants in foods. In contrast, a wider range of colourants is described by Gandhi[51] in a review entitled 'Vegetable dyes'. Originally dyes were used for colouring textiles and the origins of these compounds are given. Thus wood and bark from various trees yield a range of yellow, red, blue and black colours which are normally combined with mordants (salts of various metals, e.g. iron, chromium, aluminium and tin) when dyeing cloth to create a fast dye. Fermentation of the leaves of the leguminous plant *Indigofera* produces indigo, formerly an important article of commerce. Similarly, woad (a blue dye) is produced by fermentation of leaves from *Isatis* spp. and henna is also derived from a leaf source. Roots and tubers yield the red pigment madder and a yellow pigment morindone as well as the familiar orange–red dye from turmeric, long used to colour food. Of the flower sources, perhaps saffron is the best known. It is derived from crocus stigmas and about 4000 of these are required to produce one ounce of dye. Other sources are seeds

TABLE 5
NOVEL PLANT SOURCES OF NATURAL COLOURANTS

		Reference
General reviews		
Potential of plant material as a source of food colour		50
Vegetable dyes		51
Natural dyes used to colour food products		52
Natural food colourants		53
Use of raw materials of vegetable origin as a source of food dyes		54
Natural food colours		55
Naturally occurring colourants		56
Biochemistry of the production of natural colourings of vegetable origin		57
Colourants from by-products		
Source	*Colour*	
Cocoa beans	Red	58
Cocoa bean shells	Brown	59
Cocoa bean shells	Brown	60
Citrus waste	Orange/yellow	61
Tamarind seed coats	Brown	62
Shea nut meal	?	63
Seed cases (chestnut, beech, Japanese oak)	Brown/red–brown	64
Sunflower seed husks	Red	65
Hydrolysate of vegetable material	Brown	66
Gardenia extracts		
Stable yellow food colouring agents		67
Hydrolysed extract plus primary amine gives red colour		68
Extract plus protein enzymically modified to food colour		69
Extract boiled with protein gives blue/purple colour		70
Aspergillus or *Rhizopus* grown on *Gardenia* extracts gives blue pigment		71
Use of green extract in canned food		72
Other sources		
Source	*Colour*	
Beefsteak plant (*Perilla frutescens*, Crispa)	Yellow/red	73
Perilla plant	Red	74
Indigo plant	Indigo	75
Purple corn	Red	76
Red cabbage	Red	77
Violet sweet potato	Violet	78
Persimmon	Brown	79

TABLE 5—contd.

Source	Colour	Reference
Cranberry	Red	80
Miracle fruit	Red	81
Pokeberries	Red	82
Sambucus ebulus Linnaeus	?	83
Alcea rosea	Red	84
Hollyhock petals	Red	85
Hollyhock petals	Red	86
Butea frondosa L.	Yellow	87
Morning glory	Purple/red	88
Morning glory	Purple/red	89
Paprika	Red	90
Yellow beet	Yellow	90a
Grapes (tissue culture)	Red	91
Willow (purpurinidin glycoside)	Orange	92

(bixin), resins (gamboge) and lichens (responsible for the characteristic colours of genuine Harris tweed).

Kasumov and Kuliev[52] describe about fifty local Russian plants which are recommended as sources of food colourants. They include fruits such as elderberries and blackcurrants as well as flower petals (rose, poppy) and other sources such as grape pulp and onion skins. In a book on natural food colourants, Kharlamova and Kafka[53] review sources of red, yellow and green colourants and give some details on their production and chemical composition as well as a chapter on physicochemical methods for the control of colour in colourants. Other reviews[54,55] follow a similar pattern, while a review on the application of natural colourants in the pharmaceutical industry contains information on light stability.[56] Of more interest is a book entitled *Biochemistry of the Production of Natural Colourings of Vegetable Origin*.[57] The use of fermentation, thermal and chemical processes for the production of food colourants from tea leaves and mixtures of tea and red beet is described. It appears that tea polyphenols stabilise the red beet colour by forming complexes and perhaps through inhibition of degradative enzymes. Certainly control of the oxidative enzymes in fresh tea leaves yields dyes with green, yellow or brown colours. Food colours of orange, rose, red and black can also be made. The tea–red beet dyes are not degraded at high temperatures and the colour is pH independent. Polyphenolic compounds may sometimes impart a bitter taste to foods, but it is claimed that the products were organoleptically acceptable and their shelf life was also satisfactory.

2.3.2. Colourants from By-products

Colourant production from by-products has the advantages that there is normally an abundance of the source, it is cheap and in a defined state (e.g. meal, pulp). Further, treatment of the by-product reduces waste and enhances the profitability of a process. Both cocoa beans[58] and cocoa bean shells[59,60] have been treated to extract red and brown pigment respectively. Cocoa beans contain anthocyanins which, during fermentation and roasting, are oxidised and polymerised to give cocoa its characteristic taste and brown colour. However, extraction of roasted cocoa beans with an aqueous alkaline solution gave rise not to a brown colour but to a red pigment.[58] Extraction of cocoa bean shells[59] with acidified ethanol yielded a material with both flavouring and colouring potential. A variation of this process in which an initial acid treatment at 50 °C was followed by neutral or basic extraction gave a brown colour.[60] Because of the intimate relationship between colouring and flavour in cocoa, it would seem that a colourant from this source would also possess the characteristic flavour.

The citrus industry produces large amounts of waste and the extraction of colourants from cold pressed citrus oils has been described.[61] The colourants (presumably carotenoids) are extracted from the oil by solvent and purified. An estimate of the commercial recovery costs was that 1 lb (about 450 g) of waste could be treated for 1¢ (1977 prices). No mention is made of any bitter flavours in the extract. Attempts to extract the colour from tamarind seed coats, however,[62] necessitated a preliminary extraction with hot water or hot alkali to remove bitter flavours. Further extraction with alkaline alcohol produced a brown colourant said to be suitable for food use. The amount of this by-product produced per annum was not quoted but it would appear to be a minor source. The same can be said of a patent[63] outlining the extraction of shea nut meal to give food colourants and another patent on the suitability of chestnut, beech or Japanese oak seed cases as colourant sources.[64]

Potential production of a food colourant from a large scale source (sunflower) involves extraction of the seeds with solvents.[65] A few varieties out of the 150 tested contained a red anthocyanin in the black husk. No details of yield are given and since only a few sunflower varieties contain this pigment, it does not seem practicable.

A more widely applicable method of treating vegetable wastes to produce both colourants and flavours is contained in a patent.[66] The basic aim of the process is to decolorise an acid hydrolysate of vegetable matter by passing the solution through a semi-permeable membrane. A light coloured liquid passes the membrane while a dark brown coloured liquid is retained. It is suggested that the retained solution might be used as a food colouring agent.

2.3.3. Gardenia *Extracts*

There are various references to the use of *Gardenia* extracts of different colours as food colourants, and for convenience they are grouped together. A stable yellow colourant from *Gardenia* was stabilised by mixing with sugars (e.g. lactose and dextrin) and spray drying the mixture. This was then refluxed with acetone, filtered and the residue dried to give the stabilised yellow pigment.[67] Similarly, a patent describes stabilisation of *Gardenia* extract by hydrolysis and reaction with a primary amine to give, in this case, a red substance.[68] The same reaction was reported to proceed under the influence of an enzyme in another patent but no details of the colour formed or its stability are given, although it was claimed that the natural origin of the colour precluded any doubts about the safety of the colourant.[69] Using soybean legumin protein as the source of the primary amine and a solution of genipin derived from *Gardenia*, a blue/purple pigment was produced when the solution was boiled for 2 h.[70] A blue pigment can also be manufactured by the aerobic culture of *Aspergillus* or *Rhizopus* spp. on *Gardenia* fruits.[71] When pigment formation has reached a maximum, an ethanol extract of the culture yields a blue pigment. It is also reported that a green colour can be obtained from *Gardenia*[72] and this is suitable for colouring a canned product. Colour stability was increased by adding vitamin C.

2.3.4. *Other Sources*

A variety of fruits, vegetables and flowers have been studied as potential sources of colourants. Investigations on the beefsteak plant (*Perilla frutescens* Crispa)[73] showed that the aerial parts of the plant contained a yellow flavonoid and a red anthocyanin that could be separated by ion-exchange chromatography. Ishikura[74] also detected anthocyanin in *Perilla*. The plants may be used for colouring purposes or as food in their own right. It is claimed[73] that the extraction process is economic on a commercial basis.

Following earlier mention of the traditional sources of dyes, it is interesting to note that a patent exists for the use of indigo as a food colourant.[75] Dried indigo plant and two dried herbs were mixed in alkaline solution and heated at 40 °C for 1 h. The resulting mixture was centrifuged and the supernatant further treated by adding wheat flour and adjusting the pH to 11 with calcium oxide. Centrifuging produced a supernatant containing the concentrated colouring agent. The effects of the added herbs on the stability of the colour are not clear but it is claimed that addition of herbs makes the colourant more healthy.

Extraction of pigments from coloured strains of vegetables yields a light-stable red pigment from purple corn[76] and red cabbage[77] and a violet pigment from violet sweet potatoes.[78] While these are straight extractions of pigments, a process for producing a brown colour from persimmon[79] polymerises the phenolic compounds (flavonoids, catechin and leuco-anthocyanins) to form a polyphenol not found in the whole fruit. The product is water soluble, light and heat resistant and is claimed to be safe, presumably because of its natural origin. In fact the polymerisation is most likely induced by alkaline conditions during the process.

Fruits offer a rich variety of colours and that from cranberries[80] seems to be more stable than other preparations. Below pH 4 a red colour is observed and the extract has been used to colour jams and beverages with a shelf-life of 6–12 months. Similarly miracle fruit (*Synsepalum dulcifum* Schum.)[81] yields a red colourant suitable for carbonated (acid) beverages. In the presence of organic acids, especially malic, degradation was rapid. A Russian patent describes the extraction of a red food dye from ripe pokeberries,[82] but gives little indication of the properties of the product. The relatively high amounts of anthocyanin and the lack of alkaloids suggested that the plant *Sambueus ebulus* L.[83] could be a suitable source of colourants. Besides anthocyanins, polyphenols, sterols and triterpenes were identified but the toxicity of the extract measured by LD_{50} tests was low at 1200 mg/kg.

Flowers are an obvious source of colourants and red dyes from *Alcea rosea*[84] and hollyhocks[85,86] have been described. A yellow chalcone isolated from *Butea frondosa* was shown to consist mainly of isobutrin which was poorly stable in the presence of SO_2 and ascorbic acid but showed good pH stability and resistance to heat and light.[87]

Perhaps the most promising colourant from flowers is that derived from 'Heavenly Blue' morning glory. Extraction and analysis of the pigment showed that the anthocyanin peonidin 3-(dicaffeylsophoroside)-5-gluco-side was the major component[88] and it retained its colour through the pH range 2–8.[89] The colour changes from purplish/red at acid pH to blue around neutrality but, unlike other anthocyanins, the blue colour is said to be stable at neutral pH. Certainly in the flower itself the pH of the cell sap is around neutrality although subtle pH changes have been noted as the purple/red buds (pH 6·5) open over a 4 h period to give light blue flowers (pH 7·5).

High purity extracts from paprika[90] have also been prepared and suggested as food colourants, but the yellow pigment vulgaxanthine from yellow beets was found to be quite heat labile thus limiting its usefulness in food.[90a]

Finally, mention must be made of a source which is not novel—grapes—but the method of production—tissue culture of grape varieties—certainly is novel.[91] The callus induced from the anther of grape plants is transplanted to a liquid culture medium and cultured aerobically. Pigment is then extracted from the culture which can be manipulated to give maximum colour yield during growth by adding various chemicals to the medium or irradiating with light.

2.4. Feasibility of Novel Sources

The volume of patent literature concerning novel microbial, animal and plant sources of colourants indicates the potential of the field but, in fact, few of the proposals are workable. Many pigment extracts are no better than the presently available natural pigments and the availability and/or economics of the source material or extraction procedure causes rejection of others.

The author's view is that microbial production of pigments is unlikely in the near future due to the high production and extraction costs and possible legislative problems. Animals offer us the porphyrin nucleus in several guises but unless a friendly stabilising ligand can be found or altered porphyrins containing other metal ions are allowed (see Section 5 on stabilisation) they will only be of use in meat products, most of which are already adequately coloured.

Although plants offer a wide range of pigment colours, few appear to be sufficiently stable to warrant further development work. After all the investigations into different plants, it seems very unlikely that a 'super-pigment' with all the required properties will be discovered. Even if it is, the likelihood is that it will exist in some rare species which will require considerable investment for large-scale production. The attraction of manipulating plant cells in liquid culture or plant genes in association with micro-organisms is great until the cost of such methods of production are considered.

Of the many pigments listed in Tables 1, 4 and 5 probably those with the best chance of success are the stable anthocyanins, e.g. that from morning glory,[88,89] or purpurinidin glycoside[92,93] and some of the polyphenolic compounds formed under alkaline conditions,[57,79] the potential of which is discussed in Section 5. Doubtless patents will still be taken out on possible sources of novel colourants but the chances of finding the perfect answer seem as remote as some of the source plants.

3. STABILITY OF NATURAL COLOURANTS IN FOODS

Having considered novel sources, the next approach to be discussed is the stabilisation of natural colourants in food. Many attempts have been made to retain coloration by adding chemicals or adapting processing conditions (Table 6). For a detailed examination of the many parameters that affect natural colourant stability in food, the reader is referred to the review by Engel[94] which thoroughly covers all aspects of the use of anthocyanins, carotenoids and beet pigments in food systems. The sources of these three pigments together with their chemistry, reaction with food components, applications and limitations are chronicled and discussed. A further series of publications from the Leatherhead Food Research Association examines specific applications such as the use of beetroot red and canthaxanthin in bacon and sausage[95] and the colouring of confectionery products with copper chlorophyll,[96] red beet extract,[97] grape anthocyanin,[98] paprika,[99] annatto,[100] canthaxanthin,[101] β-carotene and apocarotenal,[102] cochineal,[103] riboflavin[104] and turmeric extracts.[105] The above reviews were written specifically for the information of the food industry and are extremely practical in contrast to the vagueness of some patents and the limitations of model systems favoured by scientists trying to isolate the exact cause of instability. Similarly two papers on the stability and use of natural colours in foods describe the utilisation of anthocyanins, β-carotene and riboflavin[106] and red beet powder, copper chlorophyll and cochineal[107] in foods.

A series of papers under the general heading 'Chemistry of natural food colours' contains sections on anthocyanins,[108] chlorophyll,[109] betanin,[110] annatto[111] and cochineal[112] which will be of interest to those using these colourants in foods. A review of the role of anthocyanins in food products was published by Hrazdina[113] and a general article on the effects of processing on the colour of fruit and vegetables outlines the general principles required for maximum colour retention during processing.[114]

A few specific reports are worthy of mention as they compare the stability of natural colourants against a synthetic colour[115,116] and report a flavour

TABLE 6
STABILISATION OF NATURAL COLOURANTS IN FOODS

	Reference
Use and stability of natural colourants in foodstuffs	
General review	94
Beetroot red and canthaxanthin in bacon and sausage	95
Copper chlorophyll in confectionery products	96
Red beet extract in confectionery products	97
Grape anthocyanin in confectionery products	98
Paprika pigments in confectionery products	99
Annatto in confectionery products	100
Canthaxanthin in confectionery products	101
β-Carotene and apocarotenal in confectionery products	102
Cochineal in confectionery products	103
Riboflavin in confectionery products	104
Turmeric in confectionery products	105
Review of anthocyanins, β-carotene and riboflavin in foods	106
Review of red beet powder, copper chlorophyll and cochineal	107
Anthocyanins: Occurrence, extraction and chemistry	108
Copper chlorophyll in food	109
Occurrence, chemistry and application of betanin	110
Extraction and chemistry of annatto	111
Extraction and chemistry of cochineal	112
Anthocyanins and their role in food products	113
Effects of processing on colour	114
Stability of phytolaccanin, betanin and FD & C Red No. 2	115
Grape pigments in beverages and desserts	116
Stability of grape anthocyanins in a carbonated beverage	117
Ascorbic acid	
Improves anthocyanin stability	118
Review of ascorbic acid and action in foods	94
Bleaches anthocyanins	119
Stabilises *Gardenia* extracts	72
Isoascorbic acid stabilises red beet pigment	120
Isoascorbic acid stabilises phycocyanin	121
Ascorbic acid plus caramel stabilises betalaine	122
Stabilises pink colour in cider	123
Metal ions	
Reviews effects of metal ions in food	94
Stability and colour of raspberry anthocyanins	124
Effect on colour of strawberry puree	125
Effect on colour of cranberry juice	126
Role in discoloration of canned pears	127

(*continued*)

TABLE 6—*contd.*

	Reference
Metal ions—contd.	
Effect of borate on elderberry anthocyanin colour	128
Elderberry anthocyanins	129
Neutral salts	
Reviews chemistry of anthocyanins and salts	108
Measurement of wine anthocyanins	130
Effects of salts on grape anthocyanins	131
Stabilisation of anthocyanins by salts	132
Organic acids	
Effect on pigments of miracle fruit	81
Effect on grape pigment	133
Formulation for changing beverage colour	134
Photoprotection	
Reviews effect of light on colour stability	94
Flavonoid sulphonates protect anthocyanins	135
Flavonoid sulphonates protect anthocyanins	136
Flavonoid sulphonates protect rubrolone	137
Protection of pigments from *M. anka*	138
Miscellaneous	
Morin stabilises paprika pigments	139
Inhibitor prevents fading of paprika	140
Encapsulation and stabilisation of paprika	141
Stabilisation of laccaic acid	142
Natural colours in maraschino cherries	143
Tannin stabilises blackcurrant juice colour	144
Phycocyanin stabilised by gelatin	145
Factors affecting betanin stability	145a

side-effect of using natural colourants.[116] Thus the stability of phyto-laccanin, betanin and FD & C Red No. 2 (amaranth) was tested in dessert gels, and amaranth was found to be more stable.[115] Again, in a comparison between amaranth and grape pigments, the synthetic colourant was superior and it was found that the natural colourant imparted a detectable flavour to the product although it was quite acceptable in this instance. Factors affecting the stability of natural colourants have been determined in model systems (see for example Palamidis and Markakis[117]) but, as is obvious in the following section, there are conflicting reports. In a complex system such as food, it is difficult to determine which are the primary causes of degradation and which are secondary results of these primary reactions.

3.1. Effect of Additives

3.1.1. Ascorbic Acid and Derivatives

Ascorbic acid has been claimed as a stabiliser for natural colourants and conversely, its presence has been cited as the cause of pigment degradation. With anthocyanins, ascorbic acid sometimes has a protective effect, e.g. when it absorbs available oxygen and thus prevents oxidation of the anthocyanin. In other cases, enzymic attack on ascorbic acid yields hydrogen peroxide which oxidises and decolorises the anthocyanins. Hence addition of ascorbic acid to food products will not necessarily stabilise the colour. A summary of the chemistry of anthocyanin and ascorbic acid is given in the 'Background of the invention' section of US Patent 4 208 434,[118] and on pages 16–20 of the review by Engel.[94]

Poei-Langston and Wrolstad[119] described the effect of ascorbic acid on the colour of an anthocyanin–flavonol model system. It was found that ascorbic acid had a statistically significant effect on anthocyanin loss due to bleaching of the pigment. With *Gardenia* extract however, ascorbic acid increased the stability of the pigment when used as a colouring agent for canned foods.[72]

Besides ascorbic acid itself, its isomer isoascorbic or erysorbic acid has been used, as have various derivatives of vitamin C. Red beet pigments were stabilised with isoascorbic acid[120] when a concentration of 0·1 % was found to improve colour retention. Similarly, isoascorbic acid was among a number of antioxidants which had a beneficial effect on the keeping-quality of food coloured with phycocyanin.[121] The level used in this case was 0·005 %. A mixture of caramel, ascorbic acid and betalaine was found to produce an enhanced red colour useful for food especially in chewing gum[122] and addition of vitamin C (200–300 mg/litre) to a pink-coloured cider stabilises the colour.[123] Because of the problems sometimes encountered when adding ascorbic acid to anthocyanin pigments, Iacobucci and Sweeny[118] devised a method of incorporating ascorbic acid derivatives into a food so that they were available as vitamins but their form prevented degradation of the pigments. Either of the enolic hydroxy groups on ascorbic acid was substituted with a sulphone, phosphate or ethyl group to give a range of derivatives. The esters, such as the 2-O-phosphate, 2-O-benzoate and 2-O-sulphate have been shown to be equivalent to ascorbic acid in terms of vitamin potency. The 2-O-ethylated derivatives are stable to autoxidation and show vitamin C activity albeit at one-fiftieth of the potency of ascorbic acid.

Because of the different chemical nature of colourants and the different physical and chemical environments that foods provide, the general use of ascorbic acid to stabilise natural colourants is not recommended. Only after consideration of each individual case should the use of ascorbic acid be contemplated.

3.1.2. Effect of Metal Ions

Traces of some metal ions, notably copper and iron, have a catalytic effect on the oxidation of ascorbic acid which in turn leads to degradation of anthocyanins. Anthocyanins containing an *ortho*-dihydroxy grouping chelate metal ions which may alter the colour of the anthocyanin. In canned products anthocyanins of this type may act as anodic depolarisers and react with stannous ions leached from the tin plating by acids.[94] Since the stannous ions are effectively removed from solution by chelation they contribute no charge and acceleration of corrosion is the result. The effect of metal ions on the colour and/or stability of food products has been the subject of several investigations. Coffey and co-workers[124] studied the stability of the pure anthocyanin cyanidin-3-glucoside and a raspberry juice extract when treated with tin and aluminium ions. Chromatography (HPLC) indicated that a complex was formed with Sn^{2+} and raspberry juice but not with pure cyanidin-3-glucoside. However colorimetric values suggested that complexes were forming both with Sn^{2+}/cyanidin-3-glucoside and Al^{3+}/cyanidin-3-glucoside mixtures. The stability of the products was determined during storage at 24 °C and 38 °C at pH 2–4. Tin tended to increase colour degradation while aluminium darkened the colour.

A related study on the effect of metal ions on the colour of strawberry puree[125] also showed that anthocyanin degradation occurred in control and tin-containing test samples. However, it was noted that the colour remained in the treated samples despite the breakdown of some anthocyanin and moreover, bisulphite has no bleaching effect on the tin-treated samples. Similarly the effect of metal ions in the water supply on the colour of cranberry juice cocktail was studied using colour measurement.[126] The colours produced by metal ions are not always desirable and pink discoloration in canned pears[127] has been attributed to interaction of tin and anthocyanins.

The coloration of anthocyanins by metal ions when a phenolic *o*-dihydroxy group chelates the ion has been used as a test for the adulteration of wines with elderberry juice.[128,129] Elderberries contain anthocyanins with chelating powers while grapes contain mainly malvin—a substituted anthocyanin. In glycine buffer at pH 9·23 both sets of pigments are blue, but in borate buffer at the same pH, the elderberry anthocyanins are bright red due to a complex with the borate ion while the grape anthocyanin remains blue.

3.1.3. Effect of Neutral Salts

The dilution of an anthocyanin solution causes loss of colour and a linear relationship between dilution and optical density is not always observed. This has been attributed to self-association of anthocyanins.[108] It has been recommended[108,130] that in the spectrophotometric analysis of anthocyanins, short path length cells should be used if necessary to avoid dilution of anthocyanin solutions. In a grape juice system,[131] inorganic salts were found to increase the colour of the anthocyanin (measured at 520 nm) at pH 3 due to 'an increase in available pigment'. The cause of the increase was not stated. Sodium chlorate produced the greatest colour increase followed by $NaNO_3$, NaBr, NaCl and Na_2SO_4. The use of neutral salt solutions of high molarity (4 M) to extract anthocyanins has been suggested[132] to prevent losses during isolation.

3.1.4. Effect of Organic Acids

Red anthocyanin pigments from miracle fruit were isolated and tested in carbonated beverages in combination with organic acids.[81] Pigment degradation occurred with all acids and malic acid caused the most rapid degradation. In grape juice[133] organic acids increased the optical density at 520 nm and there was a linear relationship between the number of carbon atoms on the carboxylic acid and the logarithmic value of E_{520}. Maleic acid caused the greatest increase and also increased the colour stability as did valeric acid. Malonic and oxalic acids increased the colour initially but fairly rapid decolorisation occurred on storage.

The known colour variation of anthocyanin pigment with pH has been utilised in a patent for coloured beverages.[134] The pigment is formulated in a powder containing coated organic acid (or coated alkaline salt). On addition of water, the pH gradually changes as the coating dissolves and consequently the colour of the drink changes.

3.1.5. Photoprotection

Light does accelerate the degradation of natural colourants, especially anthocyanins, but it is of secondary importance compared to the losses of anthocyanin due to the effect of heat and/or oxidation.[94] Anthocyanin pigments had doubled resistance to sunlight fading when flavonoid sulphonates were used as copigments.[135,136] Various sulphonated flavonoids were used and all produced a bathochromic shift of between 1 and 50 nm. A flavonoid sulphonate (quercitin 5' sulphonate) also prevents discoloration of the pigment rubrolone by sunlight.[137] Stabilisation of the red pigments from *Monascus* with various phenolic compounds was attempted[138] but only 1,4,6-trihydroxynaphthalene prevented photo-bleaching of the pigments which were *N*-glycosyl derivatives of rubropunct-amine and monascorubramine.

3.1.6. Miscellaneous Additives

Loss of colour in paprika was prevented by addition of the flavonoid morin[139] or by addition of the products of the browning reaction between different sugars or between sugars and amino acids.[140] In the former case, morin at concentrations under 500 ppm was more effective than rutin or quercetin while in the latter case, inhibition of colour loss occurred when the browning products were incorporated into paprika-coloured foods at levels of 0.005–0.5%. Paprika oleoresin was stabilised by mixing the pigments (dissolved in oil) with an aqueous solution containing 60% corn syrup solids and 1% polypeptone, vacuum drying and granulating.[141] The granules contained about 12% oil in which the pigment was dissolved and no discoloration was noted during storage at 60°C for 20 days. Laccaic acid was stabilised by admixture with alum and tartrate after which the powdered mixture was used to colour fish cake.[142]

Control of the filling process was claimed to be essential in colouring maraschino cherries with natural colours.[143] The food was adjusted to a sulphur dioxide content of 30 ppm and pH 7 prior to covering with syrup and vacuum exhausting. Colour was then added and the container sealed. Addition of tannins to blackcurrant juice greatly improved the antho-cyanin stability when added at levels of 0.4–1.0 g/litre[144] and addition of gelatin to stabilise phycocyanin in foods and beverages has also been reported.[145] Factors affecting the stability of betanin in model food systems were investigated[145a] and it was found that decreasing the water activity or adding citric acid or EDTA (10 000 ppm) increased betanin stability.

3.1.7. Conclusion

While additives can improve the colour stability of natural pigments in specific cases, there are no general guidelines for their use. Thus ascorbic acid and metal ions can stabilise colour in some situations but their use in unfavourable conditions may actually increase the rate of degradation. Some organic acids may be beneficial, but others enhance instability and the concentrations and/or nature of inorganic salts used to improve the stability of natural colourants are such as to limit their application. Photoprotection using flavonoid sulphonates is possible, but what is the status of the sulphonates? Once again a solution to the problem is dogged by chemical, legislative and economic considerations.

4. STABLE FORMS OF NATURAL COLOURANTS FOUND *IN VIVO*

Attempts to stabilise natural colourants in food as described in the previous section appear to be largely unsuccessful. An alternative approach is to study the form in which the colourants exist in nature. Some of the stable forms of natural colourants found *in vivo* owe their stability to their chemical structure which is *per se* stable, while others are stabilised by association with other compounds. Mention has already been made of some stable anthocyanins isolated from plant sources. Purpurinidin glycoside[92] extracted from willow is one of these compounds that has the useful property of resisting bleaching by sulphur dioxide whereas most anthocyanins are readily bleached. It has been shown that 4-substituted flavylium salts are resistant to bleaching[146] and purpurinidin glycoside is thought to be a dimer linked through the 4 position.[92] In other words it is the natural form of a compound which has been shown by unnatural means to be stable. The anthocyanin extracted from 'Heavenly Blue' morning glory is also a particularly stable form and is described as peonidin 3-(dicaffeylsophoroside)-5-glucoside.[88,89] This particular anthocyanin has a very stable quinoidal base which is somehow stabilised by the interaction between the acyl group and the B ring of the anthocyanin. Other blue pigments of this form have also been discovered.[108] The quinoidal base exhibits colour from pH 2–8 although the hue varies from purplish red at acid pH to blue at pH 8.

Other flowers have been studied and it is now realised that the colour of flowers is not due to extremes of pH but to complexes of anthocyanin at the normal cell sap pH of 3·5–5·5.[108] Careful extraction of the blue colour of cornflowers revealed that it was a charged complex which was easily disrupted by acid and contained pectin.[147] Similarly a complex isolated from the syrup of canned blueberries was shown to contain anthocyanin[11] (glycosides of delphinium and petunidin, 4 %) plus a high proportion of polysaccharide resembling pectin (60 %) and a small amount of proteinaceous material (2·8 %). Some metal ions were present, notably aluminium, calcium, iron and potassium, but no tin was detected (ash— 2·1 %). The complex had a molecular weight between 77 and 490 × 10⁶ daltons.

Apart from natural sources which contain stable natural colourants, there are also some foods where the colour is known to be stable. The red colour of strawberry jam persists even after several years storage and it has been shown that the pigment composition alters with time.[148] Initially the colour is due to monomeric anthocyanins which, on processing and storage, are converted into polymeric forms which retard pigment degradation and stabilise the colour. Similarly some red wines exhibit remarkably bright colours even after prolonged storage. It has been established that during maturation the monomeric anthocyanins are polymerised maintaining the red colour, giving body and removing the raw taste of young red wines (see for example References 148 and 149). The polymerised forms also resist bleaching by sulphur dioxide[150] and may therefore be useful as food colourants. Studies on the level of polymers in wine have shown that after one year, 30–40 % of the pigment is present as polymer and after five years, the pigment is totally polymeric.[151] The exact nature of the polymeric material is still unclear but it is probably a mixture of phenolics (including anthocyanins) and nitrogenous compounds such as amino acids.[152]

The stable forms described above are either natural colours or colours which are present in well-known foods that have been consumed for centuries. Under present legislation this would seem to be as acceptable as grape anthocyanins or copper chlorophyll, but their large-scale production presents problems in that the source material is either in short supply or expensive. These examples of stabilised forms of colourants which are derived from accepted sources may be of use when considering the next section.

5. STABILISED FORMS OF NATURAL COLOURANTS

The mimicking of the native environment in which a natural colour exists is just one way of producing a stabilised form. In this case, the method of stabilisation can be considered 'natural' whereas some of the modifications proposed on the following pages are distinctly synthetic. This section concentrates on the stabilisation of flavonoids and porphyrins. Since these two classes of compounds are widely available, considerable effort has been expended to make them more stable and thus increase their use as food colourants.

5.1. Flavonoids

5.1.1. Chemical Features Affecting Stability

This class of natural colourant consisting of flavonoids, anthocyanins and aurones potentially provides the greatest range of colours for food use but the compounds, especially the anthocyanins, tend to be unstable thus limiting their application. Thanks to some fundamental work on the chemistry of the flavonoids, the structural features which confer stability on the molecule are more or less understood. For detailed reviews on anthocyanin chemistry the reader is referred to recent work by Timberlake[108] and Timberlake and Bridle.[93] The basic structure of anthocyanin is given in Fig. 3. It is known that hydroxylation of the nucleus at positions 5 and 7 tends to stabilise the molecule whereas hydroxylation at position 3 renders it more labile.[153] Similarly, hydroxy substitution in the B ring leads to instability but this is overcome if the groups are methoxy rather than hydroxy.[153] The substitution of hydroxy groups by sugars or acyl groups also increases stability.[154] Timberlake and Bridle[146] found that substitution of the anthocyanins at position 4 (a position not normally substituted) with methyl or phenyl groups conferred stability on the molecule.

Bearing in mind these known facts of anthocyanin chemistry, what can be done to improve anthocyanin stability taking into account the fact that any process must still maintain the 'naturalness' of the colourant? Firstly, it is possible to specify the desirable features of an anthocyanin for food use e.g. methoxylated B ring, glycosylated or acylated hydroxy groups. It is a fortuitous coincidence that the largest single source of anthocyanin, grape skins (equivalent to 10000 tonnes per year[108]) contain as their major

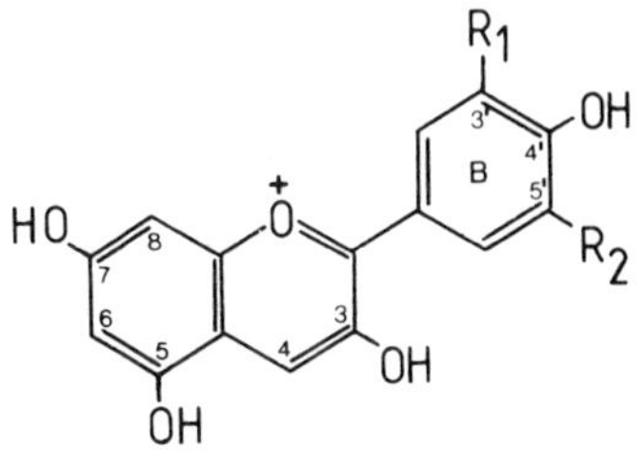

FIG. 3.   General structure of anthocyanin showing numbering system.

pigment malvidin which is one of the more stable anthocyanin derivatives. The acyl and glycosidic substituents of malvidin, besides stabilising the molecule, also give it good water solubility.

With a specification in mind, one could perhaps scan novel sources for suitable derivatives. Considering the large number of novel sources studied there are few which show much promise and those that do are generally available in limited amounts. Is it therefore feasible to consider some synthetic approach to the ideal anthocyanin? Substitution at position 4 would provide stability, but how can this be achieved by natural means, especially as no enzyme seems to operate at this location? Apart from the fact that an enzyme needs to be found, the cost of isolating the system and then treating anthocyanins with it is likely to be prohibitive. Thus even with a fairly clear idea of the 'ideal' anthocyanin, natural means of attaining it are not easy to achieve. However, the above discussion has only considered the possibilities with monomeric anthocyanins. Some degree of substitution at position 4 can be achieved through dimerisation (as in the naturally occurring purpurinidin glycoside) and the mechanism of condensation, both of which are discussed later.

5.1.1.1. Self association. In solution anthocyanins are known to self associate[108] and this is thought to stabilise the molecule by physicochemical means. The exact effect of self association on stability is not known but the nonlinear increase in absorbance that it produces is a useful property (a tenfold increase in concentration increases the absorbance by a factor of 20[108]).

5.1.1.2. Complex formation. Metal ions have been implicated in the development of flower colour and they particularly affect those anthocyanins with an *o*-dihydroxy grouping. In nature, anthocyanins probably exist in a complex form which contains metal ions and macromolecules. For instance, stannous ions form a complex with raspberry juice extract[124] although in model systems containing the main raspberry anthocyanin (cyanidin-3-glucoside), no complex was observed thus suggesting that complex formation requires additional components.

Addition of metal ions to stabilise isolated anthocyanins in food products is frequently counterproductive as they also partake in side reactions which can destroy the anthocyanin nucleus. An interesting example of stabilisation appeared originally as a test for wine adulteration with elderberries.[128] In glycine buffer at pH 9·23 both elderberry and grape anthocyanins are blue but, in borate buffer at the same pH, elderberry

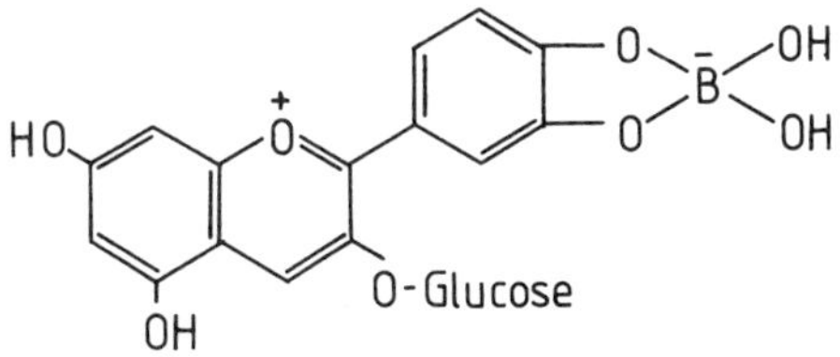

FIG. 4. Postulated structure of the borate complex formed with elderberry anthocyanins. After Wobisch and Schneyder.[128]

anthocyanins remain red due to complex formation with borate (Fig. 4). Thus wine can be readily tested for the presence of elderberry juice. Preliminary experiments in this laboratory confirmed the original findings, but attempts to form a stable complex with ions more suited to food use than borate were unsuccessful.

The formation of an inclusion complex of anthocyanins with cyclodextrin has also been reported.[155] The anthocyanins callistephin and chrysanthemin were added to a 1 % solution of β-cyclodextrin at pH 2. After 60 min the absorbance at 498 nm was 51·2 % of the original value and at 512 nm 64 %. α-Cyclodextrin had no effect on chrysanthemin and only a slight effect on callistephin. The decreased absorbance was reversed when the solutions were acidified to pH < 0·05 showing that the loss of colour was reversible and suggesting that an inclusion complex had formed. The authors further suggested that the inclusion complex protected the anthocyanin from degradation. Considering that anthocyanins probably exist naturally as complexes, it is surprising that so little published work is available on this potential method of stabilisation.

5.1.1.3. Copigmentation. This term describes another state in which anthocyanins exist in nature i.e. intimately mixed with other phenolic compounds. In fact combination of anthocyanins and flavonoids in the correct ratio and at the correct pH produces the spectra observed in flowers and this explains the multitude of colours which exist at the pH of cell sap. This phenomenon not only affects the colour of the anthocyanin but also helps stabilise it against light, which is not surprising considering the stability of flower colours to sunlight. For this reason, processes for stabilising anthocyanins with a variety of flavonoids have been patented. Solutions of apigenin, primetin, tricin, rutin or myrecitin were prepared with water, propylene glycol or glycerine as the solvent.[156] Anthocyanin was then added and the copigmented product was reported to be of stable composition, resistant to light degradation and to possess good brightness and colour. A similar patent application[157] described copigmentation of anthocyanins by mixing them with gallic, digallic or tannic acids dissolved in methanol, ethanol, ethylene or propylene glycol and acetone at 10–60 °C and pH 2–5. The copigments were found to be light resistant.

Timberlake and Bridle[158] reported that the colour of anthocyanins was augmented when mixed in solution with acetaldehyde and catechin. Of the many aldehydes and ketones tested with mixtures of catechin and anthocyanin at pH 3·5, acetaldehyde was the most effective and the different properties of the product were attributed to condensation between catechin and anthocyanin with the acetaldehyde acting as the bridge between the two. Condensation reactions are further discussed in the next section.

Work by Hrazdina[159,160] on the copigmentation of anthocyanins showed that the colour intensity and the stability of the anthocyanin–rutin complex were greater than with anthocyanin alone. The pH at which complexing takes place depends on the nature of the anthocyanin. For 3-acylglucosides, pH 4–4·5 was suitable whereas pH 3·1 was preferable for 3,5-diglucosides. Early work by Harborne[161] explained the nature of the blue colour of irises which is due to copigmentation between mangiferin and anthocyanins. Copigmentation generally produces blue or mauve colours.

5.1.1.4. Condensation. Whereas copigmentation is generally thought to be the association of molecules without the formation of covalent bonds, condensation implies that covalent bonds are formed with the liberation of water. Condensation reactions in anthocyanins take place naturally during the production of jam or the maturation of wine when monomeric constituents undergo polymerisation and produce pigments which are more stable than monomeric forms (especially to sulphur dioxide discoloration). The mechanism of condensation of synthetic flavylium salts has been studied by Jurd and the same author has characterised the products obtained by the condensation of flavylium salts with phloroglucinols,[162] catechin[163] or themselves[164] (see Fig. 5). The structures of the products are of interest because it has already been shown that modifications at certain loci on the anthocyanin nucleus benefit stability. The condensation of flavylium salts with phloroglucinol gave colourless products due to the position of the covalent linkages. Phloroglucinol links to C2 and C4 of the anthocyanin and it is the linkage at C2 which leads to loss of colour in the same way that binding of —OH (carbinol form) or sulphur dioxide at C2 causes decolorisation. This type of linkage is of no

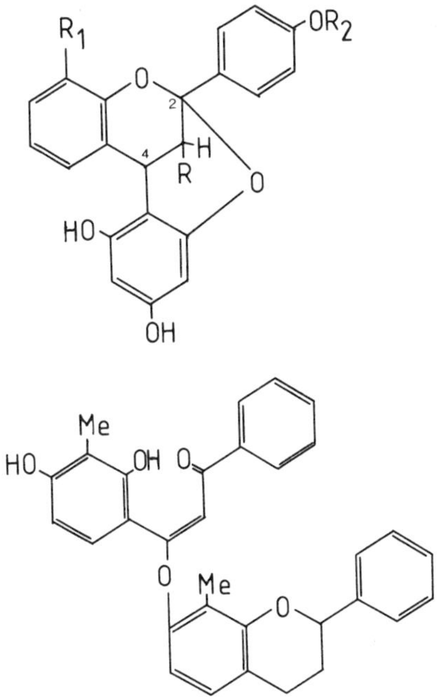

FIG. 5. Proposed structure for condensation products of flavylium salts with phoroglucinol (above)[162] and self condensation (below).[164]

use when the aim is to produce stable anthocyanins possessing colour characteristics. Condensation of a synthetic flavylium salt with catechin however, produced a red/orange colour, albeit as a precipitate, and this is due to a different kind of linkage, namely between C4 of the flavylium salt and C8 or C6 of the catechin. In this case C2 remains unsubstituted. Dimerisation of flavylium salts is also effected through C4 to C8 or C4 to C6 linkages.[164] While these experiments with synthetic compounds are important in the understanding of condensation reactions, they will not produce *natural* colourants. Synthetic derivatives are a convenient tool for the chemist but are unlikely to be accepted as 'natural colourants' for food use. Several reports on the production of food colourants by means of condensation reactions have appeared. Most of them have not used anthocyanins but have used other polyphenolic compounds and the reaction that occurs is essentially that of enzymic browning. Catechin can be dimerised by atmospheric oxygen either under alkaline conditions or by the enzyme polyphenoloxidase.[165] Further exposure to oxygen and heating causes the dimers to polymerise. Catechin is colourless but the dimer exhibits a pleasant orange/red colour which turns browner as polymerisation continues. The colour will survive a retort cycle at normal food pH and it is only sensitive to extremes of pH.[166] Another property of the dimer is that it readily adsorbs to macromolecules and, in its preparation, the enzyme polyphenoloxidase is in fact partially inactivated due to this binding. In a food product containing several varieties of macromolecules, the dimer will attach itself to the product and colour the food rather than the surrounding liquid.

Two books published in the USSR[53,57] describe how fermentative and thermal/chemical processes can produce novel food colours from tea and red beet. Manipulation of the tea fermentation yields yellow, green or brown dyes and mixing the tea polyphenols with red beet extracts gives a red dye. The polyphenols stabilise the beet pigments and they are not degraded at high temperatures; moreover their shelf life is reported to be good. There appear to be no flavour negatives despite the astringent nature of tea polyphenols and the authors suggest that the inclusion of substances that have vitamin P activity improves the nutritional quality of the food.

The same basic idea is also described in two Japanese patents which give some novel sources of phenolic substances that may be polymerised to give dyes. Thus a brown polyphenolic colouring agent which is water soluble, heat resistant and safe was prepared by reacting the phenolic components of persimmon in neutral or alkaline conditions.[79] Alternatively, chestnut, beech or Japanese oak seed cases yield a polyphenolic material that gives a brown or red/brown colour when heated in neutral or alkaline solutions.[64]

This method of producing stable colourants has many attractions. Firstly it is a totally natural, accepted reaction responsible for enzymic browning in fruits and tea production. The products therefore have been widely used over a long period of time without any obvious signs of toxicity. Production of the colourant is facile requiring atomospheric oxygen and either alkaline conditions or an enzyme, polyphenoloxidase, which is widely distributed in nature. As in tea fermentation, it may not be necessary to isolate the phenolic compounds and the enzyme before reaction. Rather, simple mixing of crude sources may produce the desired effect. It seems likely that precise control of the reaction conditions could yield various colourants and their binding power to macromolecules could be used to advantage during synthesis to prevent inactivation of the enzyme. A further possibility would be to use mixtures of anthocyanins and polyphenols to produce novel colours by natural means.

5.1.1.5. *Chemical modifications.* Although chemical modification is probably unacceptable in the preparation of natural colours, there are some patented processes which improve the stability in food. The reduction of naturally occurring flavanones (after acetylation) gives flavans which may be of use as food colours.[167] Reduction of flavanones with sodium borohydride followed by oxidation with benzoquinone derivatives gives 3-deoxyanthocyanindins. Again use as colourants has been suggested.[168]

5.1.1.6. Summary. The present use of flavonoids as food colourants is limited to anthocyanin extracts from grape processing. These preparations are largely unsuitable for food use by themselves. However, the preceding sections have outlined some methods which might improve their appeal. From the wide range of ideas listed, the following have been selected as they appear feasible methods of stabilisation within the constraints of retaining natural status.

1. *Complex formation.* Anthocyanins occur naturally as complexes which are relatively stable. Studies on pectin/anthocyanin complexes may be useful.

2. *Copigmentation.* In formulating a product containing anthocyanin colourants, the inclusion of a copigment would augment and stabilise the colour.

3. *Condensation.* This seems the most likely way of producing acceptable, natural colourants for the reasons stated previously. Considerable research to study the production of the polymeric colours and their stability in food products needs to be carried out.

5.2. Porphyrins

Chlorophyll is the porphyrin most widely used as a natural colourant. Its widespread occurrence in photosynthetic tissue and its lability have prompted many investigations concerning stabilisation of the molecule. Breakdown of chlorophyll occurs in one of three ways which are listed below in order of importance:

1. Loss of magnesium.
2. Loss of phytol.
3. Oxidation and allomerisation.

Loss of magnesium follows denaturation of the protecting protein in the chloroplast. Thereafter, the rate of magnesium loss is proportional to the square root of the hydrogen ion concentration. Several processing techniques to minimise chlorophyll loss involve alkaline blanching and soaking media and the best known is probably the Blair process for peas. Loss of magnesium yields pheophytin which is an olive–brown colour. Loss of phytol causes no colour change but the resulting chlorophyllide is then less stable and is also water soluble which means it is easily lost to aqueous media. Oxidation and allomerisation are changes that are most important during storage and lead to colour loss.

Attempts to stabilise chlorophyll have centred around the substitution of the normal magnesium ion, following the discovery that the 'regreening phenomenon' observed in some products is due to zinc and copper ions in the food being incorporated into the chlorophyll nucleus. Thus it is possible to substitute magnesium in the original molecule for zinc or copper by control of the conditions of thermal processing.[169] The zinc and copper derivatives maintain the basic green colour of chlorophyll but there is a slight bluish tinge which is particularly noticeable in concentrated solutions. Substitution of magnesium with copper is also practised in the preparation of the copper chlorophylls in water-soluble (without phytol) and oil-soluble forms. Logically, however, it is possible to substitute many other metal ions for magnesium. In a study on chlorophyll, Lamort[170] devoted a chapter to metal exchange in chlorophylls and claimed from spectrophotometric data to have synthesised the platinum, palladium and cobalt derivatives of chlorophyll. There are no data on the stability of these chlorophylls but experiments on the closely related tetrapyrrole system[49] have shown that many ions can be substituted and, of the ones tested, the order of stability was as follows:

$$Pt > Pd > Ni > Co > Ag(II) > Cu > Zn > Mg$$
$$> Cd > Sn > Li > Na > Ba > K > Ag(I)$$

Hence, if the order of stability in chlorophylls is the same as in the tetrapyrrole series, cobalt and nickel derivatives of chlorophyll will be even more stable than the copper derivative (platinum, silver and palladium derivatives can be disregarded because of their prohibitive costs). Whether these cobalt and nickel derivatives would be accepted as natural and whether their synthesis is feasible are questions that remain to be answered. One of the common metals missing from the above order of stability, iron, has been incorporated into phytochlorin.[171] A solution of phytochlorin in acetone was refluxed in the presence of reductants and iron salts for three hours and gave iron chlorophyll in good yield (2 g phytochlorin gave 1·9 chlorophyll). The stability of this derivative in comparison to the copper, zinc or magnesium versions is unfortunately not documented.

From the legislative point of view, iron chlorophyll would seem to have a greater chance of acceptance over derivatives such as cobalt or nickel because of the already high consumption of iron porphyrin (haem) compounds in food.

The metal ion in isolated chlorophyll is unstable because, although it is satisfactorily held by the four nitrogens of the tetrapyroole ring in one plane, it lacks ligands in the other planes. Thus it is susceptible to attack. Presumably, the protecting protein in nature wraps around the chlorophyll molecule and stabilises it by providing additional ligands in the correct planes. One consequence of this lack of ligands is that chlorophyll tends to aggregate in solutions and form stacks of molecules. This is an annoyance to scientists studying the molecule and in an attempt to prevent aggregation, the phytol chain of chlorophyll was replaced with a chain containing a heterocyclic ring.[172] This has sufficient length and flexibility to bend over and form a fifth intramolecular ligand to the magnesium ion which prevents aggregation and stabilises the molecules. While this particular method is unsuitable for food use, the principle of stabilising chlorophylls by providing stabilising ligands has received little attention.

Besides chlorophyll, there are other porphyrins that may have use as colourants. Haem is the most common but its lack of heat stability has limited its use. There are however many other porphyrin derivatives that have not been studied as food colourants although a great deal is known about their chemistry. Unlike the chlorophylls where the replacement of the metal ion changes just the hue of the green colour, porphyrins exhibit wider colour variations with a change of metal ion. Methods of preparing metalloporphyrins are available and it is claimed that 100 % conversion can be achieved in five minutes.[173] Porphyrin derivatives of zinc, copper, nickel, cobalt, iron, chromium, manganese, vanadium, mercury, cadmium, lead, tin, magnesium, barium, calcium, palladium and silver have been prepared.[173] Little is known about the colour stability of these compounds because they were not synthesised with food colourants in mind. For more information, the reader is referred to the standard work by Dolphin[48] and that of Dwyer and Mellor.[49]

As ever, the question 'are these acceptable in food?' must be asked. Certainly derivatives containing toxic metals can be discounted, but there are a number of metalloporphyrin complexes that occur naturally and their existence poses the question 'how are they biosynthesised?'. Lowe and Phillips[174] observed that the rate of incorporation of copper into protoporphyrin was increased by a factor of 25 000 when sodium dodecyl sulphate (SDS) was added and by a factor of 500 000 with SDS + 8-

hydroxyquinoline. This suggested that a micellar system was involved and in the same year the enzyme that catalyses the incorporation of iron into protoporphyrin was isolated from rat liver and its metal specificity studied.[175] Iron and cobalt were incorporated into protoporphyrin by the enzyme but other metals caused inhibition. An enzyme from erythrocytes was shown to catalyse cobalt (II) and zinc (II) incorporation into porphyrin at 2 % and 10 % of the rate observed with iron (II).[175] However, the same authors reported that the liver enzyme incorporated both cobalt (II) and iron (II) at the same rate. Thus it has been shown that cobalt derivatives of porphyrins are formed naturally by enzymes, so conceivably these compounds could be classed as natural. Obviously much more work on the stability of cobalt porphyrins versus iron porphyrins needs to be done to assess the amount of any advantage. It is worth noting that human ingestion of cobalt up to a dose of 150 mg per day is considered healthy while 500 mg per day is a toxic dose.[176]

At this point it seems appropriate to mention the production of coproporphyrin derivatives for use as food colours. A Japanese patent[177] describes the products of a reaction between the alkyl ester of coproporphyrin III and alkali metal hydroxides in various solvents. A major advantage of the process is the high degree of water solubility of the products. No data are available on their stability.

Another patent describing treatment of phycocyanin for food use is also of interest.[178] Phycocyanin when extracted from *Cyanophyta* consists of a protein plus the chromophore (phycocyanobilin) linked by a peptide group. In many applications, the protein becomes denatured and precipitates which also causes precipitation of the colour. Treatment with protease prior to use degrades the protein and prevents precipitation. Chlorophyll also occurs as a protein complex where the protein is thought to stabilise the molecule by providing additional ligands. Heating causes protein denaturation and chlorophyll is then more susceptible to attack. Whether limited proteolysis of the chlorophyll/protein complex would prevent loss of the ligands due to denaturation is an idea worthy of consideration.

5.3. Others

This section deals with natural colours other than porphyrins or flavonoids and with both chemical and physical methods of stabilisation.

Carriers are frequently used with natural colourants to aid solubility and to standardise the tinctorial power of the preparation. Dextrins are popular because of their easy solubility, but other carriers may confer benefits besides solubility on the colourant. Thus a carmine dye was prepared by adsorbing carsamine onto a carrier of finely-divided cellulose containing 2 % chitosan.[179] The preparation was dispersible in water and gave a clear carmine colour without bleeding.

Carriers have also been used to stabilise light sensitive colourants.[180] Carbonates, silicates, cellulose, starch, alginate, polyamides or polyacrylates of particle size 1–100 μm were used and the colour properties of the adsorbed pigments were maintained. The use of an alum and tartrate carrier has been claimed to stabilise the colour of laccaic acid.[142] A mixture of the dry components was powdered, dissolved in water and then used at the 10 % level to colour fish cake. The advantages of the method and the relatively high dosage are not explained. Similarly, the use of a sodium tartrate/alum/sodium bicarbonate carrier has been suggested as a means of producing stable forms of anthraquinone and carotenoid pigments for food use.[181]

Carriers have also been used to produce emulsions of natural colours.[182] A mixture of natural colour, oils and hydrophobic colloidal material (e.g. gum arabic or pectin) was emulsified and then spray dried yielding a powder that was used in colouring sucrose-containing powdered food materials. Although no mention of encapsulation was made in this paper, it seems likely that the process of spray drying an emulsion will tend to encapsulate the colour and protect it. A method for stabilising curcurmin by encapsulation has been patented by General Foods.[183] Curcurmin is destroyed at alkaline pH and thus the aim of encapsulation is to maintain the pH between 3·5 and 4·5. Mixtures of curcurmin, organic acid, buffer and a suitable encapsulating agent are spray dried to trap the colourant in an environment which favours stability. Since the stability of natural colours in living tissue is due to their immediate environment, this approach to stabilisation is both sensible and feasible because it retains the 'naturalness' of the product.

Besides carriers, other compounds can also assist in stabilisation. Phycocyanin, which as noted previously, tends to precipitate out in food systems, can be stabilised by adding gelatin to the formulation and adjusting the pH to 3·5 with citric acid.[145] This treatment prevents precipitation. Another approach is to use iron complexes of hydroxy-4-pyrone structures to give novel red colours which are claimed to be suitable for food use.[184,185] Two recent patents on the stabilisation of beet pigments have appeared. One used an ascorbic acid derivative in conjunction with sodium hexametaphosphate[186] while the other used certain processing conditions to yield a stabilised pigment.[187]

6. CONCLUSIONS

This chapter has attempted to review the means by which natural colourants may be made more stable and thus more attractive to food manufacturers. Although there is a rash of patents and papers on the subject, critical examination of these mainly technical documents reveals that the majority of processes are inapplicable because they do not meet the economic, legal or safety requirements of a natural food colourant. Of the various approaches to the problem, none provides a ready answer although some are more promising than others. Despite a wide search of novel sources throughout the world, attempts to find a naturally occurring pigment with all the desirable qualities of a food colourant have been unsuccessful. Even if the perfect colourant were found, there is still the attendant problem of securing an adequate supply. The stabilisation of natural colours in foods is an extremely complex process and although some success has been reported, each application must be considered individually and the optimum solution achieved largely by trial and error experiments. Stabilisation by mimicking the local environment of colourants *in vivo* is appealing because of the 'natural' character of the method but little is known about the subject at the moment. Colourants can be stabilised by a number of means and there are some ideas which appear to meet the primary criteria. Hopefully, research in these areas will determine whether these colourants are superior to those already available always bearing in mind the non-technical constraints that food colourant research imposes. In the short term the combination of careful processing and acceptable stabilising additives seems the only practical solution.

ACKNOWLEDGEMENT

I am indebted to the editor, Mr J. Walford, for his advice and encouragement during the preparation of this chapter and for allowing me access to the computer search of Chemical Abstracts and Derwent.

APPENDIX

Literature sources searched:

Food Science & Technology Abstracts (*FSTA*)
Keywords—Colorant, pigment
Hand search, 1977–August 1982

Chemical Abstracts (CA)
Keywords—Color, food, natural, pigment
Computer search, 1979–July 1982

Derwent
Keywords—Color, food, natural, pigment
Computer search, 1979–June 1982

REFERENCES

1. Walford, J., 'Towards the future', in Developments in Food Colours—1, Ed. J. Walford, 1980, Applied Science, London.
2. Havsteen, B., Z. Lebensmitt. Untersuch. u. Forsch., 1980, 170, 36.
3. Marini-Bettolo, G. B., Conv. Int. Poliphenol, 1975, 1–25. CA, 1977, 86, R28517Y.
4. Singleton, V. L. and Kratzer, F. H., 'Toxicity of plant phenolics', in Toxicants occurring naturally in food, 1973, National Academy of Science, Washington, DC.
5. Boyd, E. M., 'Tannic acid', in Toxicity of pure foods, 1976, CRC Press, Cleveland.
6. DeEds, F., 'Flavanoid metabolism', in Comprehensive Biochemistry, Vol. 20, Eds. M. Florkin and E. H. Stotz, 1968, Elsevier, Amsterdam.
7. Bjeldanes, L. F. and Chang, G. W., Science, 1977, 197, 577.
8. Zloch, Z., Ceskoslovenska Gastroenterologie a Vyziva, 1977, 31, 207. FSTA, 1978, 10, 9A555.
9. Kojima, K., in Chemical Toxicology of Food, Eds. C. L. Galli, R. Paoletti and G. Vettorazzi, 1978, pp. 319–27, Elsevier, Amsterdam.
10. Coulson, J., 'Miscellaneous naturally occurring colouring materials for foodstuffs', in Developments in Food Colours—1, Ed. J. Walford, 1980, Applied Science, London.
11. Van Teeling, C. G., Cansfield, P. E. and Gallop, R. A., J. Food Sci., 1965, 36, 1061.
12. Williams, H., Euphytica, 1977, 26, 841.
13. Barritt, B. H. and Torree, L. C., J. Amer. Soc. Hort. Sci., 1975, 100, 98.
14. Barritt, B. H. and Torree, L. C., Hort. Sci., 1975, 10, 526.
15. McClelland, C. W., 'Economic constraints on the use of naturally derived food colours', in Current Aspects of Food Colourants, Ed. T. E. Furia, 1977, CRC Press, Cleveland.
16. Holmes, A. W. and Jarvis, B., Application of Biotechnology to the Food Industry—An Appraisal, Leatherhead Food RA Report, 1981.
17. Mitsubishi Petrochemical Co. Ltd, 'Monascus pigment production', Japanese Patent, 1980, 80 78 061. CA, 1980, 93, 202709u.
18. Hiroi, T., Shima, T., Suzuki, T., Tsukioka, M. and Ogasawara, N., Agr. Biol. Chem., 1979, 43, 1975.
19. Manchand, P. S., Whalley, W. B. and Chen, F-C., Phytochem., 1973, 12, 2531.

20. Wong, H-C. and Koehler, P. E., *J. Food Sci.*, 1981, **46**, 589.
21. Haas, G. J., Herman, E. B. and Lugay, J. C., 'Method for imparting red color to animal food', US Patent, 1977, 4 031 250.
22. Chang-sik Kim, Sook-Hee Rhee and Il Kim, *Korean J. Food Sci. & Tech.*, 1977, **9**, 277. *FSTA*, 1979, **11**, 6T249.
23. Moll, H. R. and Farr, D. R., 'Red pigment and process', US Patent, 1976, 3 993 789.
24. Yamanaka, S., Shimizu, E. and Takinami, K., *Int. Congress Food Sci. & Tech. Abstracts*, 1978, 238. *FSTA*, 1979, **11**, 2T94.
25. Shepherd, D. and Carels, M. S. C., 'Red pigment production', UK Patent, 1979, 1 539 494.
26. Toyo Jozo Co. Ltd, 'Food colouring', Japanese Patents, 1979, 78 006 003 and 78 006 004. *FSTA*, 1978, **10**, 12T437 and 12T438.
27. Yamaguchi, Y., Ito, H., Watanaba, S., Yoshida, T. and Komatsu, A., 'Water soluble *Monascus* pigment', US Patent, 1973, 3 765 906.
28. Hiroit, 'Edible yellow pigments from *Monascus*', Japanese Patent, 1981, 81 006 263.
29. Broder, C. U. and Koehler, P. E., *J. Food Sci.*, 1980, **45**, 567.
30. Niigata Ken, 'Edible natural red dyestuff', Japanese Patent, 1981, 81 029 987. *FSTA*, 1982, **14**, 5T256.
31. Wasilewski, S., *Proc. European Meeting of Meat Research Workers*, 1979, **25**, 12.2:1–12.2:2.
32. Fujimoto Seiyaku, 'Natural colouring agents', Japanese Patent, 1979, 79 037 965. *FSTA*, 1980, **12**, 6T333.
33. Mishiev, P. Ya., Martynenko, E. Ya. and Egorov, I. A., *Vinodelie i Vinogradarstvo SSSR*, 1980, **6**, 15. *FSTA*, 1981, **13**, 8H1277.
34. Institut Francais du Petrole, 'Blue food colouring material from blue–green algae', French Patent, 1980, 2 453 199. *FSTA*, 1982, **14**, 7T343.
35. Hoshino, K., Yabuki, M. and Ishikawa, S., '*Nocardia* pigment for food colouring', Japanese Patent, 1977, 77 41 348. *FSTA*, 1978, **10**, 6T185.
36. Ratledge, C., 'Lipids and fatty acids', in *Economic Microbiology*, Vol. 2, Ed. A. H. Rose, 1978, Academic Press, London.
37. Lin, C. W. and Lai, D. J., *J. Chinese Agric. Chem. Soc.*, 1979, **17**, 54. *FSTA*, 1980, **12**, 10S1797.
38. Lin, C. W. and Lee, R. C., *J. Chinese Agric. Chem. Soc.*, 1981, **19**, 37. *FSTA*, 1982, **14**, 6S1055.
39. Hood, L. L., 'Color stabilised product and process', US Patent, 1977, 4 001 446.
40. Hood, L. L., 'Color stabilised semi-moist food and process', US Patent, 1978, 4 089 983.
41. Pavlovskii, P. E., Fedorova, G. A. and Murav'eva, N. N., *Proc. European Meeting of Meat Research Workers*, 1978, **24**, K12:1–K12:5. *FSTA*, 1980, **12**, 8S1490.
42. Murav'eva, N. N., Fedorova, G. A. and Pavlovskii, P. E., *Myasnaya Industriya SSSR*, 1977, **5**, 32. *FSTA*, 1978, **10**, 8S1067.
43. Roberts, P. C. B. and Lecluse, W. J., 'Colouring of protein fibres', UK Patent, 1978, 1 524 712.
44. Culioli, J., Noel, P. and Goutefongea, R., *Sciences des aliments*, 1981, **1**, 169. *FSTA*, 1981, **13**, 12G840.

45. Kanner, J. and Juven, B. J., *J. Food Sci.*, 1980, **45**, 1105.
46. Koizumi, C. & Nonaka, J., *Bull. Japan Soc. Sci. Fisheries*, 1980, **46**, 373. *FSTA*, 1981, **13**, 2R78.
47. Nippon Suisan Co. Ltd, 'Red pigment', Japanese Patent, 1977, 77 48 191. *FSTA*, 1978, **10**, 7T267.
48. Dolphin, D., in *The Porphyrins*, Vols 6 and 7, 1979, Academic Press, London.
49. Falk, J. E. and Phillips, J. N., 'Coordination chemistry of pyrrole pigments', in *Chelating agents and metal chelates*, Eds. F. P. Dwyer and D. P. Mellor, 1964, Academic Press, London.
50. Henry, B. S., *Tropical Science*, 1980, **21**, 207.
51. Gandhi, V., *Botanica*, 1979, **29**, 52.
52. Kasumov, M. A. and Kuliev, V. B., *Izv. Akad. Nauk. Az. SSSR, Ser. Biol. Nauk.*, 1981, **4**, 126. *CA*, 1982, **96**, 102655S.
53. Kharlamova, O. A. and Kafka, B. U., in *Natural Food Colourants*, Moscow, 1979. *FSTA*, 1981, **13**, 10T558.
54. Sud'ina, E. G. and Lozovaya, G. I., *Pischevaya Promyshlennost*, 1979, **4**, 31. *FSTA*, 1980, **12**, 11T533.
55. Krishnamurthy, N., Shivashankar, S., Sampath, S. R., Nagarathna, K., Ravindranath, B., Shankaranarayana, R., Lewis, Y. S. and Natarajan, C. P., *Proc. 1st Indian Convention Food Scientists & Technologists*, 1979, **7.2**, 74. *FSTA*, 1979, **11**, 12T602.
56. Auslander, D. E., Goldberg, M., Hill, J. A. and Weiss, A. L., *Drug and Cosmetic Industry*, 1977, Nov./Dec.
57. Bokuchava, M. A., Pruidze, G. N. and Ul'yanova, M. S., in *Biochemistry of the Production of Natural Colourings of Vegetable Origin*, 1976, Tbilisi, USSR. *FSTA*, 197, **10**, 6T224.
58. Morinaga Co. Ltd, 'Red pigments', Japanese Patent, 1977, 77 48 190. *FSTA*, 1978, **10**, 7T266.
59. Eggen, I. B., 'Berry-like flavoring', US Patent, 1979, 4 156 030. *FSTA*, 1980, **12**, 1T21.
60. Hasegawa, K. K., 'Natural colouring material obtained from cacoa bean shell', Japanese Patent, 1977, 77 023 753.
61. Anon., *Proc. Int. Soc. Citriculture*, 1977, 808.
62. Hasegawa Kanzo, 'Brown food colouring agent from tamarind seed coats', Japanese Patent, 1981, 81 145 955. *CA*, 1982, **96**, 102774e.
63. Oura, M., Tsumara, H. and Kubota, H., 'Coloring matter for foods', US Patent, 1980, 4 229 483.
64. Ezaki Glico K. K., 'Food grade brown pigment', Japanese Patent, 1977, 77 109 529.
65. Pifferi, P., 'Red dye', UK Patent, 1979, 1 544 654. *FSTA*, 1980, **12**, 1T6.
66. Huster, L. B. and Guggenbuhler, M., 'Process for the treatment of an acid hydrolysate of vegetable matter and products obtained', UK Patent, 1981, 1 584 916.
67. Kako Honsha K. K., 'Stable yellow food colouring agents', *Japan. Kokai*, 1980, 80 108 464. *CA*, 1980, **94**, 064083c.
68. Taito, K. K., 'Red pigment for textiles, food and medicines prepared from iridoid compound and primary amine', Japanese Patent, 1977, 77 151 145.
69. Taito, K. K., 'Pigment produced by enzymatic action on fruit extract and protein', Japanese Patent, 1977, 77 158 842.

70. Okuyama, H., Toyama, R. and Sanada, Y., 'Food colouring agent', *Japan. Kokai*, 1977, 77 53 934. *CA*, 1977, **87**, 100865a.
71. Hasegawa Kanzo, 'Blue food colouring agent from Gardenia fruits', *Japan. Kokai*, 1979, 79 152 026. *CA*, 1980, **92**, 196401y.
72. Kawaguch, T., Katsuo, H. and Sogabe, Y., *Tokushima-ken Shokuhin Kako Shikenjo Kenkyu Hokoku*, 1980, **27**, 16. *CA*, 1982, **96**, 102696f.
73. San-Ei Chemical Industries, 'Colouring materials from beefsteak plants'. Japanese Patent, 1981, 81 151 767. *CA*, 1982, **96**, 161159f.
74. Ishikura, N., *Agric. Biol. Chem.*, 1981, **45**, 1855.
75. Shiode Hakuichi, 'Indigo blue food colouring agent', Japanese Patent, 1979, 79 39 413. *CA*, 1980, **92**, 145295j.
76. Wakabayashi, T., Yasuda, T. and Tadamasa, H., 'Food colouring agent from purple corn', Japanese Patent, 1977, 77 21 586. *CA*, 1977, **87**, 199478m.
77. Schewfelt, R. L. and Ahmed, E. M., *Food Prod. Dev.*, 1977, **11**, 52. *FSTA*, 1978, **10**, 5J553.
78. San-Ei Chemical Industry K. K., 'Violet pigment', Japanese Patent, 1981, 81 17 061. *FSTA*, 1982, **14**, 2T81.
79. Ezaki Glico K. K., 'Brown colouring agent from persimmon', Japanese Patent, 1976, 76 115 967.
80. Ambrosoli, A., *FSTA*, 1979, **11**, 2J283.
81. Buckmire, R. E. and Francis, F. J., *J. Food Sci.*, 1978, **43**, 908.
82. Abutalybov, M. G., Aslanov, S. M., Gorchieva, Sh. E., Novruzov, E. N. and Farkhadova, M. T., 'Method of obtaining a red food dye from ripe pokeberries', USSR Patent, 1977, 574 455. *FSTA*, 1978, **10**, 3T62.
83. Aynyanov, I., Popov, A., Ivanova, B., Dinkov, D., Petkov, V. and Manolov, P., *Rivista Italiana Essenze, Profumi, Piante Officinali, Aromi, Saponi, Cosmetici, Aerosol*, 1979, **61**, 114. *FSTA*, 1982, **14**, 8J1150.
84. Salikhov, S. A. and Idriskhodzhaev, U. M., *Khlebopekarnaya i Konditerskaya Promyshlennost'*, 1978, **8**, 23. *FSTA*, 1979, **11**, 6T258.
85. Kasumov, M. A., Kerimov, Yu. B., Babaev, R. A. and Isaev, N. Ya., 'Method of obtaining a red food colourant', USSR Patent, 1979, 704 971. *FSTA*, 1980, **12**, 8T408.
86. Kafka, B. V., Salikhov, S. A., Sultankhodzhaev, A. S. and Askarov, M. A., 'Method of obtaining a red food dye', USSR Patent, 1977, 571 491. *FSTA*, 1978, **10**, 3T61.
87. Oke, M. S., Thomas, P. and Shrinkhande, A. J., *J. Food Sci.*, 1980, **45**, 746.
88. Asen, S., Stewart, R. N. and Norris, K. H., *Phytochem.*, 1977, **16**, 1118.
89. Asen, S., Stewart, R. N. and Norris, K. H., 'Stable foods and beverages containing the anthocyanin peonidin 3-(dicaffeylsophoroside)-5-glucoside', US Patent, 1979, 4 172 902.
90. San-Ei Chemical Industry K. K., 'High purity paprika pigment production', Japanese Patent, 1981, 81 041 665.
90a. Singer, J. W. and Elbe, J. H., *J. Food Sci.*, 1980, **45**, 489.
91. Meito Sangyo Co. Ltd, 'Production of red pigment by tissue culture of grapes', *Japan. Kokai*, 1980, 80 118 392.
92. Bridle, P., Stott, K. E. and Timberlake, C. F., *Phytochem.*, 1973, **12**, 1103.
93. Timberlake, C. F. and Bridle, P., 'Anthocyanins', in *Developments in Food Colours—1*, Ed. J. Walford, 1980, Applied Science, London.

94. Engel, C., Leatherhead Food RA Scientific and Technical Surveys, 1979, No. 117.
95. Barke, S., Leatherhead Food RA Technical Circular, 1981, No. 721.
96. Dodson, A. G. and Beacham, J., Leatherhead Food RA Technical Circular, 1981, No. 722.
97. Dodson, A. G. and Beacham, J., Leatherhead Food RA Technical Circular, 1981, No. 723.
98. Dodson, A. G. and Beacham, J., Leatherhead Food RA Technical Circular, 1981, No. 732.
99. Dodson, A. G. and Beacham, J., Leatherhead Food RA Technical Circular, 1981, No. 733.
100. Dodson, A. G. and Beacham, J., Leatherhead Food RA Technical Circular, 1981, No. 734.
101. Dodson, A. G. and Beacham, J., Leatherhead Food RA Technical Circular, 1981, No. 735.
102. Dodson, A. G. and Beacham, J., Leatherhead Food RA Technical Circular, 1981, No. 736.
103. Dodson, A. G. and Beacham, J., Leatherhead Food RA Technical Circular 1981, No. 737.
104. Dodson, A. G. and Beacham, J., Leatherhead Food RA Technical Circular, 1981, No. 738.
105. Dodson, A. G. and Beacham, J., Leatherhead Food RA Technical Circular, 1981, No. 739.
106. Kearsley, M. H. and Rodrigue, N., J. Food Technol., 1981, 16, 421.
107. Kearsley, M. W. and Katsabox, K. Z., J. Food Technol., 1980, 15, 501.
108. Timberlake, C. F., Food Chem., 1980, 5, 69.
109. Humphrey, A. M., Food Chem., 1980, 5, 57.
110. Harmer, R. A., Food Chem., 1980, 5, 81.
111. Preston, H. D. and Rickard, M. D., Food Chem., 1980, 5, 47.
112. Lloyd, A. G., Food Chem., 1980, 5, 91.
113. Hrazdina, G., Lebensmitt. Wiss. u. Technol., 1981, 14, 283.
114. Adams, J. B., Nut. Food Sci., 1981, 69, 12 and 70, 17.
115. Driver, M. G. and Francis, F. J., J. Food Sci., 1979, 44, 518.
116. Clydesdale, F. M., Main, J. H., Francis, F. J. and Damon, R. A., J. Food Sci., 1978, 43, 1687.
117. Palamidis, N. and Markakis, P., J. Food Sci., 1975, 40, 1047.
118. Iacobucci, G. A. and Sweeny, J. G., 'Color stabilisation', US Patent, 1980, 4 208 434.
119. Poei-Langston, M. S. and Wrolstad, R. E., J. Food Sci., 1981, 46, 1218.
120. Bilyk, A., Kolodij, M. A. and Sapers, G. M., J. Food Sci., 1981, 46, 1616.
121. Kao Soap K. K., 'Phycocyanin stabilised with antioxidant', Japanese Patent, 1981, 81 005 143.
122. van Praag, M. and Duijif, G., 'Use of red caramel colour for augmenting or enhancing the color of natural red dyestuffs', US Patent, 1978, 4 118 516. FSTA, 1979, 11, 7T298.
123. Simard, R. E. and Beaulieu, F., Can. Inst. Food Sci. Tech. J., 1980, 13, 178. FSTA, 1981, 13, 8H1317.

204   A. J. TAYLOR

124. Coffey, D. G., Clydesdale, F. M., Francis, F. J. and Damon, R. A., *J. Food Prot.*, 1981, **44**, 516.
125. Wrolstad, R. E. and Erlanson, J. A., *J. Food Sci.*, 1973, **38**, 460.
126. Starr, M. S. and Francis, F. J., *J. Food Sci.*, 1973, **38**, 1043.
127. Chandler, B. V. and Clegg, K. M., *J. Sci. Food Agric.*, 1970, **21**, 315.
128. Wobisch, F. and Schneyder, J., *Monatsheft*, 1952, **83**, 478.
129. Saller, W. and DeStefani, C., *Weinberg u. Keller*, 1960, **7**, 45. *CA*, 1960, **54**, 16736f.
130. Somers, T. C. and Evans, M. E., *J. Sci. Food Agric.*, 1977, **28**, 279.
131. Ohta, H. and Osajima, Y., *J. Japanese Soc. Food Sci. Tech.*, 1978, **25**, 73.
132. Goto, T., Hoshino, T. and Ohba, M., *Agr. Biol. Chem.*, 1976, **40**, 1593.
133. Ohta, H. and Osajima, Y., *J. Japanese Soc. Food Sci. Tech.*, 1978, **25**, 78.
134. Kawakami Kagaku Kog, 'Variable colour drinks', Japanese Patent, 1980, 80 015 769.
135. Sweeny, J. G., Wilkinson, M. M. and Iacobucci, G. A., *J. Agr. Food Chem.*, 1981, **29**, 563.
136. Iacobucci, G. A. and Sweeny, J. G., 'Process for enhancing the sunlight stability of anthocyanic pigments', US Patent, 1981, 4 285 982.
137. Iacobucci, G. A. and Sweeny, J. G., 'Process for enhancing the sunlight stability of rubrolone', US Patent, 1981, 4 285 985. *FSTA*, 1982, **14**, 7T363.
138. Sweeny, J. G., Estrada-Valdes, M. C., Iacobucci, G. A., Sato, H. and Sakamura, S., *J. Agr. Food Chem.*, 1981, **29**, 1189.
139. San-Eli Chemical Industries, 'Prevention of fading of paprika pigment by morin', Japanese Patent, 1977, 77 119 648.
140. Hasegawa, K. K., 'Colour fading inhibitor for paprika', Japanese Patent, 1981, 81 041 259.
141. Ono, F., *J. Japanese Soc. Food Sci. Tech.*, 1979, **26**, 346.
142. Goto, R., 'Stabilisation of laccaic acid with alum and tartrate', *Japan. Kokai*, 1977, 77 108 061.
143. Jordan, J. K., 'Process for coloring maraschino cherries with natural colors', US Patent, 1978, 4 115 595.
144. Simard, R. E., Bourzeix, M. and Heredia, N., *Sciences des Aliments*, 1981, **1**, 389.
145. Dainippon Ink and Chemicals Inc., 'Gelatin stabilisation of phycocyanins in foods and beverages', *Japan. Kokai*, 1979, 79 076 867. *CA*, 1979, **91**, 139165e.
145a. Pasch, J. H., *Dissertation Abstracts Int.*, 1978, **B38**(11), 5263. *FSTA*, 1980, **12**, 2T95.
146. Timberlake, C. F. and Bridle, P., *Chem. & Ind.*, 1968, 1489.
147. Bayer, E., *Angew. Chem. Intern. Ed. Engl.*, 1966, **5**, 791.
148. Little, A. C., *J. Food Sci.*, 1977, **42**, 1570.
149. Somers, T. C., *Nature*, 1966, **209**, 368.
150. Somers, T. C., *Phytochemistry*, 1971, **10**, 2175.
151. Getov, G., Frtsov, K. and Simov, N., *Lozarstvo i Vinarstvo*, 1978, **27**, 27.
152. Valuiko, G. G., Mekhtiev, U. D., Ivanyutina, A. I. and Moravek, T. I., *Vinodelie i Vinogradarstvo SSSR*, 1978, **7**, 12. *FSTA*, 1979, **11**, 10H1618.
153. Okta, H., Akuta, S. and Osajima, Y., *J. Japanese Soc. Food Sci. Tech.*, 1980, **27**, 81.
154. Timberlake, C. F. and Bridle, P., *Chem. & Ind.*, 1966, 1965.

155. Yamada, T., Komiya, T. and Akaki, M., *Agr. Biol. Chem.*, 1980, **44**, 1411.
156. San-Ei Chemical Industries, 'Colour stable anthocyanin/flavonoid composition', Japanese Patent, 1980, 80 013 771.
157. Nippon Coka Cola K.K., 'Anthocyanin/tannic acid is light resistant', Japanese Patent, 1981, 81 035 968.
158. Timberlake, C. F. and Bridle, P., *J. Sci. Food Agric.*, 1977, **28**, 539.
159. Scheffeldt, P. and Hrazdina, G., *J. Food Sci.*, 1978, **43**, 517.
160. Williams, M. and Hrazdina, G., *J. Food Sci.*, 1979, **44**, 66.
161. Bate-Smith, E. C. and Harborne, J. B., *Nature*, 1963, **198**, 1307.
162. Jurd, L. and Waiss, A. C., *Tetrahedron*, 1965, **21**, 1471.
163. Jurd, L., *Tetrahedron*, 1967, **23**, 1057.
164. Jurd, L., *Tetrahedron*, 1972, **28**, 493.
165. Craven, M. R., Ledward, D. A. and Taylor, A. J., *Sci. Food Agric.*, 1981, **32**, 847.
166. Gaisford, S., Undergraduate thesis, 1980, University of Nottingham, Faculty of Agricultural Science.
167. Iacobucci, G. A. and Sweeny, J. G., 'Flavan derivatives', UK Patent, 1979, 1 552 403.
168. Iacobucci, G. A. and Sweeny, J. G., 'Process for the preparation of 3-deoxyanthocyanidins', UK Patent, 1979, 1 552 402.
169. Jones, I. D., White, R. C., Gibbs, E., Butler, L. S. and Nelson, L. A., *J. Agric. Food Chem.*, 1977, **25**, 149.
170. Lamort, C., *Rev. Ferment. Indust. Aliment.*, 1956, **11**, 84.
171. Nisshin Flour Mill K.K., 'Iron chlorophyllin alkali metal salts', Japanese Patent, 1981, 81 053 587.
172. Denniss, I. S. and Sanders, J. K. M., *Tetrahedron Lett.*, 1978, **3**, 295.
173. Adler, A. D., Longo, F. R., Kampas, F. and Kim, J., *J. Inorg. Nucl. Chem.*, 1970, **32**, 2443.
174. Lowe, M. B. and Phillips, J. N., *Nature*, 1961, **190**, 262.
175. Labbe, R. F. and Hubbard, N., *Biochim. Biophys. Acta*, 1961, **52**, 130.
176. Smith, E. L., 'Cobalt', in *Mineral Metabolism*, Eds. C. L. Comar and F. Bronner, Vol. II, Part B, 1962, Academic Press, London.
177. Nippon Oil K.K., 'High purity coproporphyrin III alkali salt production', Japanese Patent, 1980, 80 076 881.
178. Dainippon Ink Chem. K.K., 'Alcohol resistant phycocyanin preparation', Japanese Patent, 1980, 80 077 890.
179. Sanyo Kokusaku Pulp, 'Adsorbed carmine dye', Japanese Patent, 1981, 81 041 667.
180. Parke Davis & Co., 'Stabilisation of light sensitives by adsorption onto highly dispersed adsorbent', US Patent, 1981, 4 268 265.
181. San-Ei Chemical Industries, 'Anthraquinone and carotenoid food colour stabilisation', Japanese Patent, 1981, 81 139 561. *CA*, 1982, **96**, 084386y.
182. Ajinomoto General Foods K.K., 'Spray dried natural colourants', Japanese Patent, 1982, 82 16 675. *CA*, 1982, **96**, 161161a.
183. General Foods Corp., 'Stabilisation of curcurmin', European Patent, 1981, 0 037 204.
184. Scarpellino, R., 'Coloring food with iron complexes', US Patent, 1977, 4 018 907. *CA*, 1977, **87**, 004312x.

185. Parliment, T. H., 'Stabilisation of iron complex colours', US Patent, 1977, 4 018 934. *CA*, 1977, **87**, 004313y.
186. Int. Flavors & Fragrances Inc., 'Red beet stabilised with ascorbic acid derivative and sodium hexametaphosphate', UK Patent, 1982, 2 003 375.
187. Poisson, J., 'Stabilised pigment', US Patent, 1980, 4 238 518, *FSTA*, 1981, **13**, 11T592.

Chapter 6

ADVERSE REACTIONS TO FOOD ADDITIVES AND COLOURS

K. MILLER and S. NICKLIN

*British Industrial Biological Research Association,
Carshalton, Surrey, UK*

SUMMARY

Symptoms characteristic of food intolerance have been described following exposure to chemicals used to colour, flavour or preserve foods, drugs and cosmetics. Tartrazine is the colour most frequently implicated, usually in subjects who react to acetylsalicylic acid. The prevalence of tartrazine sensitivity is not known, but figures of 1 in 10 000 have been suggested— remarkably low, given the exposure. Intolerance to tartrazine does not appear to be mediated by inhibition of prostaglandin synthesis or reagenic antibody production. Clinical studies on selected subjects indicate a high degree of cross-reactivity to a wide range of food colours. These individuals generally appear to belong to a select group that is atopic or exhibits multivalent allergic or idiosyncratic responses to a variety of ingested and inhaled material. Whether food colours are able to initiate a state of intolerance or whether they act only on previously sensitised individuals is not known, and can only be resolved by future research into this area.

1. INTRODUCTION

Adverse reactions to certain foods are a long recognised occurrence. Urticaria due to tomatoes and strawberries or vomiting and diarrhoea on eating shellfish are well known examples. The complexity of western diet,

207

however, often prevents identification of the offending substance. Moreover, various natural and synthetic additives are used to improve the appearance of foods, to assist in their palatability and to ensure the intensity and uniformity of colour the consumer has come to expect in certain foods. The consumer is therefore exposed to a high number of chemicals as part of the normal diet. Several commonly used food colours, preservatives and antioxidants have been implicated as the causative agents in adverse reactions to ingested food in certain individuals. Whether food additives are able to initiate a response, however, or whether they only provoke a reaction in predisposed or sensitised individuals is not resolved.

The most commonly described reactions to ingested food are urticaria, angio-oedema and respiratory symptoms. Other symptoms are sometimes so vague as to be almost impossible to define, for example nausea, abdominal distention, irritability and headaches. Clinical descriptions and the terms used for classification of untoward reactions also vary widely, so that there is uncertainty as to a generally acceptable definition of food 'allergy'. The vocabulary used by scientists and immunologists is not the same as the one used by clinicians and the general public. Recently several attempts have been made to clarify the terminology used by clinicians and the general public. Both the First Food Allergy Workshop[1] (1980) and the EEC Commission Working Group[2] (1981) have suggested standard nomenclatures, although the terms chosen by each group differ in some respects.

The Food Allergy Workshop recommends that the term *food intolerance* be used to describe all abnormal reactions to foodstuffs. This term would include both allergic and non-allergic adverse responses, and should be used when the underlying mechanism is unknown, whereas the term *food idiosyncrasy* would be used when non-allergic mechanisms are involved. Lactase deficiency in the gut, resulting in lactose intolerance, is an example of an idiosyncratic response: fat intolerance in biliary tract disease is another example. Symptoms resembling allergic reactions, but which are not elicited by immunological phenomena, would also fall under this heading. Reactions to strawberries and shellfish, mentioned earlier, would be idiosyncratic responses because the symptoms are caused by substances which cause the release of histamine from mast cells and circulating basophils without the involvement of IgE antibody.

The EEC Working Group prefer to maintain the term adverse reactions and use the terms intolerance and idiosyncratic reactions to describe abnormal but non-immune responses to a foreign substance, which in the case of an idiosyncratic reaction is 'determined by a particular

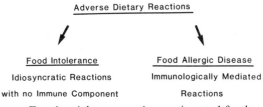

FIG. 1.   Adverse reactions to ingested food.

characteristic of certain individuals'. Both agree, however, that terms such as food allergy, or food allergic disease, should be used only when there is proof that an immunological component is involved (Fig. 1). Ideally the diagnosis of allergy would rest on the demonstration of specific antibodies or lymphocytes sensitised to the causative substance, but in practice this can be difficult to prove, where, as in food allergy, there is a lack of purified antigens. The diagnosis of food allergic diseases therefore often rests upon the clinical documentation of symptoms after repeated challenges following periods when the patient is symptom free on a diet in which the suspected food or food chemical is eliminated.

The diagnosis of food allergy is rendered still more difficult in that the same patient may manifest both allergic and idiosyncratic responses during a battery of provocation tests, and for each response the symptoms may be the same.[3] A patient may also, although initially reactive to a certain additive, become tolerant after a given period of time, and no longer react.[4] A return to normal tolerance of food additives, in fact, occurs naturally in many patients after a few weeks or months on an additive-free diet.[5]

1.1. Types of Allergic Reactions

Similarly to other types of allergic reactions, different immunological manifestations occur in food allergic responses. Types of allergic responses have been grouped into four general categories by Coombs and Gell according to the mechanisms involved.[6] In this system, allergic reactions are grouped into four general types, designated Types 1–4 (Fig. 2). Immediate hypersensitivity-type allergic reactions refer to those responses which occur within minutes or hours of contact with antigen and are always associated with antibody production. This group includes Types 1, 2 and 3.

Type 1 reactions are produced by the release of histamine and other vasoactive substances when antigen combines with antibody bound to the surface of mast cells and basophils. The cytophilic antibody which produces the release of these mediators is often designated by the older

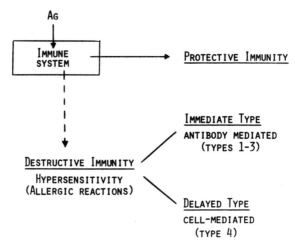

FIG. 2. Hypersensitivity reactions.

term, reaginic antibody or reagin. Species variation exists within the type of reaginic antibody formed, that is whether it is IgE, IgG_1 or IgG_4, and the type of mediator released during anaphylaxis. In man the major class of reaginic antibody is IgE and the mediator histamine. The molecular basis of IgE-mediated allergic reactions is well understood and there have been several fairly recent reviews.[7,8] The effects of this type of hypersensitivity can be seen either locally, as with swollen lips from ingestion of nuts, or systemically, as with skin rashes from certain foods. The most common cutaneous symptoms are urticaria and angio-oedema, both of which have been described in reports of adverse reactions to food colours.

Type 2 hypersensitivity reactions occur when antibody reacts either with a cell surface or with antigen bound to the cell surface of host tissues. If the antibody is complement fixing, cell lysis will take place. This type of hypersensitivity can be seen in response to certain drugs, for example penicillin. Thus, small traces of penicillin, sometimes found in milk of penicillin-treated cows, may produce allergic reactions in individuals previously sensitised to this antibiotic by skin contact or drug therapy.[9]

Type 3 hypersensitivity reactions are caused by complement fixation, which follows the formation and deposition of antigen–antibody complexes at some reaction site. The reaction typically occurs several hours after eating and specific IgG antibodies are generally present. Several cases of milk sensitivities have been described which fulfil the criteria of this type of reaction.[10,11] Clinical symptoms may include asthma, rhinitis, pallor, headache, vomiting and diarrhoea.[12] Some forms of allergic reactions to chocolate, eggs and peanuts appear similar to Type 3 reactions, but further proof is needed.

Delayed type hypersensitivity (Type 4) is so termed because of the relatively longer period of onset, generally 24–48 h, although the onset of symptoms may occur 6–24 h after ingestion of food. This response is independent of serum antibody and is mediated by specifically sensitised T lymphocytes. These T cells have specific markers on their surface which recognise the antigen deposited at a local site, for example the skin or the gastro-intestinal mucous membrane, and then produce mediators which cause tissue damage. The best known example of delayed type hypersensitivity reactions is contact sensitivity where, as a rule, low molecular weight substances are involved. Low molecular weight substances in food, including some food additives, apparently are able to act like haptens and react with tissue proteins before exerting their effects. Benzoates added to many foodstuffs as preservatives may give rise to exacerbations of eczema in individuals who have a delayed type hypersensitivity to compounds of comparable chemical structure present in cosmetics, pharmaceuticals and topically applied medicaments.[13]

1.2. Food Intolerance

Some forms of food intolerance have recently been described and identified more precisely. The term *pseudo-allergy* has been proposed for those conditions which have symptoms identical to those of an immediate Type 1 allergic response, but are caused by non-specific histamine response.[14] The source of histamine could be histamine-rich foods, histamine-releasing foods or micro-organisms in the colon which synthesise histamine. The statement that pseudo-allergies are always associated with a functional impairment of the digestive mucosa and the response initiated by a relatively large quantity of one category of food is of particular interest. Some patients with food intolerance to those foods that are eaten daily (and often in large amounts) are described as being sensitive to trace amounts of chemicals, such as insecticides, colouring material and other substances, whether they be in the food or in the environment.[15]

Other investigations have demonstrated an association between increased levels of the prostaglandins and abdominal symptoms after ingestion of specific foods,[16] suggesting that in some cases of food intolerance, local inflammatory mediators would be released from the gut and disseminated in the blood stream. Mussels, milk and peanuts have been identified as the causative agents in individual patients.[17] If prostaglandins and histamines transmit their effect to distant organs they might also be responsible for the cutaneous reactions, headaches and other symptoms described in some groups of patients.

1.3. Atopy

Food allergic reactions may occur in both non-atopic and atopic subjects. Atopy is a non-specific hypersensitivity state and atopic subjects respond to a number of environmental, inhalant and ingested antigens by an IgE response. Atopic individuals (about 10 % of the population) are generally hypersensitive to several substances.[18] In a large clinical study of children with fish allergic disease, characterised by asthma and urticaria, the majority of children were found to have multivalent allergies and were also hypersensitive to inhalants such as house dust, pollen and fungi.[19]

The pattern of allergies differs from patient to patient, but in adult life nearly all people who manifest atopic disease are sensitive to human dander and house dust.[20] From various studies (in which diet trials, food elimination and provocation methods were used) it appears that at least 10 % of children under the age of 6 with asthma, rhinitis and atopic dermatitis may show clinical symptoms of atopy after challenge with food, whereas the incidence is 1–3 % in older atopic individuals.[21] Thus food may provoke or lead to an aggravation of atopic symptoms in a small percentage of the population. The mechanisms involved in both allergic and non-allergic adverse response to ingested material are complex, interdependent on other factors, and not well understood.

Symptoms characteristic of food intolerance have been described following exposure to chemicals used to colour, flavour or preserve foods, drugs and cosmetics. Most compounds used in the formulation of drugs and several used in cosmetics have been selected because of their toxicological clearance for safety-in-use as food additives.

2. FOOD ADDITIVES

2.1. Tartrazine

Tartrazine (FD & C Yellow No. 5) is the colour most frequently implicated in food-intolerance studies, usually in subjects hypersensitive to acetyl-salicylic acid (ASA). The chemical structure of the tartrazine molecule has features similar to those of benzoates, other azo compounds, pyrazole compounds and the hydroxy-aromatic acids which include salicylates. It is known that the azo group can be reduced in the intestine and liver,[22] indicating one of the several routes through which the compound could be conjugated to form a potentially antigenic hapten structure.[23] That tartrazine itself is not reactive is indicated by a clinical study where ingestion of the colour reproduced signs of asthma and urticaria in susceptible individuals, whereas skin tests failed to elicit an adverse reaction.[24]

Tartrazine is added to many pharmaceutical products as well as to foods and soft drinks and indeed, the majority of reports on adverse reactions are confined to pharmaceutical preparations. The first report of intolerance to tartrazine appeared in 1959, and described three patients, each of whom reacted to a corticosteroid product containing tartrazine.[25] One of the patients had a history of intolerance to acetylsalicylic acid and the second was known to be 'violently' sensitive to drugs of coal-tar origin, suggesting that some degree of cross-reactivity may occur at a clinical level. Cross-reactivity between ASA and tartrazine was demonstrated in a later case report, where a number of sensitisation tests were carried out on the patient.[25] The occurrence of cross-reactivity to a number of chemicals was strengthened by a report that seven ASA-sensitive patients who reacted to tartrazine also showed significant intolerance to 4-hydroxybenzoic acid.[26] Further evidence for cross-reactivity was demonstrated in an investigation of 52 patients with recurrent urticaria or angio-oedema, together with 33 control subjects.[27] In addition to tartrazine, the subjects were tested with various other azo dyes and food preservatives (Fig. 3). The dyes included amaranth, Sunset Yellow FCF and Ponceau 4R, and whilst no definite pattern for the reaction to the different azo colours was seen, 27 patients reacted to some azo dyes at dosages similar to those applied for tartrazine. Several other investigators have reported that patients reacted to different azo dyes during provocation tests.[28,29]

There is no evidence at present that these reactions are mediated through specific IgE antibodies normally implicated in Type 1 or sensitised reactions. Tartrazine has been shown to induce specific IgG antibody production when bound to a protein carrier and administered systemically to rabbits.[30] The demonstration that a tartrazine conjugate is antigenic when injected and gives rise to a normal humoral response in an animal model does not imply that it can provoke an allergic response.

Recent findings have, however, demonstrated that there may be an association between clinically identified intolerance to tartrazine and an antigen-specific IgD.[31] Little is known of the functional properties of circulating IgD, although surface membrane-bound IgD is involved in

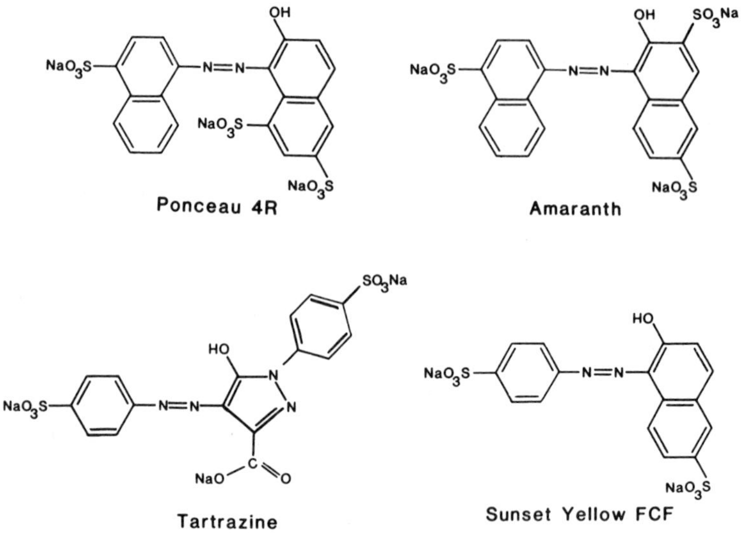

Ponceau 4R

Amaranth

Tartrazine

Sunset Yellow FCF

FIG. 3. Azo dyes used in food.

lymphocyte maturation. The antigen specificity for IgD described hitherto has been for autologous tissue substances such as nuclear antigens[32] and for insulin.[33] This is the first time IgD antibody to a low molecular weight chemical has been reported.

The specificity of the IgD anti-tartrazine antibodies found in the above-mentioned study was to the sulphophenyl portion of the tartrazine molecule, and the azo and pyrazol portions of the molecule were found not to participate as antigenic determinants. Many synthetic dyes, as well as detergents and other chemicals present in the environment, contain sulphonated benzene groups, and therefore the nature of the sensitising agent cannot be identified. The majority of the tartrazine-sensitive patients also had high total serum IgE levels, indicative of allergies to a variety of substances. Whether immunological mechanisms other than those commonly involved in drug and food allergy play a role in adverse reactions to food additives, particularly in hypersensitive individuals, can only be clarified by further investigations.

2.1.1. Association Between ASA- and Tartrazine-intolerance

Adverse reactions to tartrazine occur most commonly in subjects who are sensitive to ASA. Between 10 and 40% of aspirin-sensitive patients, depending on the test protocol followed,[34,35,36] respond to tartrazine with

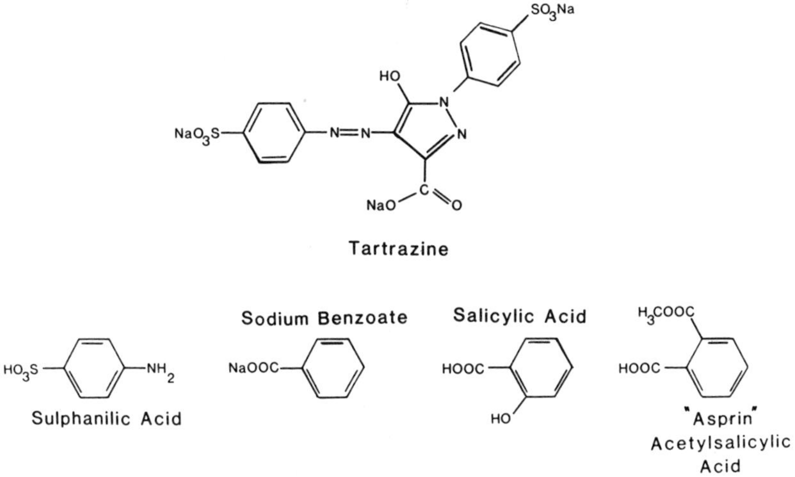

FIG. 4. Structural comparison of cross-reactive compounds.

reactions ranging from severe asthma to urticaria and mild rhinitis. Anaphylaxis has been reported in two cases[37] but it rarely occurs as a consequence of ingestion. In the majority of subjects, intolerance to ASA does not seem to involve immunological mechanisms, although there is published evidence to suggest that allergic reactions play a part in some ASA-sensitive patients.[38]

Apart from ASA, exposure to salicylates in the diet is a common experience. Salicylates are present in a number of vegetables and fruits, notably peas, rhubarb, bananas and grapes. Many of the natural salicylates are stable and appear unchanged in food products such as preserves and wine. A range of synthetic salicylates is also used to flavour sweets, ice-cream, soft drinks and cake mixes. The chemical similarity of these materials with aspirin (Fig. 4) poses a possible explanation for the cross-reactivities seen in ASA-sensitive patients.

A major breakthrough in the understanding of the mechanisms involved in ASA-intolerance came with the discovery that aspirin can inhibit protaglandin synthesising enzymes via the cyclooxygenase pathway.[39] The inhibition of the prostaglandins is associated with the release of bronchoconstrictive mediators from mast cells. Abnormal blocking of prostaglandin E2, which is a bronchodilator, has also been proposed as a possible explanation.[40] Patients with aspirin-sensitive asthma have also been found to have idiosyncratic reactions to other non-steroidal antiinflammatory drugs that are able to inhibit prostaglandin synthesis.[41] Thus a close correlation between the prostaglandin system and adverse reactions to aspirin appears to exist in certain individuals.

No effects of tartrazine on the inhibition of prostaglandin pathways have been observed.[42,43] This is not an unexpected finding, as was tartrazine to inhibit cyclooxygenase pathways the cross-reaction between tartrazine and aspirin ought to have occurred much more commonly. There has been one report suggesting that the response to both ASA and tartrazine seen in patients with chronic urticaria is due to some non-specific effect on the production of metabolites leading to the development of urticarial weals.[44] No evidence for this postulate is presented, pointing to the need for studies on the influence of ASA and tartrazine on pharmacological mediator release or formation. All that can be stated at the present time is that a substantial proportion of aspirin-sensitive individuals do react to tartrazine, and that intolerance to tartrazine does not appear to be mediated by inhibition of prostaglandin synthesis or reagenic antibody production.

2.2. Other Food Colours

Investigations so far suggest that tartrazine is the most commonly implicated food colour in patients with adverse reactions to ingested materials. Some allowance, however, must be made for the selective usage of the colours as well as for the frequency of testing for responses to other synthetic colours in clinical trials. Amaranth, Sunset Yellow FCF, and Ponceau 4R have all been implicated in adverse reactions in patients with chronic urticaria.[26,45] From investigations on patients with chronic urticaria who were tested for their responses to a range of food colours[46] it has been calculated that 17% of patients would show positive reactions to Sunset Yellow FCF, 16% to Allura Red AC, 15% to Ponceau 4R, 14% to Brilliant Blue FCF, 12% to erythrosine, 11% to tartrazine and as high as 26% to the natural food colour annatto. These studies on selected groups of patients all point to a high degree of cross-reactivity or co-sensitivity to a wide range of food colours.

Cross-reactions with other dietary components must also be considered in the case of food-intolerant individuals. Such components include not only preservatives such as benzoic acid, but also synthetic food flavourings, antioxidants and stabilisers.

One of the earliest reports of intolerance apparently mediated by a new dietary additive was the aptly called 'Dutch margarine syndrome'. The cause of this disease was attributed to a new margarine emulsifier promoted in West Germany (1958) and The Netherlands (1960). Susceptible individuals developed urticaria-like lesions 2–24 hours after ingesting the new brand of margarine. Mali and Malten[47] believed that the disease was a food allergy but also suggested that the ailment attributed to the margarine preparation may also have appeared spontaneously. This seems unlikely, however, due to the particular distribution of the disease associated with the launching of the new margarine product. The Dutch margarine syndrome therefore could be considered the first report of intolerance to a new emulsifier.

2.3. Antioxidants
In more recent years the safety of food antioxidants and preservatives has also been considered in terms of their potential to provoke adverse reactions in sensitive individuals.[48,49] The use of gallate esters, for example, has given rise to both concern and controversy with regard to their potential allergenicity and continued use as food antioxidants. Lauryl gallate in particular was implicated in topically elicited dermatitis in workers exposed to materials containing this product.[50,51] The reactions appeared to be specific for individual gallate esters; skin tests with lauryl gallate applied at 0·2 % evoked a positive reaction in sensitive individuals, whereas propyl gallate failed to elicit a reaction.[52] Following the repeated cutaneous application of 0·1 % n-octyl gallate solution a positive reaction occurred in 13 out of 445 volunteers (overall incidence 2·9 %).[53] The use of n-octyl gallate as an antioxidant in beer therefore caused particular concern, in view of the large risk of exposure index associated with the consumption of this beverage. Oral mucosa tests conducted using beer containing 20 ppm n-octyl gallate produced strong positive reactions in individuals previously sensitised by the cutaneous application of this agent. Non-sensitised individuals did not react. In 1974 WHO[54] expressed concern over the continued use of n-octyl gallate. Nevertheless it is important to point out that strong reactions were seen to occur only in 'contact sensitised' individuals, either working with or repeatedly challenged with these agents. It is also important that in experimental animal studies the repeated ingestion of even potent contact sensitising agents has been shown to lead to a state of immunological tolerance.[78] In this condition the animal is effectively protected from initiating an adverse reaction.[56] Kahn et al. (1974)[55] provided evidence to suggest that this could occur also with gallate esters. The experiments demonstrated that guinea-pigs previously exposed to propyl gallate by the oral route failed to react when the same material was subsequently administered by injection.

These observations, taken together with the results from other experimental animal studies, explain the lack of recorded illness in the majority of the population, but offer no explanation for the occasional reports of adverse responses in sensitive individuals. One must therefore conclude that, in the majority of the population, oral ingestion of additives like gallate esters leads to tolerance, yet at the same time accept that some individuals will react adversely. Butylated hydroxytoluene (BHT) and butylated hydroxyanisole (BHA) are also widely used antioxidants. Interest in these agents stems from the fact that 14–15% of patients suffering from chronic urticaria also reacted against these additives,[11] suggesting that individuals sensitive to one substance also tend to react to a variety of other substances.

2.4. Preservatives

Amongst the preservatives under suspicion are the benzoate derivatives. These also are the most frequently cited additives in tartrazine-/aspirin-sensitivity studies. The wide range of observed reactivity (between 3 and 44% of selected patients) appears to be due to similar chemical structures shared by the azo dyes, aspirin and benzoate molecules. It would also appear to explain why patients suffering from chronic urticaria and aspirin-associated asthma tend to improve when fed diets free from azo colours and preservatives.[29,73–76]

2.5. Food Flavours

Reactivity to food flavours is also recognised in 'food additive'-intolerant patients.[77] Peru balsam and its products have been suspect flavouring agents for many years. Peru balsam is an oleoresin obtained from *Myroxylon pereirae*, a tree which grows mainly in Central America. Crude resin extracts contain 50–60% cinnamein, an ester of cinnamic and benzoic acid, and approximately 28% resin, styracine and vanillin. The balsam has had considerable use in perfumes, flavours, toilet waters, etc. Peru balsam oil is the refined form of the resin obtained after solvent extraction or distillation. The oil contains large amounts of benzyl benzoate and benzyl cinnamate.

The parent resin balsam of Peru has been demonstrated to be a contact allergen in a number of studies.[57–59] Cross-reactions have also been reported to occur between the balsam and resorcinol monobenzoate[60] and Poplar resins.[61] As benzyl benzoate and benzyl cinnamate are constituents of Peru balsam[63] cross-sensitivity with both cinnamon and benzoic acid can occur.[63] It has also been suggested that previous sensitisation with vanillin or cinnamate could explain some of the many positive patch test reactions to Peru balsam seen in individuals who have apparently not previously been exposed to this substance.[61] Cinnamon oil, which is widely used in foods and pharmaceuticals, can also elicit skin reaction in subjects previously sensitised to this flavour.[62]

2.6. Other Food Additives

Modern processed, packaged and canned foods and beverages all contain a range of 'hidden' ingredients. Evidence suggests that patients with multiple food- or chemical-intolerance syndromes usually improve on diets containing only natural unprocessed ingredients. However, even selected diets do not guarantee protection, since inadvertent exposure can still occur. Fresh fruits and vegetables and 'health food' products at first sight appear ideal for additive-intolerant individuals; however, patients can still react to these products because of unexpected processing/packaging procedures. Almost all commercially produced fruit and vegetables have been exposed to inseciticides or fertilisers, many of which remain on the product and can cause reactions in intolerant individuals.[64,65]

Cosmetic alteration of fruit should also be treated with caution. The addition of azo dyes to maintain the 'natural colour' of fruit products is commonly practised in the canned fruit, preserves and fruit juice industry.[66] Even with 'fresh' foods, the appealing shine on fruits and vegetables is often the result of precoating with vegetable mineral oils or petrochemically derived waxes.[67,68] These chemicals are not water soluble and so not easily removed. Peeling will obviously result in reduced exposure, but it is not practical to peel green peppers, for example. Furthermore, all commercially dried fruits are treated with sulphur dioxide unless otherwise stated on the packet.[69]

Drugs may also be present in foodstuffs. Salicylates have been discussed above. However, a variety of other drugs are employed in preventing biological deterioration of food. Frozen fish is often dipped in antibiotics before freezing to retard spoilage. Eggs may be dipped in penicillin solution; the penicillin penetrates the shell and so can contaminate the contents. Processed chickens may also be contaminated: antibiotics, coccidiostats and hormones are often added to chicken feed and can sometimes be detected in the final product.[70] During processing and packing eviscerated chickens are also sometimes placed in ice baths containing antibiotics to prevent bacterial growth.[71] Penicillin and tetracycline have been found on occasion contaminating dairy products.

Drug-sensitive patients are obviously put at risk by the traces of these materials that may remain in the marketed products.

Medical products commonly contain hidden additives; as their function is unrelated to the medicinal or drug component their presence in the product is not necessarily stated. A given tablet or capsule, in addition to often being colour coded by a suitable azo dye, may also contain starch as a filler derived from a range of unidentified sources (corn, potato, sorghum, arrowroot, tapioca, etc.).[72] Medications often also contain a binder such as calcium or magnesium stearate.[72] Both fillers and binders act as carriers, not only for the drug but also for the associated artificial colours and flavours used in the product. It is therefore not at all surprising that many of the adverse reactions to food colours are often first recognised following exposure to a colour in a medicinal product.

3. HYPERKINESIS

Over the past years the Feingold treatment of hyperkinesis has achieved some degree of popular fame.[79] Briefly, his principal hypotheses are that hyperkinesis is due to an inborn chemical reaction affecting the nervous system of certain genetically predisposed children, and that salicylates as well as synthetic food colours and flavours are the causative agents. These hypothesis depended on the empirical observations made by Paul Feingold with patients under his therapeutic regime and on elimination diets designed to be low in salicylates and free of food additives (Table 1). Return to ordinary diet was said to result in immediate return to the hyperkinetic condition by those children who showed marked improvement on the elimination diet. Early studies appeared to support this hypothesis, but were severely criticised in that both subjects and investigators knew when the diet was administered.[80] It seems likely that the favourable results reported anecdotally for the Feingold diet may be attributable to the change in the family's lifestyle necessitated by adherence to the diet, and the resultant changes in the hyperactive child's role in family life. Recent data evaluating the relationship between hyperactivity, salicylates, artificial food colours and flavours indicate that the symptoms of the vast majority of hyperactive children are not related to additives in their diet.[84,85] On present evidence it seems that hyperkinesis, or hyperactivity, cannot be considered a disease or a syndrome, but is in fact a symptom with a variety of causes which needs to be treated by a multi-disciplinary cooperative effort involving home, school and family doctor.

TABLE 1
THE FEINGOLD DIET

These foods are to be *eliminated* from diet.

Cereals and Grain Products
All breakfast cereals with artificial colours or flavours
All cakes, cookies, pastries, sweet rolls, doughnuts, breads, etc., with artificial flavours or colours (i.e. from bakery)
Manufactured pie crusts
Frozen baked mixes
Prepared poultry stuffing

Fruits
Almonds
Apples
Apricots
Berries—blackberries, blueberries, boysenberries, gooseberries, raspberries, strawberries
Cherries
Currants—grapes and raisins or any products made of grapes (e.g. wine, wine vinegar, jellies)
Nectarines
Oranges
Peaches

Vegetables
Tomatoes and all tomato products
Cucumbers (pickles)

Protein Sources
Meats
  Bologna, luncheon meats[a]
  Salami
  Frankfurters
  Sausage[a]
  Meat loaf[a]
  Ham, bacon, pork[a]
  All barbecued types of chicken
  All turkey prepared with basting, called 'self-basting'
Frozen fish fillets that are dyed or flavoured—fish sticks or patties, dyed or flavoured
Dairy Products
Manufactured ice cream or ice milk unless label specifies no synthetic colouring or flavouring
Coloured cheeses (i.e., processed or yellow or orange)
All instant breakfast drinks and preparations
Flavoured yogurt
Prepared chocolate milk
Coloured butter

(*continued*)

TABLE 1—*contd.*

Beverages
Cider
Wine
Beer
Diet drinks
Tea, hot or cold
All carbonated beverages

Miscellaneous
Sherberts, ices, gelatins, junkets, puddings with artificial flavour or colouring
Powdered pudding, jello, and drink mixes
All dessert mixes
All manufactured candy—hard or soft
Oleomargarine
Prepared mustard
All mint-flavoured and wintergreen-flavoured items
Gum
Oil of wintergreen
Cloves
Jam or jellies made with artifical colours or flavours
Soy sauce, if flavoured or coloured
Cider vinegar
Wine vinegar
Commercial chocolate syrup
Barbecue flavoured potato chips
Catsup
Chilli sauce

Sundry Items
Aspirin, Bufferin, Excedrin, Alka-Seltzer, Empirin, Empirin Compound, Anacin
Vitamins
All toothpastes and toothpowder
All mouthwashes
All cough drops
All throat lozenges
Antacid tablets
Perfumes

---

[a] When flavoured or coloured.
Based on Appendix I, presented in 'Food additives and hyperkinesis: a controlled double blind experiment'.[116]

A double-blind crossover trial on 15 hyperkinetic children found some improvement on the Feingold diet, but pointed out that any major intervention into the dietary habits of a family would produce behavioural effects, regardless of the specific diets.[81] A double-blind crossover study to obtain objective laboratory and classroom observational data, in addition to subjective parent–teacher ratings on hyperactive children under control and experimental diet conditions, yielded no support for the Feingold hypothesis.[82] Another double-blind crossover trial on 22 hyperkinetic children, aged between four and eight years, showed a statistically significant improvement in the mothers' ratings of the children's behaviour, but these results were not substantiated by results from objective tests.[83]

4. MECHANISMS

The mechanism responsible for producing sensitisation to food colours and additives is unknown. Although more fundamental research is required to establish a complete understanding of the phenomenon, some of the factors thought to be involved in predisposing individuals to food intolerance are discussed below.

It is apparent from a number of studies that a range of antigenic dietary components gain access to the body across an intact mucosal surface.[86,87] This natural process of persorption usually leads to a state of unresponsiveness, even to subsequent parenteral exposure to the same antigen.[56] The individual is said to be immunologically tolerant and, as such, is prevented (protected) from initiating potentially damaging hypersensitivity reactions. Research has shown that in the majority of individuals a gut-associated immunological regulatory system exists to prevent adverse reactions acting at the level of the gut. In most individuals therefore oral intake of food antigens/additives leads to specific and prolonged tolerance. However, it appears that in individuals predisposed to allergic diseases the tolerance response is either not effective or does not occur. This failure to achieve tolerance is currently believed to be one of the major underlying causes of dietary allergic disease (see Fig. 5).

Clinical and laboratory observations emphasise that allergen avoidance in infancy is important, not only in terms of the immaturity of mechanisms for limiting allergen absorption, but also because of the risk that patterns of response may be established in genetically susceptible infants which will lead to persistent allergic disorders. Exclusive breast feeding, for example, greatly reduces the chance of a child developing eczema (cow's milk

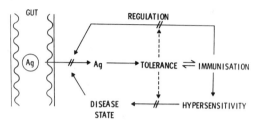

FIG. 5.   Immunological interactions in the gastrointestinal tract.

intolerance syndrome).[88] In childhood at least, the critical events in infant sensitisation apparently hinge upon the 'open' neonatal gut allowing greater than normal antigen access, thus exposing the developing immune system to new food antigens. In the adult, the immune system is mature and the gut less permeable. Nevertheless, there are a number of defects which can lead to the excessive absorption of food allergens. There is good evidence that IgA, an antibody secreted into the gastrointestinal tract, controls the absorption of dietary components. Food antigens induce the formation of the specific secretory IgA which can complex with antigen within the intestinal lumen and reduce antigen absorption.[89] Individuals who are unable to produce and secrete IgA are less effective in limiting antigen absorption and, as such, are more susceptible to dietary allergy syndromes.[90]

There are also a variety of ways in which the anatomical barrier of the gut may be damaged, thus allowing greater antigen access.[91] Changes may occur due to the breakdown of tight junctions between cells which normally form a very efficient seal between gut wall cells at the lumenal surface. This breakdown has been portrayed as a failure in the normal gate mechanism which regulates the absorption of antigen. Factors which can affect cell to cell contacts and facilitate antigen entry include intestinal infection,[92] non-specific inflammation of the gastrointestinal mucosa due to disease processes, e.g. ulcerative colitis, inflammatory bowel disease,[93,94] and ingestion of various vasoactive drugs. The vasodilatory and irritant effect of alcohol is well known. Aspirin and indomethacin are also both known to cause intestinal/gastric damage.[95,96] Damage to the gut wall not only increases antigen access, but because of the associated inflammatory response, causes the accumulation of immunologically competent cells.

Less obvious, but nonetheless important factors include the quantity and form of food eaten; whether it was contaminated with pathogens or bacterial endotoxins; how well cooked the food was is also important— hard-boiled eggs are much less likely to evoke a response than raw or partly cooked eggs. The gut may also be in a refractory state due to a previous allergic reaction elicited by other allergens.

Histamine can also cause a dramatic increase in the permeability of the gut wall. This is particularly important in patients suffering from urticaria, who may have abnormal histamine release or sensitivity to histamine. Furthermore, the ingestion of foods either naturally rich in histamine (cheese, beer, canned food, fish and meat) or capable of releasing histamine directly from mast cells (e.g. fish, tomato, egg white, strawberries and chocolate) can also cause vasodilation and increase the absorption of antigenic molecules from the gut lumen.

However, uptake of antigen under these conditions is only part of the story. It is clear that individuals must be atopic or predisposed to make adverse responses to food colours and additives before true intolerance develops. It would appear that genetic factors may predispose individuals to a number of diseases, and this may also hold true for certain food-intolerance syndromes. There are, for example, suggestive links between the HLA haptotype (gene) coded AI B8 and atopic eczema,[97] and between HLA B8/DW 3 and gluten sensitivity.[98] However, in the main, studies of genetic factors relating to host susceptibility have not yet demonstrated convincing associations with increased frequency of specific HLA-antigens.[99] This failure may perhaps be due to the paucity of evidence so far accumulated.[100] However, even in ankylosing spondylitis (where the association between HLA and disease is convincing) 10% of caucasian patients presenting the disease lack the diagnostic B27-antigen. Indeed, recent experimental evidence suggests that there may well exist a whole class of non-HLA linked genes that also control immune responses to foreign substances.[101] Until these areas have been explored, genetic testing for susceptibility to ingested materials remains of only restricted value.

Genetic factors can only come into play following the appropriate exposure to the environmental stimulus. Development and/or the environmental pressures must be superimposed upon a genetic pre-disposition before an intolerance disease can appear. A predisposition to dietary intolerance is obviously a real phenomenon, but at this point in time we remain unclear as to how this operates.

There is therefore a real need for research to be carried out on both the epidemiology of and the basic mechanisms concerned in the adverse reactions to food additives. At present there is no suitable animal model to assess the allergic potential of new food additives. The present methods assess additives for their activity as contact-sensitising agents and, as such, measure delayed hypersensitivity reactions. Results from such studies have no real relevance to reactions to ingested compounds, since these are, in the main, antibody-mediated reactions.

5. FREQUENCY OF ADVERSE REACTIONS

It is apparent from the previous sections that the precise assessment of food allergy or intolerance is difficult, since diagnosis depends on subjective methods associated with clinical screening tests and the interpretation of a patient's previous history. The consequence of this is widely varying estimates of prevalence. Ogle and Bullock[102] suggested that between 0·3 % and 20 % of children suffer from, or have suffered from, some form of dietary-intolerance disorder. Juhlin[103] suggests that between 3 % and 44 % of selected adult additive-intolerant patients gave a positive reaction on challenge with benzoates. The wide range of incidence in these studies reflects the effects of selective bias and different diagnostic criteria employed in the various studies, and emphasises the difficulty in establishing a useful estimate of prevalence.

If we consider defined food allergies, 'cow's milk intolerance' is the most common allergy in young children. Bahna[104] quotes the prevalence as between 0·2 % and 7·5 %. In a similar survey involving 400 infants monitored from birth to two years of age, the incidence of milk intolerance was determined to be about 0·5 %.[105] In older children (aged between 5 and 12), 6·6 % presented some history of clinically recognised food intolerance. The commonest symptoms were urticaria, followed by hayfever, headaches, stomach ache, asthma, vomiting and diarrhoea in descending order of frequency. In these studies it was possible to work with a defined population, reasonably precise clinical histories and, in the case of milk intolerance, a defined antigen. When it comes to assessing the frequency of allergy or intolerance to food additives, however, the problem is considerably more difficult. This is because a number of colours and additives are often used in conjunction, and appear in a wide variety of foodstuffs. As cross-reactivity between various colours and additives also occurs, a given individual may not know what particular food or food component triggers the allergic reaction. Studies concerning reactivity to food additives have therefore been somewhat restricted to selected populations and, in the main, to patients attending hospital for the treatment of 'allergy-like' diseases. These studies cannot present true estimates of prevalence, since it is impossible to extrapolate from a given selected group to the general population. They do, however, give an indication of the importance of a given condition, at least in clinical terms, and highlight those additives which may be responsible for food allergy or intolerance syndromes. To obtain an approximate figure for the prevalence of additive-associated disease, Juhlin[103] reviewed the literature for relevant information and, in conjunction with his own data, attempted to calculate the frequency of additive-induced allergic responses. All results refer to selected patient studies. In patients with chronic urticaria 33–50 % of individuals tested reacted to one or more food additives. Of the additives employed in the provocation tests tartrazine produced a reaction in 5–46 % of those tested, other azo dyes gave from 5–20 % positives. Amongst the preservatives considered benzoate derivatives produced positive reactions in between 3 and 44 % and the antioxidants butylated hydroxytoluene (BHT) and butylated hydroxyanisole (BHA) yielded an incidence of 14–15 %. In a study by Mikkelsen[106] reactions to individual food colours yielded the following percentages: amongst 61 patients suffering from chronic urticaria and/or angioneurotic oedema 11 % reacted to tartrazine, 17 % to Sunset Yellow FCF, 16 % to Allura Red AC, 9 % to amaranth, 15 % to Ponceau 4R, 12 % to erythrosine and 14 % to Brilliant Blue FCF. In the same study the natural colour annatto, a commonly used colour in butter and edible fat products, was also studied. Challenge was performed with a dose equivalent to the amount present in 25 g of butter. Twenty-six patients in the group reacted within about 4 h of ingestion, indicating that natural food colours may also induce intolerance reactions as frequently as synthetic dyes. In the same study 30 % of patients reacted to aspirin and 15 % to sodium benzoate. There was, however, no pattern of cross-reactivity between the azo dyes and the natural annatto extract. Intolerance to aspirin/salicylates and cross-reactivity with azo dyes and benzoates appears repeatedly in the literature. Juhlin[103] found that between 8 and 44 % of aspirin-intolerant asthmatics also reacted to tartrazine and 14 % were also sensitive to benzoates. Amongst asthmatic children, of 32 studied 1 in 3 reacted to aspirin and 1 in 5 to tartrazine and/or benzoates.[107] Nevertheless, Vedanthan et al.[108] tested 54 asthmatic children, aged 10–17 years, for reactivity to tartrazine and found no responders. Weber et al. (1979)[109] investigated 45 asthmatic patients and found only three who reacted to commonly employed colour agents. Although this is equivalent to an incidence of 5–6 %, it must be emphasised that the subjects were selected to include individuals with a history suggestive of food sensitivity. Concern is also raised by the study of Østerballe et al.[110] who, in their initial study, suggested that almost a quarter of children with asthma showed intolerance to azo dyes, aspirin and benzoates. However, on retest in a double-blind trial only 6·5% of the children reacted. It has been estimated that in every 10 million people about 40 000 will show intolerance to aspirin (0·4%), 6000 to tartrazine (0·06%) and 5000 to benzoates (0·05%). In France sensitivity to tartrazine was estimated to be between 0·03%[11] and 0·15%.[112] A recent study in Denmark[113] employed a more systematic approach. The frequency of asthma, chronic rhinitis and chronic urticaria was assessed in the general population over 16 years of age and determined to be in the order of 3·8%, 1·9% and 0·5% respectively. The frequency of adverse reactions to food additives within each incidence group was then determined by reference to previous case histories and previous provocation tests. It was concluded that 0·01–0·1% of the population were sensitive to both tartrazine and benzoates. These figures are in the same order as those suggested by Juhlin,[103] and are endorsed by the findings of MacCara[114] who, although cautious concerning the relevance of prevalence figures, suggests that the incidence of tartrazine sensitivity in the general population is of the order of 1 in 10 000. When one considers that almost everyone in the population has probably been exposed to tartrazine at some time or another, sensitisation to tartrazine occurs only rarely and presumably only in predisposed individuals.

6. CURRENT STATUS

There is little doubt that intolerance to food additives occurs in a small minority of the population. These individuals generally appear to belong to a select group that is atopic or exhibits multivalent allergic or idiosyncratic responses to a variety of ingested and inhalant material. Tartrazine is the colour most frequently incriminated and, depending on the protocol followed, between 10% and 40% of patients sensitive to aspirin respond adversely to tartrazine. The prevalence of tartrazine sensitivity is not known, but figures of 1 in 10 000 have been suggested—remarkably low, given the exposure.

Whether food colours or other food additives are able to initiate a state of intolerance, or whether they act only on previously sensitised individuals, can only be resolved by future research into this area. The EEC Commission Working Group[2] have suggested a number of lines of investigation, including attempts to identify specific differences in immunological parameters between individuals who respond adversely to food additives and those who do not. Some of the lines of research that are suggested however (a study of HLA antigens being a case in point), would be associated with great and possibly insurmountable practical difficulties. The Working Group considered that consumers have the right to know what ingredients they are exposed to in foods as well as in drugs and cosmetics, and that all additives present should be clearly and specifically listed on product labels. The views expressed by the Working Group have recently been endorsed by the Scientific Committee for Food.[115]

REFERENCES

1. *Proc. First Food Allergy Workshop*, 1980. Medical Education Services, Oxford.
2. *Report of a working group on adverse reactions to ingested additives*, III/556/81-EN, 1981, Commission of the European Communities, Brussels.
3. Soothhill, J. F., in *The Mast Cell—Its Role in Health and Disease*, Eds. J. Pepys and A. M. Edwards, 1979, p. 387, Pitman Medical, Tunbridge Wells.
4. Bedford, B. and Wade-West, S., *Brit. Med. J.*, 1983, **286**, 148.
5. Ros, A. M., Juhlin, L. and Michaëlsson, G., *Brit. J. Derm.*, 1976, **95**, 19.
6. Coombs, R. R. A. and Gell, P. G. H., in *Clinical Aspects of Immunology*, Eds. P. G. H. Gell, R. R. A. Coombs and P. J. Lachmann, 1975, p. 761, Blackwell, Oxford.
7. Katz, D. H., *J. Allergy Clin., Immun.*, 1978, **62**, 49.
8. Aas, K., *Allergy*, 1978, **33**, 3.
9. Wicher, K., Reisman, R. E. and Arbesman, C. E., *J. Am. Med. Ass.*, 1969, **208**, 143.
10. Matthews, T. W. and Soothhill, J. F., *Lancet*, 1976, **ii**, 893.
11. Sandberg, D. H. and Bernstein, C. W., *Pediat. Res.*, 1972, **6**, 383.
12. Galant, S. P., Bullock, J. and Frick, O. L., *Clin. Allergy*, 1973, **3**, 363.
13. Fisher, A. A., *Contact Dermatitis*, 1967, Lea & Febiger, Philadelphia.
14. Moneret-Vautrin, D. A., in *The Mast Cell—Its Role in Health and Disease*, Eds. J. Pepys and A. M. Edwards, 1979, p. 431, Pitman Medical, Tunbridge Wells.
15. Gerrard, J. W., in *The Mast Cell—Its Role in Health and Disease*, Eds. J. Pepys and A. M. Edwards, 1979, p. 416, Pitman Medical, Tunbridge Wells.
16. Buisseret, P. D., Youlten, L. J. F., Heinzelmann, D. I. and Lessof, M. H., *Lancet*, 1978, **i**, 906.
17. Lessof, M. H., Buisseret, P. D., Merrett, T. G., Merrett, J., Wraith, D. G. and Youlten, L. J. F., in *The Mast Cell—Its Role in Health and Disease*, Eds. J. Pepys and A. M. Edwards, 1979, p. 406, Pitman Medical, Tunbridge Wells.
18. Hedström, V., *Arch. Allergologi*, 1958, **12**, 153.
19. Aas, K., *Arch. Allergy*, 1966, **29**, 346.
20. Bleumink, E., in *Immunology of the Gastro-Intestinal Tract*, Ed. P. Asquith, 1979, p. 195, Churchill, London.
21. Gonzalez de la Reguera, I., Inigo, J. F. and Gehling, A., *Dermatologica*, 1971, **143**, 288.

22. Jones, R., Ryan, A. J. and Wright, S. E., *Fd Cosmet. Toxicol.*, 1964, **2**, 447.
23. Roxen, J. J., Ryan, A. J. and Wright, S. E., *Fd Cosmet. Toxicol.*, 1967, **5**, 645.
24. Chafee, F. H. and Settipane, G. A., *J. Allergy*, 1967, **40**, 65.
25. Lockey, S. D., *Allergy*, 1959, **38**, 206.
26. Juhlin, L., Michaëlsson, G. and Zetterström, O., *J. Allergy Clin. Immun.*, 1972, **50**, 92.
27. Michaëlsson, G. and Juhlin, L., *Brit. J. Derm.*, 1973, **88**, 525.
28. Green, M., *Ann. Allergy*, 1974, **33**, 274.
29. Thunel, P. and Granholt, A., *Dermatologica*, 1975, **151**, 360.
30. Johnson, H. M., Peeler, J. T. and Smith, B. G., *Immunochemistry*, 1971, **8**, 281.
31. Weliky, N. and Heineo, C., *Clin. Allergy*, 1980, **10**, 375.
32. Watson, I., Heineo, D. C., Rose, B. and Boatello, A., *Clin. Res.*, 1969, **17**, 362.
33. Devey, M., Sanderson, C. D., Carter, D. and Coombs, R. R. A., *Lancet*, 1970, **ii**, 1280.
34. Vedanthan, P. K., Menon, M. M., Ball, T. D. and Bergini, D., *J. Allergy Clin. Immun.*, 1977, **60**, 8.
35. Settipane, G. A., Chafee, F. H., Postman, I. M., Levine, M. I., Saken, J. H., Barrick, R. M., Nicholas, S. S., Schwartz, H. J., Honsiger, R. W. and Klein, D. E., *J. Allergy Clin. Immun.*, 1976, **57**, 541.
36. Stenius, R. S. M. and Lemola, M., *Clin. Allergy*, 1976, **6**, 119.
37. Desmond, R. E. and Trantlein, J. J., *Ann. Allergy*, 1981, **46**, 81.
38. de Weck, A. L., *Int. Arch. Allergy*, 1971, **41**, 393.
39. Vane, J. R., *Nature (New Biol.)*, 1971, **231**, 232.
40. Settipane, G. A., Chafee, F. H. and Klein, D. E., *J. Allergy Clin. Immun.*, 1974, **51**, 190.
41. Szczeklik, A., Gryglewski, R. J., Czerniawska-Mysik, G. and Zmude, A., *J. Allergy Clin. Immun.*, 1976, **58**, 10.
42. Gerber, J. C., Payne, N. A., Velz, O., Nies, A. S. and Oates, F. A., *J. Allergy Clin. Immun.*, 1979, **63**, 289.
43. Vargraftig, B. B., Bessot, J. C. and Pauli, G., *Respiration*, 1980, **39**, 276.
44. Warin, R. P. and Smith, R. I., *Brit. Med. J.*, 1982, **284**, 1443.
45. Lockey, S. D., *Ann. Allergy*, 1977, **38**, 206.
46. Juhlin, L., *Brit. J. Derm.*, 1981, **104**, 369.
47. Mali, J. W. H. and Malten, K. E., *Acta derm.-vener.*, 1961, **46**, 123.
48. Johnson, F. C., *Crit. Rev. Fd Technol.*, 1966, **2**, 267.
49. Food additives and contaminants committee, *Report on the antioxidants in Food Regulations 1966 and 1974*, 1974, Ministry of Agriculture, Fisheries and Food, London.
50. Bruckhardt, Von, W. and Fierz, U., *Dermatologica*, 1964, **129**, 431.
51. Brun, R., *Berufsdermatosen*, 1964, **12**, 281.
52. Brun, R., *Dermatologica*, 1970, **140**, 390.
53. Industrial Biotest Laboratories, 1971. Report IBT F9655, IBT P8473 and IBT No. 8473, IBT, Illinois.
54. World Health Organisation, *Tech. Rep. Ser. Wld Hlth Org.*, 1974, No. 539, WHO, Geneva.
55. Kahn, G., Phanuphak, P. and Claman, H. N., *Archs. Derm.*, 1974, **109**, 506.
56. Challacombe, S. J. and Tomasi, T. I., *J. Exp. Med.*, 1980, **152**, 1459.

57. Jahassohn, J., *Handbuch der haut-und geschlechtskrankheiten*, 1932, Springer Verlag, Berlin.
58. Wood, H. C. and Osol, A., *The Dispensary of the United States of America*, 23rd edn, 1943, Lippincott, Philadelphia.
59. Rudner, E. J., Santen, F. J. and Appleyard, T. N., *Contact Dermatitis*, 1975, **1**, 277.
60. Jordan, W. P., *Archs Derm.*, 1973, **108**, 278.
61. Rotlenberg, H. W., *Archs Derm.*, 1967, **95**, 381.
62. Mitchell, J. C., *Archs Derm.*, 1971, **104**, 49.
63. Opdyke, D. L. J., *Fd Cosmet. Toxicol.*, 1974, **12** (Suppl.), 951.
64. Randolph, T. G., *Human Ecology and Susceptibility to the Chemical Environment*, 1962, p. 65, Charles C. Thomas, Springfield.
65. Frazier, C. A., *Coping with Food Allergy*, 1974, pp. 58–9 and 298, Quadrangle/The New York Times Book Company, New York.
66. Coulson, J., 'Synthetic organic colours for food', in *Developments in Food Colours—1*, Ed. J. Walford, 1980, pp. 47–96, Applied Science, London.
67. Furia, T. E. (Ed.), *Handbook of Food Additives*, 1968, p. 252, The Chemical Rubber Company, Cleveland.
68. Randolph, T. G., *Human Ecology and Susceptibility to the Chemical Environment*, 1962, pp. 71 and 115, Charles C. Thomas, Springfield.
69. Randolph, T. G., *Human Ecology and Susceptibility to the Chemical Environment*, 1962, p. 116, Charles C. Thomas, Springfield.
70. Winter, R., *Poisons in your Foods*, 1969, pp. 42–3, USA General Publishing Company Ltd, New York.
71. Furia, T. E. (Ed.), *Handbook of Food Additives*, 1968, p. 188, The Chemical Rubber Company, Cleveland.
72. Lockey, S. D., *Ann. Allergy*, 1971, **29**, 461.
73. Ros, A. M., Juhlin, L. and Michaëlsson, G., *Brit. J. Derm.*, 1976, **95**, 19.
74. Warin, R. P. and Smith, R. I., *Brit. J. Derm.*, 1976, **94**, 401.
75. Douglas, H. M. G., *Dermatologica*, 1977, **154**, 308.
76. Rudski, E., *Dermatologica*, 1977, **64**, 163.
77. August, P. J., in *Proc. of the First Food Allergy Workshop*, 1980, pp. 76–81, Medical Education Services, Oxford.
78. Chase, M. W., *Proc. Soc. Exp. Biol. Med.*, 1946, **61**, 257.
79. Feingold, B. B., *Introduction to Clinical Allergy*, 1973, Charles C. Thomas, Springfield.
80. Wessey, J. S., *Med. J. Aust.*, 1976, **2**, 281.
81. Conners, C. K., Yoytte, C. H. and Southwark, D. A., *Pediatrics*, 1976, **58**, 154.
82. Harley, J. P., Ray, R. S. and Tomasi, L., *Pediatrics*, 1978, **61**, 818.
83. Levy, F., Dumbrell, S. and Hobbes, G., *Med. J. Aust.*, 1978, **1**, 61.
84. Stase, F. J., Whelan, E. M. and Sheridan, M., *Pediatrics*, 1980, **66**, 521.
85. Mathes, J. A. and Gittelman, R., *Archs Gen. Psychiat.*, 1981, **38**, 714.
86. Le Fevre, M. E. and Joel, D. D., *Life Sci.*, 1977, **21**, 1403.
87. Walker, W. A. and Isselbacher, K. J., *Gastroenterology*, 1974, **67**, 531.
88. Saarinen, U., Kajosaan, M., Buckman, A. and Siimes, M., *Lancet*, 1979, **ii**, 163.
89. Swarbrick, E. T., Stokes, C. R. and Soothhill, J. F., *Gut*, 1979, **20**, 121.

90. Cunningham-Rundles, C., Brandeis, W. E., Good, R. A. and Day, N. K., *Proc. Nat. Acad. Sci.*, 1978, **75**, 3389.
91. Furguson, A., in *First Food Allergy Workshop*, 1980, p. 28, Medical Education Services, Oxford.
92. Harrison, M., Kilby, A., Walker-Smith, J. A., France, N. F. and Ward, C. B. S., *Brit. Med. J.*, 1976, **1**, 150.
93. Bendixen, G., *Gut*, 1969, **10**, 631.
94. Jewel, D. P. and Truelove, S. C., *Gut*, 1972, **13**, 796.
95. Shaw, D. H., *J. Dent. Res.*, 1976, **55**, 1133.
96. Del Soldato, P. and Meli, A., *Proc. Soc. Exp. Biol. Med.*, 1978, **158**, 525.
97. Soothhill, J. F., Stokes, C. R., Turner, M. W., Norman, A. P. and Taylor, B., *Clin. Allergy*, 1976, **6**, 305.
98. Dansset, J. and Svejgaard, A. (Eds), *HLA and Disease*, 1977, Munksgaard, Copenhagen.
99. Evans, C. C., Lewinsohn, H. C. and Evans, J. M., *Brit. Med. J.*, 1977, **1**, 603.
100. Bodmer, W., *J. Roy. Coll. Phys.*, London, 1980, **14**, 43.
101. Rosenstreich, D. L., *Nature*, 1980, **285**, 436.
102. Ogle, K. A. and Bullock, J. D., *Ann. Allergy*, 1977, **39**, 8.
103. Juhlin, L., *Brit. J. Derm.*, 1981, **104**, 364.
104. Bahna, S. L., *Ann. Allergy*, 1978, **41**, 1.
105. Freier, S. and Kletter, B., *Clin. Pediat.*, 1970, **9**, 449.
106. Mikkelsen, H., Larsen, J. C. and Tarding, F., *Archs Toxicol.*, 1978, Suppl. I, 141.
107. Syvanen, P. and Beckman, A., *Abstract Nordic congress of allergology*, 1978, p. 58, Munksgaard, Copenhagen.
108. Vedanthan, P. K., Menon, M. M., Bell, T. D. and Bergin, D., *J. Allergy Clin. Immun.*, 1977, **60**, 8.
109. Weber, R. W., Hoffman, M., Raine, D. A. Jr and Nelson, H. S., *J. Allergy Clin. Immun.*, 1979, **64**, 32.
110. Østerballe, O., Taudorf, E. and Haahr, J., *Ugeskr. Laeg.*, 1979, **141**, 1908.
111. Moneret-Vautrin, D. A., Grilliat, J. P. and Demange, G., *Med. et Nut.*, 1980, **16**, 171.
112. Pellegrin, A., *Ann. Intern. Med.*, 1979, **130**, 211.
113. Poulsen, E., 1980, Toxicology Forum, Aspen, Colorado.
114. MacCara, M. C., *Can. Med. Ass. J.*, 1982, **126**, 910.
115. *Report of the Scientific Committee for Food on the sensitivity of individuals to Food Components and Food Additives*, Oct. 1981, Ministry of Agriculture, Fisheries and Food, London.
116. Conners, K. C., Goyette, C. H., Southwick, D. A., Lees, J. M. and Andrulonis, P. A., *Pediatrics*, 1976, **58**, 154.

Chapter 7

FUTURE TRENDS

F. J. FRANCIS

Department of Food Science and Nutrition, University of Massachusetts, Amherst, USA

SUMMARY

There is an obvious worldwide trend towards the use of natural or nature-alike colourants rather than synthetic compounds for food use. A survey of the patent literature for the years 1971–75 compared with 1976–81 shows a doubling of the total patents for food colourants. Patents in the carotenoid, anthocyanin, betacyanin and haemoglobin type pigments more than doubled, whereas the patents on synthetic compounds were equal. The applications for crude plant extracts and novel plant pigments, such as those from Monascus, *showed considerable increase. This general trend may reflect worldwide perceived toxicological concerns and the uncertainties in toxicological methodology. Hopefully, as our research continues, the concerns will abate, and the above trends may be short term. Possibly, the pressures on efficient food utilisation in an increasing world population will reverse the trends over a longer time period.*

1. INTRODUCTION

The opportunity to speculate on future trends in food colourants is tempting and fascinating. In my opinion, developments will, in the near future, be driven mainly by perceived uncertainties with safety of food additives. Further distant in time, the developments will, I hope, be influenced more by a better understanding of sound scientific principles in food safety, food acceptance, food production, and food, nutrition and public health delivery systems. Before attempting to interpret the effect of developments in the above areas, it may be of interest to tabulate world-wide interest in this area. There are many ways of doing this such as pertinent legislation, literature citation surveys, usage of colourants, etc., but I will confine my attention to the patent literature. This, at least, gives an indication of what some workers consider to be important and economically feasible. There are obviously some ambiguities in this approach since some developments are patented in several countries and not all developments are patented. Actual usage may not follow practices in the recent patent literature. Even with these uncertainties, several interesting trends have developed.

2. THE PATENT SITUATION

Table 1 lists the number of patents by country of origin. Not surprisingly, the list is dominated by countries with a high degree of interest in the development of processed foods. There are no 'warm weather' countries on the list. This again is not surprising in view of the tendency of countries with year-round growing conditions to rely more on a fresh-food economy. The necessity for food preservation with its attendant possibilities for

TABLE 1

FOOD COLOURANT PATENTS LISTED BY
COUNTRY OF REGISTRATION, 1971–81

Country	Number
USA	50
Japan	48
Britain	28
West Germany	21
Russia	17
Switzerland	11
France	9
The Netherlands	5
Canada	1
Israel	1
Total	191

Source: International Food Information Service (IFIS). Food Science and Technology Abstracts.

TABLE 2
FOOD PATENTS LISTED FOR APPLICATIONS
RATHER THAN PIGMENT PREPARATION,
1971–81

Application area	Number
Confectionery	12
Plant products	11
Animal products	9
Edible casings	8
Dairy products	7
Dry mixes	7
Baked goods	3
Miscellaneous	8
Total	65

Source: IFIS.

manipulating food makes the use of colourants, and actually, most additives, more economically feasible and more desirable in the colder countries. Table 1 also reflects the degree of sophistication of the food industries, with some notable exceptions (e.g. Scandinavia, Italy).

Table 2 lists the patents which primarily describe applications to types of foodstuffs. The applications are spread across the range of major foods with emphasis on animal and dairy products including edible casings for sausage-type products. Only five are for fruits and vegetables: one each for cherries, raisins and green peas, and two for general use. The others in the plant product group were soy (3), popcorn (2) and coconut (1). Baked goods were low with only three applications listed.

Table 3 is more interesting from the point of view of trends because the type of pigment in the patent applications is listed for two periods, 1971–75 and 1976–81. The synthetic colourant area shows eight and nine patents in the two periods, but this interpretation is misleading because it involves mainly two countries, the US with two applications in the first period and seven in the second, and Britain with two in each. The seven US patents in the period 1975–81 include five from the linked polymer concept of the Dynapol company. This company ceased operations in 1982, but the colourants already developed will probably be marketed. There is relatively little patent interest in the development of the synthetic colourants as portrayed by the FD & C list of certified colourants. Four countries (Russia, West Germany, The Netherlands and Japan) had one application each in the 1971–75 period and none in 1976–81. Again, this is not

TABLE 3
FOOD COLOURANT PATENTS FOR PIGMENT PREPARATIONS, 1971–81

Type of pigment	Number of patents		
	1971–75	1976–81	Total
Carotenoids	6	14	20
Synthetic colourants	8	9	17
Anthocyanins	4	11	15
Turmeric, carmine, paprika, annatto, chlorophylls	3	8	11
Monascus	0	9	9
Caramel	6	2	8
Betacyanins	3	5	8
Iron compounds	3	5	8
Plant hydrolysates	0	7	7
Haemoglobins	2	4	6
Carotenoid extracts	0	4	4
Miscellaneous	5	8	13
Total	40	86	126

Source: IFIS.

surprising since these countries show a high degree of concern over the use of food colourants.

The interest in carotenoid colourants more than doubled in the two periods. This development is even more apparent when the zero and four patents for carotenoid extracts are added to the list. This sequence of events is obviously related to the success of the Hoffman-La Roche company in marketing the 'nature-alike' carotenoid colourants. The other two well-known natural colourant groups, the anthocyanins and the betacyanins, also showed a doubling in the two periods. Possibly this reflects a desire to use 'natural colourants'. The doubling of the haemoglobin-type compounds is probably a reaction to the nitrite/nitrosamine controversy and a desire to use natural meat colourants. Indeed the possibility of using stabilised haemoglobin and myoglobin compounds is very attractive. However, any modification of the pigment molecule would constitute a new compound and obviously should be subjected to toxicological testing for safety.

The nine patents (Japan, 5; Switzerland, 3; Britain, 1) associated with pigments of the Monascus group indicate the breadth of interest in this new colourant, and probably we shall see more developments in this area. The eight patents (US, 3; West Germany, 2; Britain, 1; Japan, 1; Russia, 1) for caramel indicate a long-standing and continuing interest. The increasing interest in iron compounds, excluding the haem types (US, 4; Japan, 3; France, 1) is surprising since these relate more closely to synthetic colourants than to the 'naturals'. Perhaps the association with iron strikes a sympathetic chord with the nutrition fraternity. Probably the desire for natural colourants is reflected in the increased interest in annatto, carmine, paprika, turmeric and chlorophylls (Japan, 6; US, 2; West Germany, 1; Russia, 1; Israel, 1). The same interest is reflected in the development of plant hydrolysates (US, 3; France, 2; Britain, 1; West Germany, 1). The above trends indicate quite clearly that the research developments and applications are directed towards the 'natural' or 'nature-alike' compounds and away from the synthetics. Whether these trends will continue poses an interesting question. In my opinion, they will continue in the short term (up to 10 years) but not in the longer term. My major reason for this conclusion is that most of the safety considerations should be resolved in the next decade. A secondary consideration is the need to utilise food more efficiently in a nutrition/public health system. Another consideration is the need to maximise food availability in a world with an increasing population.

3. THE NEED FOR COLOURANTS

The desire for food colourants has been very much in evidence for many generations. The aesthetic and psychological background for this statement is presented very well in Chapter 3. In my opinion, the need for food colourants is patently obvious. The only question remaining is the source of colourants. This poses some very interesting scientific, economic and philosophical questions.

Consumers seem to have an intrinsic belief that compounds produced in nature are probably safer for human consumption as opposed to new compounds created in research laboratories. Undoubtedly, 10 000 years of association with agriculture has fostered this opinion. Yet, clearly this is scientifically untenable. Compounds such as botulinum toxin, the hallucinogenic compounds in ergot, the toxins in mushrooms, aflatoxins in cereals, etc., are very dangerous. A long list of compounds found in nature[1,2] have very dubious benefits for mankind. This situation is accepted with the caveat that we have learned to distinguish the hazards and can avoid them. Perhaps so, but new ones are being discovered all the time. Actually the rate of discovery of hazardous compounds seems to be increasing, particularly in the microbiological area. There is every indication that this trend will continue. A second argument is presented that over the years, human beings have developed detoxification mechanisms to handle compounds of dubious safety in nature. In view of the millenia taken for mankind to evolve, it is difficult to imagine that appropriate detoxification systems could be developed in 25–50 generations.

The public concern with synthetic compounds versus compounds produced in nature has led to some interesting economic decisions. One of the most successful of these decisions was that developed by Hoffman-La Roche concerning the four carotenoid colourants, namely β-carotene, apocarotenal, canthaxanthin and the esters of apocarotenoic acid. These compounds are synthesised by the company, yet because they occur in nature, they are termed 'nature-alike'. Clearly this was a business decision by the company since carotenoid extracts of a wide variety of plants (e.g. palm oil, carrot oil) were available for commercial exploitation. They decided to go the synthetic route for a number of good scientific reasons. Not the least of these reasons was that they could control and specify the purity of the preparations offered for sale. Obviously they could control the supply and apparently the economic cost of synthesis was within reach. In view of the public acceptance and apparent success of this group of colourants, obviously this was a sound decision. However they clearly are synthetic compounds. The caveat that they are also found in nature serves to blur the distinction between synthetic and natural compounds. Perhaps this is as it should be.

A different approach has been adopted with the other two major groups of plant colourants, the anthocyanins and the betacyanins. There are no synthetic products on the US market or even concentrated formulations. Apparently the cost of synthesis is too high, as is the cost of concentration. Another factor in the development of colourant concentrates for these two groups of compounds is the cost of the required toxicological data. In the US, a formulation with an increased concentration of colourant is considered to be a new product and, consequently, proof of safety has to be established. Two sources of anthocyanins can be sold legally in the US. The first is a series of preparations prepared from wine grape skins (one general name is Oenocianina). This blue formulation is allowed under the 'grandfather' clause for beverages, which is a catch-all to describe the policy under which additives which have been in the food system for a long time are allowed. The second, just recently approved[3] is a preparation from the lees in the bottoms of tanks containing juice from Labrusca type grapes. This formulation can be used for foods other than beverages. Both are obviously extracts which contain a wide variety of compounds. Two betacyanin formulations from red beets are allowed under the 'grandfather' clause. The first is whole beets or dehydrated whole beets and the second is whole or dehydrated beet juice. No colourant concentrates are allowed in the US in spite of the obvious commercial desirability and feasibility[4] because no one to date has provided the toxicological data. It is perhaps unfortunate that the rise in interest in the betalaines as colourants has coincided with the increase in concern over the nitrosamines and the nitrites. Beets are notorious accumulators of nitrates which can be a precursor of nitrites. In addition, they also contain saponins similar to the phytolaccatoxins from *Phytolacca*,[5] but in much lower quantities. In my opinion, there is no public health problem here but prudence would suggest that betacyanin concentrates from beets should undergo some toxicological testing.

The decision to market a pigment extract rather than a pure compound has some technological and philosophical disadvantages. The technological disadvantages are the variability in raw material with the attendant difficulties in standardisation and specification of the actual chemical composition of the formulation. For example, with anthocyanin extracts from grape skins, the pigments polymerise and degrade making it impossible with the present state of the art to specify the chemical composition of the formulation. The situation is further complicated by the wide array of other chemical components that go along with the pigments in the natural extracts. The philosophical considerations are that it would be very nice if we knew what we were eating. However, in spite of these apparent problems, the natural extracts do produce satisfactory colourants. This situation merely emphasises the chemical complexity of the foods in our normal diet.

4. COLOURANT SAFETY DECISIONS

The history of the permitted FD & C colourants in the US has not been one of stability. Bernard Hesse at the Bureau of Chemistry was assigned the task of evaluating the 695 different coal-tar dyes available on the world market around the year 1900. He reduced the potential candidates for food colourants in 1907 to seven (Table 4). It is coincidental that there are seven allowed today, but only two (FD & C Red No. 3 and FD & C Blue No. 2) have survived from the 1907 list. Only one new colourant, FD & C Red No. 40, has been approved in the last two decades, and there is little interest,

TABLE 4

CHRONOLOGICAL HISTORY OF FD & C COLOURANTS IN THE US

Year listed	Common name	FDA name	Colour index No.	Year delisted
1907	Ponceau 3R	FD & C Red No. 1	16 155	1961
1907	Amaranth	FD & C Red No. 2	16 185	1976
1907	Erythrosine	FD & C Red No. 3	45 430	—
1907	Orange I	FD & C Orange No. 1	14 600	1956
1907	Naphthol Yellow S	FD & C Yellow No. 1	10 316	1959
1907	Light Green SF Yellowish	FD & C Green No. 2	42 095	1966
1907	Indigotine	FD & C Blue No. 2	73 015	—
1916	Tartrazine	FD & C Yellow No. 5	19 140	—
1918	Sudan I	—	12 055	1918
1918	Butter Yellow	—	11 160	1918
1918	Yellow AB	FD & C Yellow No. 3	11 380	1959
1918	Yellow OB	FD & C Yellow No. 4	11 390	1959
1922	Guinea Green B	FD & C Green No. 1	42 085	1966
1927	Fast Green FCF	FD & C Green No. 3	42 053	—
1929	Ponceau SX	FD & C Red No. 4	14 700	1976
1929	Sunset Yellow FCF	FD & C Yellow No. 6	15 985	—
1929	Brilliant Blue FCF	FD & C Blue No. 1	42 090	—
1939	Naphthol Yellow S potassium salt	FD & C Yellow No. 2	10 316	1959
1939	Orange SS	FD & C Orange No. 2	12 100	1956
1939	Oil Red XO	FD & C Red No. 32	12 140	1956
1950	Benzyl Violet 4B	FD & C Violet No. 1	42 640	1973
1959	Citrus Red No. 2	Citrus Red No. 2	12 156[a]	—
1966	Orange B	Orange B	19 235	Withdrawn (1979)
1971	Allura Red AC	FD & C Red No. 40	16 035	—

Source: National Academy of Sciences, *Food Colors*, 1971, Nat. Acad. Sciences, Washington, DC, p. 43.

[a] Food use limited to the colouring of oranges not intended to be used for further processing at a level not exceeding 2 ppm by weight.

apart from the linked polymer concept, in introducing new synthetic colourants. Table 4 refers only to the US and the lists are different for other countries, but the concept of potential safety or harm is common to all.

The colourants were singled out in the US for toxicological testing by a number of consumer groups during the world-wide activism movement of the 1960s and 1970s. The colourants were visible symbols of a highly processed food delivery system. It has been suggested that the criticism directed towards the colourants was really aimed at the 'junk food' concept. The colourants were judged as tools which made it possible for manufacturers to produce 'junk food'. Obviously this criticism could be directed at many additives but the colourants were very visible and judged by some to be merely cosmetic. Regardless, their safety was questioned and more toxicological data were requested. Together with the non-caloric sweeteners, the colourants received the dubious honour of being the most studied compounds in the US food supply.

The concept of testing for the safety components in the food supply was also undergoing serious changes. For example, in 1950, about 50 compounds known to cause cancer in man were recognised. Today the list is at least 5000. The study of potential carcinogens is an extremely important, and very popular, area of research so there is every indication that the list of suspected carcinogens will continue to grow. The detection of potential carcinogens is, itself, an area of considerable debate. Long-term animal testing for tumour production is the traditional approach. This usually requires the selection of the species of animal most susceptible to tumour production by a specific compound, and feeding studies over several generations. There are two major problems with this approach. The first is that usually very large dosages have to be fed in order to get a response from the animal. A positive response is necessary in order to have an experiment since negative data do not carry much weight. The high dosages require extrapolation to dosages which would reasonably be expected in the marketplace. This introduces an uncertainty. The second problem is that the animal data have to be interpreted in human terms. This introduces a second uncertainty. There are a number of statistical methods for extrapolating from high to low dosages and from animal to human data, but the choice of which method to choose is far from clear. In the worst case scenario, the estimates of the risk may differ by a factor of 200 000. This degree of uncertainty does not inspire confidence in the methodology.

Fortunately the means to reduce the degree of uncertainty are being developed. Whole batteries of tests with bacteria, protozoa, etc., provide additional evidence. Also, knowledge about the mode of attack on DNA, the channels of detoxification, the interaction with other compounds in the biological systems, dose-related phenomena and organ specificity, will allow investigators to choose more appropriate estimations of risk. As our knowledge of this incredibly complicated interplay of events increases, it will be possible to evaluate toxicological risks more realistically. More accurate estimations of risk should help to alleviate perceived concern over the safety of the food colourants.

5. THE NUTRITION LABELLING PROGRAMME

The development of knowledge in human nutrition has been accompanied by increasing endeavours to translate this knowledge into terms understandable by the general public. Unfortunately we eat food, not nutrients. Public education to translate foods into nutrients has taken many paths in different countries. The current approach in the US is to try to persuade the public to eat at least one portion from each of five food groups per day. If this advice is followed, it would be difficult indeed to be malnourished except possibly from too many calories. The five food group classification is serving well, but it is simplistic. There are many foods which do not clearly fit into one group. For example, a taco (a Mexican product, essentially a meat and vegetable mixture in a thin, crisp, unleavened bread) is represented by three groups, meat, vegetables and cereals. This is a relatively simple interpretation which can easily be resolved by consumers since the components are recognisable. However, how does one recognise the nutrient composition of 'Space Bars' or granola bars? The further we go down the road towards 'engineered' (or 'civilised' as opposed to 'natural') foods, the less able is the consumer to judge the nutrient content of the foods. There was a movement in the US in the 1960s, that, understandably, the consumer deserved a better deal. This led to the world's largest experiment in consumer nutrition education—the nutrition labelling programme. A voluntary, nationwide programme was instituted to encourage manufacturers to put the nutrient content on the label. No longer would a consumer have to consult a table of nutritional values to estimate the nutritive value of a particular food. The response of manufacturers was, predictably, mixed, but over 50 % of the foods in the marketplace now have nutritional labelling. The response of consumers was not exactly overwhelming either, but it is a forward step. It will take a long time to raise the degree of consumer awareness, or concern, to the possibilities of judging nutrient intake. In my opinion, it will come in time.

The introduction of nutritional labelling together with ingredient labelling, and the five food group concept means that two systems of nutrition education are being pursued at the same time. The simultaneous approach has provided some interesting developments. It has served to expose some of the more absurd nutritional claims for some particular foods. It has always been a source of frustration to nutritionists to read absurd claims. The frustration is still there as portrayed by popular diet books, media claims, etc., but at least the actual nutrient content is there on the label for all to see and, hopefully, read. There were some surprises, indeed, when some of the popular 'natural' foods were exposed to the unbiased efforts of the food analysts.

The introduction of nutritional labelling should make it possible to introduce and justify, from a nutritional viewpoint, novel foods. It is absolutely essential that nutritional justification be a prime consideration for government legislation in this area. Prevention of fraud is not the least of the necessities. Probably the introduction of national nutritional goals is the most important, and it would be made much easier with good public awareness of nutrient content of food. This approach is bound to blur the distinctions between the primary sources of food and their nutritional content. It should reduce public concern about natural food. Obviously, it will not address the extremely important concept of food aesthetics, but that is another story.

6. A FOOD/NUTRITION/PUBLIC HEALTH DELIVERY SYSTEM

Every country would like to provide the best nutrition/public health system possible within the constraints of economic possibility. The US is no exception, but the expectations are straining the resources. The spectacular developments just in the instrumentation available for diagnosis and treatment are putting intense pressure on the budgets of many health delivery systems. This had led to spiralling increases in the cost of medical care delivery. Politically, it is very popular to search for approaches to curtail the ever-increasing costs. One simplistic approach for curbing the spiralling costs has been suggested. All one has to do to lower the costs of treatment for chronic degenerative diseases is to improve the general nutritional state. This is translated into better diets; and we have seen a number of examples.[6-8]

The political appeal for the possibility of reducing health care costs merely by changing the diet should not be underestimated. This can be accomplished in a myriad of ways involving the supply and type of food. National nutrition policies have an appeal akin to motherhood and make an excellent rallying slogan. Whether they will be effective with our present state of knowledge remains to be seen, but it is certain that, in one form or another, they will be in evidence. National nutritional policies with the goals stated above will blur the distinctions between the original sources of food.

7. NUTRIENT DATA BANKS

The nutritional labelling programmes and the national nutritional policy concepts have considerable appeal today because they are technically feasible. The nutritional labelling programme necessitated huge numbers of analyses and automated, computerised analytical systems have made this possible. The refinements of food production, processing and delivery information systems have made it feasible to estimate supply and demand. The missing link in the interaction between food supply and nutrient intake has been the ability to manipulate sufficient data to be able to estimate and predict nutrient intake. The nutrient data banks have filled the gap.

Perhaps one example will illustrate the organisation and use of a nutrient data bank. The University of Massachusetts[9] operates a nutrient data bank for the entire New England area. Physically, it comprises two small computers interfaced with the large computers in the University's Computer Center. The random access storage has over 5000 food items each with up to 40 nutrients. They can be indexed in any combination and corrected for serving size, edible portion, cooking loss, etc. This facility makes it possible to obtain computer read-outs on the nutrient content of individual diets for diet recall surveys or actual surveillance diets. Nutrient availability for institutions, hospitals, etc., can be obtained very quickly. The nutrient content of new combinations of foods or even new products if the components are known, can be easily calculated. This ability to interpret large amounts of data within a reasonable time is paramount to the success of any national nutrition policy.

The application of nutrient data banks, which obviously translate food to nutrients, will further serve to blur the distinctions between the original sources of food.

8. WORLD FOOD SUPPLY

World food supply has probably been the source of more speculation than any other single topic in the food and nutrition delivery system. The approach developed by Malthus over 150 years ago, namely, that

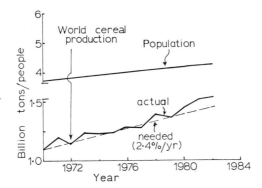

Fig. 1. World cereal production and world population for the years 1970–82. The dashed line labelled 'needed' is an FAO estimate of a desirable increase in food production per year. Note that the slope of the population curve is less than that of the cereal curve indicating that the population/food supply ratio is improving. Source: Population Reference Bureau, Intercom.

population increases geometrically while food supply increases arithmetically, is philosophically attractive but unfortunately simplistic. Neither premise is correct. Figure 1 presents a summary of world cereal production superimposed on world population. Obviously food production is keeping pace with population growth. There are obvious inconsistencies in the trend but they are short-time occurrences. Whether the 'gloomers and doomers' or the optimists are in favour depends on the particular point in the time cycle. Yet the mere statement that food production is keeping pace with population, is itself misleading. There is a problem in distribution. The countries with sophisticated agricultural practices have been increasing their production by raising yields per hectare whereas others have been raising production by bringing more land into production. There are only two major unexploited potential food production areas remaining in the world—the Amazon basin and the Sudan. Other countries, sooner or later, will have to place more emphasis on raising yields per hectare rather than relying on new land. The supply of land is obviously finite. The techniques for raising yields vary from the 'tender loving care' of family plots to the most sophisticated agribusiness concept. Yet they all require inputs in one form or another. The generation of the inputs will entail careful consideration of all priorities in the system from food production to public health. It may well be that a more efficient nutrient delivery system may be one of the less expensive alternatives. The trends in the past have been to place more emphasis on primary food production, less on prevention of storage losses, and even less on maximising the nutrient delivery system. It seems inevitable that relative costs of food will increase as demand goes up with increasing population and less productive land is brought into production. With this scenario, the priorities for inputs into the nutrient delivery system should change.

One scenario may change the conclusion of the above paragraph. There are those eternal optimists, whose faith in science is boundless, and who will say, 'that equation does not take into account the enormous untapped potential of science to provide unlimited food'. Recombinant DNA techniques will enable researchers to make a corn plant which will fix its own nitrogen thus eliminating the need for nitrogenous fertiliser. The famous 'sunbean' breakthrough in which a gene for protein storage from a French bean was transferred to a sunflower may introduce a new era in the production of plant protein. The cell fusion approaches that enable one to cross a soy bean with a Douglas fir tree have unlimited potential. Tank culture of plant, animal and microbial cells in food factories may remove, once and for all, the spectre of famine. The list goes on and on, but I am not that much of an optimist. Undoubtedly, the advances of science will help to hold down the cost of food. However, in my opinion, the inexorable increase in population will increase the pressure on the food delivery system. If the pressures as described above do develop, they will blur the distinction between natural and processed food.

9.   CONCLUSIONS

A survey of the patent literature over the past decade indicates quite clearly a trend towards the use of natural colourants at the expense of the synthetics. This trend is probably due to perceived fears of safety and will probably continue—perhaps for another decade. The safety issue is based on present-day knowledge and more realistic appraisals of safety are bound to be available in the near future. With this knowledge, the public may be more concerned with the source of food than with the cost, safety, quality, nutrient content and aesthetic appeal of the food.

A number of developments may minimise the importance of the source of food. These include better data on food safety, nutritional labelling, national nutritional policies for better public health delivery, nutrient data banks, and last but not least, the population/food supply situation. All of these will exert pressure to make the food supply, nutrient content and public health delivery system more efficient. The use of food colourants is one of many methods to achieve this aim. When the choice of colourants is determined by economics, with all other considerations equal, the synthetics will probably win over the naturals.

REFERENCES

1. Liener, I. E., *Toxic Constituents of Plant Foodstuffs*, 1st Edn, 1969, 500 pp. 2nd Edn, 1980, 502 pp. Academic Press, New York and London.
2. National Academy of Sciences, *Toxicants Occurring Naturally in Foods*, 1973, Nat. Acad. Sciences, Washington, DC, 624 pp.
3. *Federal Register*, 'Listing of colour additives exempt from certification', 1981, **46**(188), 29 September, pp. 47532–3.
4. von Elbe, J. H., 'The betalaines', in *Current Aspects of Food Colorants*, Ed. T. E. Furia, 1977, CRC Press, Boca Raton, FL, 93 pp.
5. Driver, M. W. and Francis, F. J., 'Purification of phytolaccanin by removal of phytolaccatoxin from *Phytolacca americana*', *J. Food Sci.*, 1977, **44**, 521–3.
6. Select Committee on Nutrition and Human Needs, United States Senate, *Dietary Goals for the United States*, 1977, 95th Congress, 1st Session. US Government Printing Office, Washington, DC, 2nd Edn, December 1977.
7. National Academy of Sciences, *Towards Healthful Diets*, 1980, Food and Nutrition Board, Nat. Acad. Sciences, Washington, DC.
8. National Academy of Sciences, *Diet, Nutrition and Cancer*, 1982, Committee on Diet, Nutrition and Cancer, Nat. Acad. Sciences, Washington, DC.
9. Samonds, K. W. Personal communication.

INDEX